Wild Wisconsin
NOTEBOOK

James Buchholz

Prairie Oak Press
A SUBSIDIARY OF TRAILS MEDIA GROUP, INC.

Library of Congress Catalog Card Number:2001032114
ISBN:1-879483-65-3

Design: Carol Lynn Benoit
Production: Colin Harrington
Cover Design: Flying Fish Graphics, Blue Mounds, WI
Printed in the United States of America by McNaughton & Gunn

Library of Congress Cataloging-in-Publication Data

Buchholz, James.
         Wild Wisconsin notebook / James Buchholz.-- 1st ed.
      p. cm.
   ISBN 1-879483-65-3
      1. Natural history--Wisconsin. I. Title.

   QH105.W6 B83 2001
   508.775--dc21   2001032114

Prairie Oak Press, a subsidiary of Trails Media Group, Inc.
P.O. Box 317 • Black Earth, WI 53515
(800) 236-8088 • e-mail: books@wistrails.com
www.trailsbooks.com

Dedicated to my wife Kathy
and my children Jim Jr., Krissy and Joey,
my hiking companions who helped me see
the beauty and magic of wildlife wherever
we explored the fields and forests of Wisconsin.

Contents

Introduction

The beautiful blue-and-green planet we call earth is home to us, but we are not alone. Other earthlings share the same air we breathe, the water we drink and swim in, the landscape on which we travel. We are only one part of nature's delicate and complicated web of life. Thousands of other unique species of plants and free-roaming animals blanket the world around us, all of which we collectively refer to as "wildlife."

Wisconsin is a land of natural scenic beauty, known for its outstanding wildlife-viewing opportunities. No matter where one travels in the state, from the northern forests where timber wolves howl on moonlit nights and the eerie call of loons echoes across sparkling wilderness lakes, to the aqua-blue shoreline of the Great Lakes where gulls soar over sand dunes in the fresh, cool breezes, the call of the wild still resounds loud and clear. River otters are often seen sliding down the muddy river banks along the mighty Mississippi and Wisconsin rivers, and the shrill call of bald eagles can be heard as they pluck fish from the water with their sharp talons. In the rolling landscape of the Kettle Moraine hills, hardwood forests are illuminated each spring with millions of beautiful white trilliums, while nearby thousands of Canada geese fill the skies of Horicon Marsh on their migration route north. Whether in a remote northwoods forest wilderness area, wildlife refuge, state park, urban park, or your own backyard, wildlife is always abundant in Wisconsin.

As our spinning planet orbits the sun over the course of a year, it tilts both to and from the sun, giving rise to Wisconsin's varied seasons of the year. These annual shifts in climate signal wildlife to either migrate, hibernate, or adapt to the weather changes ahead. It also creates the reliable mileposts of natural events that we anticipate each year. Biologists refer to the study of this annual progression of natural phenomena as "phenology." It includes events such as the appearance of the first wildflower or robin in spring, when we can expect fireflies to light up the blackened skies on a summer night, or when geese may be seen flying south for the winter, just as they have for uncounted generations.

This book highlights twelve representative wildlife species for each of the twelve months of the year, and reveals little-known secrets, folklore, legends, myths, superstitions, history, and current information for many of them. Introductions to the chapters describe weather patterns and wildlife activities that may be expected in each month of the year. In addition, the spring and fall equinox dates are listed, as well as those for the summer solstice and winter solstice. The traditional and colorful names for the full lunar moons, such as the wolf, thunder, frog, and blood moons, are explained, as well as during which months we can expect to see them rising in our night skies.

Although all the wildlife, both plant and animal, featured in this book inhabits or migrates through Wisconsin, most can be found in any state east of the Rocky Mountains, and many are indigenous to the entire continental United States. The timing of the phrenological events in this book are based on average Wisconsin seasons, but dates can change from year to year by as much as several weeks. In general, the onset of a natural event in nature, such as the return of robins in spring, occurs about four days later with each degree in latitude (about 70 miles) from south to north. But even within the same latitude, local weather can be affected by many other factors, including altitude, warmer south-facing hillside slopes, or by large bodies of water such as the Great Lakes, which often create mini-climates much different from the surrounding area.

In our rapidly changing world, technological advances, new ideas, inventions, institutions, and even entire governments seem to come and go at a frightening pace. Our stress-filled lives often seem controlled by the sterile indoor environments of concrete, steel, plastic, fluorescent lights, computer monitors, cell phones, answering machines, and the day-to-day deadlines we struggle to meet both at home and at work. But despite our daily preoccupation with this artificial world, it's comforting to know that the natural rhythms of the "real" world of nature continue to go on around us. Wildlife and the seasons of the year continue to march to the beat of nature's drum, just as they have for millions of years

Since the dawn of time, people have enjoyed observing and celebrating the passing seasons, along with the joy of watching and listening to the colorful array of wildlife around us. Although most of us can't abandon our busy, mostly urban, lifestyles, we can escape from time to time to explore and enjoy the natural world around us. I hope that this brief glimpse into the secret lives of the common plants and animals with whom we share this beautiful planet will inspire you, if only for a moment, to turn off the television and CD player, log off the internet, leave your e-mail unread, and hang up the cell phone. It's time to park your car and take a hike in the great outdoors to enjoy the REAL wild Wisconsin. ▲

January

JANUARY

Wisconsin's new year begins during the coldest month of winter. January was named after the Roman god Janus, who had two faces—one that looked back to the past and the other that looked ahead to the future. Despite the frozen landscape, the woods are alive with the busy antics of nuthatches, cardinals, and blue jays already enjoying the longer days and looking forward to warmer days ahead.

Great-horned owls can be heard hooting in the frosty, moonlit nights as they begin to pair and nest. The Ho-Chunk referred to January's full moon as the "bear moon," while other tribes called it the "wolf moon." Somewhere, deep inside the frozen forests, bear cubs are born warm and snug inside their mother's den, while outside a lone wolf can be heard howling far in the distance across the ice-encrusted landscape.

Then, usually by the third week of the month, a January thaw brings warm, welcome relief from the cold and signals the halfway point of winter. But all too soon, the icy winds and freezing temperatures of January return, and winter continues to run its course.

SNOWY OWLS
WINTER GHOSTS OF THE FAR NORTH

"And when it came to pass that man and animals had quarreled, the Great Spirit sailed away in disgust across the seas, to return only when they had made up their differences. So every night in the great pine forests, the snowy owl repeats his 'Koo, koo, koos—Oh I am sorry, Oh I am sorry.' "

—American Indian legend

The call of the snowy owl to Native American tribes once meant sadness and a longing for the "golden age" when man and animals lived in perfect unity. Even today, the sight of these beautiful, ghostlike visitors from the north can bring out ancient emotions in most of us. Maybe they remind us of the wild, untamed wilderness regions of the Arctic, or maybe they awaken memories of simpler

I

times. A time when our ancestors were part of the natural world—not apart from it.

The sight of a snowy owl can often cause traffic to grind to a halt on the highway or bring out the local television crew to film it for the six o'clock news. The snowy owl's seeming lack of fear of people, buildings, highways, and cities make these rare visitors from the north even more mysterious, reassuring us that not all creatures have yet to learn to fear humans.

Snowy owls visit the northern part of the United States most every year, but in greater numbers in some years than in others. Biologists have found that snowy owls are more common here in years when their natural food supply, such as Arctic hares and lemmings, is low in their native tundra region. They usually show up in our state as early as late November and stay through early March.

Snowy owls may often be seen during daylight hours, perched on the highest spot of their hunting territory. This might be the tallest tree, utility pole, a rooftop, or even a smokestack. They seem to prefer to hunt in areas similar to the wide-open Arctic landscape, including snow-covered farm fields, parks, and golf courses.

Unlike most owls that hunt only at night and are rarely seen during the day, snowy owls can be seen hunting during daylight hours. Most likely this is because they spend their summers in the Arctic regions which offer nearly three months during which the sun never completely sets at any time.

Snowy owls eat mostly small rodents such as mice and voles while in Wisconsin, but will also take rabbits, squirrels, and game birds on occasion. Our resident owls often eat only part of their prey and cache or store the rest for a later meal, but snowy owls have not learned this technique, probably because they would have a hard time finding it again in the barren, treeless, drifting snows of the Arctic. Instead, they have evolved a sort of "carryout" technique. Whatever they can't eat at a single meal, they carry along with them throughout the day, hidden under their warm, feathered feet, for a later snack.

Even though snowy owls are among the largest owls in the world, they can be difficult to spot, especially in heavy snow cover. During winters with little snow, these beautiful white birds with bright yellow eyes can really stand out against the brown landscape. Adult males have nearly pure white plumage, while younger birds and females are smaller and have black streaks in their plumage.

The sudden appearance of a snowy owl can create some fine memories for anyone who enjoys watching wildlife. While driving through Kohler-Andrae State Park in Sheboygan County a few years ago, I stopped to point out a small herd of deer to my children in the back seat. Because it was already twilight and darkness was setting in, all we could see clearly were the white "flags" of their tails as the deer slowly moved away from us. Suddenly, one of the "flags" rose into the air and sailed effortlessly to the crest of a nearby sand dune. It was a snowy owl. Like a winter ghost of the far north, this snowy owl did indeed create some fine memories. As we watched him proudly perched atop the dune, with Lake Michigan in the background, we could almost imagine the Great Spirit sailing back across the waters once again, just as the great Indian legend described so long ago.

CARDINALS
NATURE'S CHEERLEADERS

"*What cheer! What cheer! What cheer!*"
"*Birdie, birdie, birdie*"
"*Cue, cue, cue*"

Whistle these verses through your front teeth with a little gusto and you'll generate a pretty good impression of Wisconsin's most colorful bird—the northern cardinal. With some practice, you can even mimic cardinals well enough to have them call back to you, especially on bright, sunny, winter days. Among most other birds, only the male sings, and then usually only during the brief mating season in spring. But not the cardinal. Both the male and female like to sing throughout the year, except when they're molting their feathers and, for some unknown reason, again in early winter. Although the "cheer song," as it's called, is their all-time favorite, cardinals have a repertoire of some twenty-eight different songs that they can sing whenever the mood strikes them.

The male cardinal, with its brilliant scarlet-red plumage and black mask, is probably the most recognized bird in America. Females and juvenile males are less colorful, with mostly olive-colored feathers and only a fringe of red. Both the male and female have the familiar pointed crest on their head, which they can raise or lower, and powerful reddish beaks for cracking seeds. Because of the male's bright red color,

3

early colonists named the bird after the cardinals of the Catholic church, who wear red skullcaps and red robes as a symbol of their office.

Although a common bird in our backyards and forests now, it wasn't too long ago that there weren't any cardinals at all in Wisconsin. They first began to enter our state from the south around the turn of century, following major waterways including the Mississippi and the shores of Lake Michigan. The first official record of a cardinal in eastern Wisconsin didn't occur until 1922. Today, cardinals are still expanding their range northward and are becoming more common in the northern forests.

Some biologists believe that backyard feeding stations have helped the cardinal establish itself in northern climates and survive our harsh winters. Cardinals can be your best customers at the bird-feeder. They are usually the first to arrive in the morning and the last to leave, provided there aren't too many threats, such as cats, in your backyard. They prefer to eat cracked corn and sunflower seeds, which they crack open with ease. Despite their enormous appetites, cardinals can be pretty fussy as to where they dine. They don't like hanging feeders that have small perches, preferring to eat seed and corn on the ground or from a sturdy pole feeder. They often will fly away if they see you looking at them out the window.

Male and female cardinals stay paired all year and you rarely see one without the other nearby. Late in winter, you might see the beginnings of the birds' mating rituals at your bird-feeder. After spending much of the early winter being a bully and often chasing the female away from "his" feeder, the male suddenly turns into a Don Juan of the bird world. He begins to pick up seeds, crack away the hard shell, and feed the sweet nutmeat to his mate by gently placing it in her beak. This sudden show of affection may cause some bird-watchers to exclaim, "Aw, ain't that cute!" Experienced female cardinals, however, know this to be the "he-wants-something" behavior common to the males of all species, including humans, I'm told.

Cardinals are one of the earliest nesters in Wisconsin, beginning by late April. Although I have watched several pairs of cardinals over the years, I've rarely found one of their secret nesting sites. It may be because the male realizes his brilliant red plumage is easily visible to predators such as hawks and owls. To protect their young, cardinals build their nests in dense thickets such as honeysuckle shrubs, or deep inside evergreens.

A few years ago, I had the rare opportunity of watching a pair of cardinals build a nest not only in my backyard, but right outside my living-room window, only a few feet off the ground in shrubbery. After laying three eggs, the female incubated them day and night, while the male fed her on the nest. Both parents fed the young hatchlings nearly every minute of the day, a job so exhausting that cardinal parents may lose ten percent of their own body weight in the effort. On really hot days, the female instinctively stood over the young birds, shading them against bright sunlight by spreading her wings over them for hours, while the male continued to bring them insects to eat.

After the color, excitement, and glitter of the holiday season leaves our homes, and the cold, harsh reality of the long winter season sets in, it's nice to look out the window and see the cheerful, colorful cardinal brighten up the day.

If you don't have a pair of cardinals in your neighborhood, you can usually locate them in a local park. You may even want to whistle the "cheer" song to attract them. Who knows, they might even answer you. After all, "what cheer, what cheer," spring is almost here.

SNOW BUNTINGS
WINTER VISITORS FROM THE ARCTIC

In January, Wisconsin seems to get a fresh coat of white paint every few days or so, as the cold north winds and frequent snowstorms magically transform the entire state into a winter wonderland. Along with the frigid temperatures and snowdrifts comes another annual visitor from the Arctic north—the snowbirds or snow buntings. These sparrow-like birds have snow-white plumage over much of their bodies with some patches of black and brown. Snow buntings can be difficult to spot in winter, due to their snow-white coloration, but you can often see them in small flocks searching for grit along the gravel shoulders of rural highways as you drive by.

Like its human counterparts who flock to warmer southern climates in winter, snow buntings come to Wisconsin to enjoy our warm, mild, and relatively muggy winter. No, our weather can't compare to that of Florida, but to a bird that spends most of its life in the cold Arctic tundra, Wisconsin is truly a sunbelt state.

Snow buntings begin to arrive in our state early in winter. I've seen large flocks of them in open fields as far south as Milwaukee, as early as the first week of December. Although they're not that uncommon, few people actually see them because of their effective white camouflage against the winter landscape. As legend has it, the arrival of snow buntings early in the winter is a sign that bad weather is on the way.

Besides being difficult to spot because of their color, snow buntings avoid bird-feeders and rarely go near houses, preferring the windswept farm fields of rural areas. A true friend of the farmer, snow buntings feed almost exclusively on weed seeds. The birds have an interesting and very efficient feeding technique. As soon as the flock lands in a field, they disperse quickly and begin scratching in the snow for seeds while the entire flock moves in the same direction. When feeding from one side of the field to the other, those in the rear fly ahead of the ones in the front and switch back and forth until the entire area is covered.

It's hard to imagine any creature able to withstand the harsh, bone-chilling cold and winds of our Wisconsin winters without some sort of shelter, but snow buntings actually prefer the open fields with little or no cover. Unlike other birds that seek woodlands or buildings to shelter themselves from the deep freeze, snow buntings stay in open fields, using small depressions in the landscape to shield themselves from the wind. They can survive in temperatures of forty degrees below zero or colder. Buntings never perch in trees and don't even have feet designed to grasp branches, probably because trees are rare in their summer homes in the Arctic regions.

As quickly as they came, snow buntings seem to disappear over-night as the late winter thaws begin. It's almost as if they can't stand the sight of brown patches of field showing through the snow cover. By March, most of the snow buntings have begun their long journey back to the Arctic regions of Canada, Greenland, and Alaska. During the breeding season, the plumage of male snow buntings turns almost completely white, making them even more difficult to see in the snowy landscape of the Arctic. They build nests of moss, feathers, and fur and lay four to six eggs in a grass cup inside the nest. The parents incubate the eggs and raise their young in the wide-open, barren, tree-less, Arctic landscape. After the brief summer of the polar region, they begin the long trek back to their winter range in the northern part of the United States.

After a long, cold winter here in Wisconsin, most of us long for the day when the first robin appears to assure us that spring and warm weather are on the way. At the same time, far to the north, Alaskans are waiting in anticipation for the return of their own harbinger of spring —the snow buntings.

NUTHATCHES
THE UPSIDE-DOWN BIRDS

They're not your ordinary little dickey birds. You may have caught a glimpse of these tiny, fidgety birds hopping up the side of a tree, or down, or sideways, or even upside-down. Either way, up or down, it's all the same to these entertaining little comics of the bird world we call nuthatches.

Wisconsin is home to two species of nuthatches. The white-breasted nuthatch is the larger of the two and has blue-gray feathers and a white face and breast. Males sport a dark black cap. Its smaller cousin, the red-breasted nuthatch, has the same bluish feathers but sports a reddish-brown or chestnut-colored breast. It also has a striking black streak through its eye with a white eyebrow above. Both birds are permanent, year-round residents of Wisconsin and are familiar customers at birdfeeders everywhere in winter.

Nuthatches are classified as songbirds, but they don't seem too musically inclined. Their song, if you can call it that, is a loud, nasal "ank, ank" that always reminds me of a toy horn being squeezed. Like chickadees, nuthatches are friendly birds and are rarely spooked away by people watching them at the feeder. They were named by early European settlers because they reminded them of similar birds back in the old country called nut "hacks." True to their name, nuthatches do indeed hack open nuts and seeds with ease. They wedge the nuts or seeds into tree bark crevices where they whack them open with their hatchet-like bills.

For such little birds, nuthatches lay claim to huge territories of up to thirty acres, which they defend during the mating season in January or February. They can be fun to watch as they perform their elaborate courtship rituals. The male nuthatch begins by singing a monotonous "wick-a wick-a wick" song over and over for hours on end, until a female finally shows up—probably just to shut him up. Once paired, the happy couple spend days chasing each other around and around, up and down nearly every tree in the forest. After exhausting themselves with their courtship displays, the female finally selects a natural cavity in a tree and lays about eight eggs. Even at the nest site, nuthatches act in peculiar ways.

One of their odd habits, called "sweeping," occurs when they wipe their bill back and forth, as if cleaning it off, on the tree bark right outside the entrance to their nesting hole. Sometimes the sweeping is done with an insect in their beak and is repeated over and over again, often as long as fifteen minutes at a time. Nobody knows for sure why they perform this curious task, but it may be to warn or repel their archenemies—squirrels and woodpeckers.

If they're in your neighborhood, nuthatches are easy to attract to the birdfeeder. I have both white-breasted and red-breasted nuthatches at my feeders and they seem to get along fine, even feeding together at the same time. For some reason, they don't tolerate one of their own kind, however, and chase others of the same species. Nuthatches love to eat sunflower seeds and suet, but can be messy eaters. They often hop right into the middle of the feeder and thrash the seeds back and forth, spilling most of them before they choose just the right one to carry away. Although they usually fly to the nearest tree to crack the seed open and eat it, they are also known to stash seeds by stuffing them into bark crevices, coming back for them later. In the wild, nuthatches eat caterpillars, beetles, spiders, flies, and insect eggs and larva. They especially like to eat harmful forest pests such as tent caterpillars and gypsy moth larva, much to our benefit.

Few birds are as much fun to watch as the friendly, energetic nuthatches. Winter is the best time to watch as they begin to perform their bizarre mating rituals, hopping up and down tree trunks. After a few moments of watching these little clowns of the forest, you'll know why they're called the "upside-down" birds.

WHITE PINE
KING OF FOREST

"Ever eat a pine tree? Some parts are edible."

—Euell Gibbons

Remember those old TV commercials for breakfast cereal featuring well-known naturalist Euell Gibbons? I don't know if ole Euell ever sold much cereal with these corny pitches, but he did enlighten many of us to some of the wild edibles we never thought of as food before, including white pine.

For centuries, Native Americans did indeed eat white pine, or at least parts of it. The tree's inner bark, made up mostly of sugars and starch, was ground into flour and cooked with meats such as venison. White pine needles were chopped up finely and brewed into an aromatic tea rich in vitamins A and C. Although rarely used as food nowadays, white pine bark extract is still used in several cough remedies and is still classified officially as a drug in this country.

The eastern white pine is a beautiful tree with graceful, long branches and feathery needles. The tree usually grows sixty to eighty feet tall and is found throughout the Great Lakes region, including Wisconsin. One huge white pine growing in the Brule River State Forest was found to be 151 feet tall with a trunk circumference of almost 18 feet. At one time, giants such as this were commonplace throughout most of northern Wisconsin. The white pine was king of the forests from the 1840s to 1910, when at least a billion board feet of lumber were sawed from these seemingly inexhaustible forests.

Wisconsin's history is rich with stories about lumberjacks who conquered the northern forests with axe and saw and helped build the burgeoning port cities, including Chicago and Milwaukee. The lumbering era also produced tall tales about folk heroes such as Paul Bunyan, who according to legend was so large that he could fell an entire forest with one swoop of his mighty axe.

Of course, Paul Bunyan was just a mythical character, but the destruction of northern white pine forests was only too real. This man-made disaster of cutting, slashing, and burning left a landscape of charred and eroding soil from which the white pine has never recovered. Although white pine is still used in landscaping backyards and is a popular Christmas tree, the glory days of lumbering are over.

Today, when you go to the lumberyard to buy a few two-by-fours,

JIM McEvoy

9

they most likely are Douglas fir or southern yellow pine imported from the southern and western states.

Although white pine may no longer reign as king of the forest, they still stand tall as guardians, marking the gateway to the northern forest country. Where exactly the true north begins is the subject of some controversy between many city chambers of commerce, all of whom claim their town to be the "true" beginning of the northwoods. Next time you drive from the southern part of the state, watch for where the white pines start to appear on the horizon. This is what botanists call the "tension zone," an area that includes both northern trees such as white pine and southern hardwood trees. If you follow this line through the entire state it follows a massive S-shaped curve all the way from the northeastern counties to those of the northwest.

Although most all the virgin white pine forests have long been removed, you can still see some huge second-growth pine forests in the northern part of the state and even as far south as Sheboygan County, along Lake Michigan.

The king of Wisconsin's forests may never be royalty again, but let's hope that this stately and beautiful native tree remains a part of our landscape and continues to guard the gateway to the north for generations to come.

HIGHBUSH CRANBERRIES
NATURE'S SOURPUSS

Winter is the best time of the year to harvest cranberries. But where could anyone find fresh cranberries in the middle of winter, when all the cranberry bogs of northern Wisconsin have long since frozen over?

Try looking along stream banks or in lowland woods and marshes almost anywhere in the state. There you'll find a tall shrub or small tree with bright red berries hanging in clusters, called "highbush cranberry." No doubt you've seen this unique tree many times on one of your hikes in the woods or in a ditch along the roadside. It's easy to spot, especially in winter when its cheerful red berries stand out like tiny Christmas ornaments in the snowy woods.

Perhaps you've wondered why these juicy, delicious-looking berries were still hanging from their branches in winter when all the other wild fruit had long since been eaten by birds and mammals. The reason is that highbush cranberries do not ripen until they have been frozen several times. Only in late winter do they become sweet enough to eat, even for woodland birds and mammals. Occasionally I'll pick a couple berries to nibble on, but even when ripe they're really too sour to eat many fresh. Highbush cranberries are not related to the more familiar bog cranberries, but they do have the same bright red, cherry-like fruit and the same acidic flavor that can make you pucker up when you take a bite.

Although highbush cranberries are easy to identify in winter, there is a look-alike plant that has escaped cultivation and now grows wild in the woods, called Guelden rose, snowball bush, or European highbush cranberry. Its fruit is usually much too bitter to eat, even in late winter when it has ripened. Both European and American highbush cranberries have been used for centuries, not only for food but also for medicinal purposes. The tree's bark and berries have been used over the ages to treat everything from the whooping cough to mumps. Chaucer, a fourteenth-century poet, mentions highbush cranberry as a healer of scurvy due to its high Vitamin C content. He listed it among the plants that "shal be your hele" and encouraged others to "picke him right as they grow and eat hem in."

A few years ago I decided to "eat hem in" by trying a highbush cranberry jelly recipe I found. Even though my previous cooking expertise was pretty much limited to grilling hamburgers and making Jell-O, I decided to give it a try, anyway. After picking about five cups of cranberries in a driving snowstorm, I brought them home, thawed them out, and washed them. My wife was a bit apprehensive about the whole project after I read her the recipe. I guess it was the part about adding some lemon peels to help suppress the foul odor of the cranberries as they were being cooked. After letting them simmer in pot for awhile, I crushed and strained the berries to get rid of the pits and skins. Then with a little (okay, a lot) of help from my partner, we added sugar and the miracle of Sur-gel, and in no time we had several pints of clear, bright red, grade-A, authentic highbush cranberry jelly that tasted great.

There's always a special pleasure in harvesting, preparing, and eating something you can't buy at the local grocery store at any price. Whether it's fish, game, or even highbush cranberry jelly, it always tastes better right out of the wilds of Wisconsin.

EASTERN TIMBER WOLF
CALL OF THE WILD RETURNS

It was one of those rare wildlife encounters you never forget. A light snow had just started falling on a dead-still, late-winter afternoon when I saw him break cover. The lone wolf made a wild dash through the forest clearing, but slowed to a trotting gait about halfway across. At first glance, I thought it might be someone's lost German shepherd or maybe the biggest coyote I'd ever seen. But then it stopped and allowed me to get a good look. I could see its long, stretched-out, six-foot frame on a hefty eighty-pound body, oversized paws, and distinctive bushy cheek fur. This was no domestic pet, but rather the largest member of the dog family and one of the rarest animals in Wisconsin—the timber wolf.

At the time, I was a forest ranger stationed in the northern counties of Vilas and Oneida and thought I was a fairly seasoned outdoorsman. But coming face-to-face with a wild wolf, on foot in a remote wilderness area, was a humbling experience. Before disappearing into the forest, the wolf looked back and sent me a piercing glare that, nearly twenty years later, can still send chills down my spine. Later, I learned that wolves avoid people and have never caused even a single human death anywhere in the United States. I also discovered that my chance encounter with a wolf was very rare, since there were only thirty or forty wolves left in the northwoods at the time. I felt privileged for the experience.

Wolves are social animals that live in family groups called packs, with six to ten members. In January or February, the pack's dominant male and female breed and five or six pups are born in spring. Pups are born deaf and blind and weigh a mere pound, but at six weeks of age are ready to eat meat along with the adults. Studies conducted in Wisconsin revealed that wolves eat lots of mice, squirrels, muskrats, snowshoe hares, and beaver, but the majority of their diet (55 percent) is deer. Although often accused in the past of hurting deer populations in the northern forests, a single wolf can kill and eat only one deer every eighteen days or so. At this rate, all the wolves in the state together could bring down only about 900 deer a year, compared to the 300,000 deer harvested by hunters and 30,000 more killed by automobiles.

Wolves were once common in Wisconsin, although they were probably never numerous since they need large tracts of 50 to 150 square miles of wild land to survive. Before settlers started to level the forests for croplands in the 1800s, there were probably up to 25,000 wolves in the state. But raising free-roaming livestock didn't mix well with hungry wolves, so farmers lobbied the 1865 Wisconsin legislature to pass a five-dollar bounty on wolves. The program worked so well that by the early 1900s there were no wolves left in the southern two-thirds of state. Later, the bounty was raised to twenty dollars for adult wolves and ten dollars for any pups, because they were thought to be a threat to the growing popularity of deer hunting in the northern forests. By the time the bounties were finally lifted in 1957, the wolf had already disappeared from our landscape.

But the story of Wisconsin's wolves didn't end there. Through the protection of the U.S. Endangered Species Act in the 1970s, wolf populations increased in a few remote wilderness areas such as northern Minnesota. Although wolves never were reintroduced into Wisconsin by man, they came home anyway, crossing hundreds of miles of forests from our neighboring state. Today, wolves are increasing in numbers and may soon be removed from the endangered species list in Wisconsin. Despite this, the wolf's survival is a year-to-year struggle, even after more than 25 years of protection. Biologists found that about 35 percent of all adult wolves die each year, mostly due to its number one enemy—us. Despite federal penalties of up to a $10,000 fine and nine months in jail, some wolves are still shot, trapped, or killed on our highways.

In recent years, public interest in protecting wolf populations has been growing. Mail-order catalogs and department stores are bursting with wolf shirts, wolf books and videos, wolf jewelry, wolf paintings and sculptures, wolf computer mouse pads, wolves howling on classical music CD's, and on and on. Americans seem to love their wolves and seem to be willing to spend what it takes to keep them in the wild. In contrast to earlier times, when millions of taxpayer dollars were spent on bounties to get rid of wolves, many more millions are now being spent by federal, state, and private organizations, such as the Timber Wolf Alliance, in an effort to restore wolves to their former native regions throughout the country.

A few years ago, a wolf was found shot to death near Hazelhurst, the community where I lived when I first encountered the lone wolf in the wilderness forest clearing years ago. The wolf had been nicknamed "Lobo" by the biologists who had been radio tracking it since 1991. The loss of a single wolf in northern Wisconsin may not seem like an important event in the scope of our busy, mostly urban lives, but the loss seems tragic and senseless, nonetheless. Maybe it's because our ties to things wild and free are not as far away as we think. Or maybe it's the thought that without a change in society's attitude, our children may never get the opportunity to hear the eerie, lonely howl of a wolf, to experience that primordial chill down their spines in the wilds of Wisconsin.

OPOSSUMS
NATURE'S SMARTEST DUMB ANIMAL

"It hath a head like a swine, a tail like a rat and is of the bigness of a cat. Under her belly she hath a bag where she lodgeth, carrieth and sucketh her young."
—Captain John Smith Jamestown, Virginia, 1608

Although Captain John Smith's description of the opossum was written almost four hundred years ago, it is as accurate today as it was then. The opossum is surely one of nature's most unlikely-looking crea-

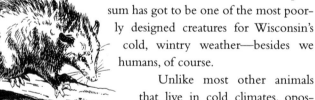

tures, with its bare feet, and a tail and ears that often suffer from frostbite. In fact, the opossum has got to be one of the most poorly designed creatures for Wisconsin's cold, wintry weather—besides we humans, of course.

Unlike most other animals that live in cold climates, opossums don't hibernate or dig underground burrows for shelter. They also don't know how to store food for the winter months, which forces them to roam the winter landscape in search of food. So how did an animal so ill-equipped to live in a northern climate manage to evolve here? The answer is simple—it didn't. Opossums were the original illegal aliens to cross the Rio Grande River many thousands of years ago, migrating from Central and South America. By the time Captain John Smith had arrived in the New World, the opossum had expanded its range northward into the New

England area, but would not make it into Wisconsin until the 1920s. Even today, this unlikely migrant continues to expand its range into Canada and even farther north to Alaska.

Opossums are not known for their high intellect. In fact, these slow-moving, dimwitted critters seem almost unaware of danger of any kind, making them an easy meal for predators such as fox, owls, hawks, dogs, and in the southern states, even man. Opossums live throughout Wisconsin both in rural and urban areas. They're mostly nocturnal, so we rarely see them except when they get into our garbage receptacles, and occasionally during the winter months when they're forced to look for food during daylight hours. Unfortunately, most of us get to see opossums only in various shapes and sizes plastered on our highways. When it comes to crossing roads, it seems opossums took lessons from skunks and are often victims of our automobiles.

Despite being dumber than a doornail and basically unresponsive to all threats, the opossum has continued to thrive and even expand its range on earth ever since the age of the dinosaurs. There seems to be two reasons for the opossum's success. They eat almost anything and they reproduce quickly. Come to think of it, these are basically the same traits that have allowed humans to be so successful.

In the wild, opossums eat grubs, worms, fruits, hornets, mushrooms, seeds, grass, carrion, or anything else that doesn't get out of its way or fight back. They're especially fond of kitchen scraps, pet food, and other snacks they can steal from our backyards. Over the years, wherever people have moved, opossums soon followed. Although opossums have the ability to store huge amounts of fat on their bodies (another similarity to man) they can also lose more than 45 percent of their weight over the winter and still survive.

Opossums are North America's only marsupials, and their reproduction system is nothing short of amazing. Female opossums are mature and ready to breed at six months of age. They give birth to their premature young after only thirteen days of pregnancy. Newly born opossum babies are only a half-inch in length, naked, and have stubs for limbs, making them look more like jellybeans than animals. Like their kangaroo cousins, baby opossums must crawl up their mother's furry belly to get into the pouch where they will attach to a nipple and complete their growth. The mother opossum often gives birth to two dozen babies, but has nipples to feed only thirteen of them. Because of this, some of the young are doomed to die of starvation at birth—a strange and seemingly cruel twist of nature that insures the survival of only the strongest young.

Another survival trick unique to the possum is faking death, better known to us as "playing possum." When threatened by a predator, the animal falls over, sticks out its tongue, emits a foul odor from a gland, defecates, and generally becomes something it hopes the predator will not want to eat. I once came across a roaming opossum near our home and attempted to coax the animal into its "playing possum" mode by cornering it as a predator might do. Instead of playing possum, however, the critter growled, raised the hair on its back, and showed me all of its fifty sharp white teeth, at which point I decided to end my experiment and take the word of others who have seen this behavior.

So the "dumbest" animal on earth has survived due to probably the "smartest" plan of all—eat anything and reproduce like crazy. No wonder they outlived the dinosaurs. Maybe they'll outlive us, as well.

BLACK BEAR
KING OF THE NORTHWOODS

My first encounter with a black bear occurred many years ago in the northwoods of Wisconsin. As a newly appointed forest ranger, one of my jobs was to work on illegal bear-baiting stations scattered throughout the Northern Highland State Forest, in Vilas County. Back then, a few unscrupulous hunters would haul bags of pastry, cookies, pies, and cakes into the forest and pile them on the ground near their tree stands. This is an unlawful baiting practice, and the wrappings of the pastry littered the woods for hundreds of yards when torn open by the sweet-toothed bears.

One day, quietly sneaking up on one of these illegal baiting stations, I heard what sounded like a hunter crawling up his tree stand. Finally, my patience would be rewarded with an arrest, I thought, as I rounded the corner of the trail to apprehend the violator. But, instead of a person, I came nose-to-nose with an enormous 500-pound black bear. Well okay, it was more like 250 pounds and several yards away. But for a kid from southern Wisconsin it seemed pretty big at the time. The bear turned and let out a few grunts and growls, after which I determined that it might be wise for me to retreat—fast.   Most likely, the bear was just as surprised as I was, and probably retreated in the opposite direction as quickly as I did—but neither of us looked back to see.

Black bears are impressive animals, our state's largest mammal. Adult males weigh about three hundred pounds, although they can grow much larger. A Wisconsin bear killed in 1963 tipped the scales at just over seven hundred pounds. Add to this their large non-retractable claws, long canine teeth, their ability to climb trees and run more than thirty miles per hour, and you can see why they are definitely the king of the forest. They have few predators except for man.

Despite their image as ravenous meat-eaters, bears actually eat mostly fruits, berries, nuts, insects, and vegetation. They do eat meat when they can get it, especially mice, squirrels, and carrion, but are not a serious threat to most other animals since they usually are not quick enough to catch them. Occasionally, bears search out easy meals at dumps, in garbage cans, farmsteads, campsites, and beehives, resulting in hundreds of complaints of bear damage each year.

Like other game animals, bears are hunted to keep their numbers in check and their populations healthy. Bears have always been hunted and trapped for their fur and meat, by both Native Americans and early settlers. In pioneer days, their fat or oil was also highly prized for frying grease, lamp oil, and as a liniment or ointment for stiff joints and muscles.

In Wisconsin, bears prefer to live in the expansive forested areas. Except for one month or so in summer, when males and females pair up for breeding, bears are solitary animals and tend to avoid each other. They move through their home range of up to twenty square miles along well-worn trails and often mark their territory by scratching the bark of trees or rubbing it with their head and back, leaving fur and scent behind as a warning to other bears.

Bears have not lived in most of the southern part of the state for almost a hundred years, now, but every few years one or two of them wander out of the northwoods and roam hundreds of miles from their normal range into the farming and urban areas of southern Wisconsin.

March is the time of year that most bears begin to stir from their winter sleep and leave their dens. Although bears fall into a deep sleep during the winter months, they don't actually go into a true hibernation and can easily be awakened if their den is disturbed. Mother bears have already given birth to their cubs in January or February, while they were in a semi-sleep. Despite being born during the coldest months of the year, the cubs come into the world with almost no fur on their tiny bodies, weighing only half a pound or less. Luckily, their snoozing mother has plenty of warm fur and lots of warm milk for them to suckle.

In early spring, bears leave their dens in search for food. Although they may not have eaten for almost four months, they don't seem to be very hungry and are still in good shape. Their first order of business, once out of the den, is to discharge their unique fecal plug and drink lots of water to get their digestive systems operating again. They then feed lightly on green sprouts, bark, buds, and other vegetation.

Although the black bear will likely never make a comeback in the heavily populated and farmed areas of southern Wisconsin, it's nice to know they're still the reigning monarchs of our northern forests and continue to be a part of Wisconsin's wild heritage.

RIVER OTTERS
THE ORIGINAL PARTY ANIMALS

"I hate them perfectly, because they love fish so well; indeed so much, that in my judgment all men that keep otter-dogs ought to have pensions from the King to encourage them to destroy the very breed of those otters."

—Izacc Walton, 1653, from The Complete Angler

Few other animals on earth like to eat fish more than river otters— except maybe fishermen. Because of this, otters have been condemned by mankind for centuries as vermin to be destroyed on sight. But our attitude towards this gentle, curious fur-bearer is changing. Yes, it's true that otters do like to eat fish. After all, nature has custom-built these animals as superb fish-catching machines with their sleek, muscular, torpedo-shaped bodies and powerful webbed feet for propulsion that few fish can match. Yet, contrary to popular belief, otters really don't deplete game fish populations in most of the rivers and lakes they populate. In fact, biologists have shown that almost a quarter of the fish they do eat are of the variety we really don't care to catch, anyway, such as suckers, mudminnows, and bullheads.

River otters were common throughout Wisconsin well into the late 1800s, but by the 1950s they were nearly exterminated from the southern half of the state due to polluted rivers, over-trapping, and habitat destruction from urban development and marshes drained for croplands. Today, otters are still rare in much of the state, but seem to be making a slow comeback as the water quality of our rivers and lakes continues to improve and more wetlands are restored.

Otters have dense, luxurious fur, and are still harvested in Wisconsin, usually in conjunction with trapping more common fur-bearers such as beaver and muskrat. Their populations are carefully monitored by biologists, and in most years trappers are limited to only two otter per season in the northern part of the state, and only one in southern Wisconsin. Occasionally, otters are seen in waters near urban areas, but don't seem bothered by all the attention they get. A few years ago, a family of otters lived in a heavily populated area along the Sheboygan River in eastern Wisconsin, where they learned to beg for handouts, providing some interesting entertainment for local residents.

But even in the northwoods, where otter populations are strong, they are never plentiful, since they need at least three square miles of good waterways to survive. Otters are known as long-distance travelers with a normal home range of sixty square miles or more. Because otters are on the go so much, searching for food from one stream to another, most of us are unaware of their presence even when they're right in our own backyard. Otters don't build permanent homes, relying on natural cavities or burrows of other animals in which to live. The longest they ever stay in one place is a few weeks in April or May when their pups are born and weaned.

River otters are members of the weasel family, but unlike their grumpy, quick-tempered cousins such as mink, skunks, and badgers, they have gentle and curious dispositions. Otters spend a lot of time just playing and frolicking in the water, wrestling, chasing, and teasing each other as a bunch of puppies or kids might do. But even when left all alone, otters can make their own entertainment by chasing their tails, sliding down riverbanks, playing with sticks and pebbles, or just swimming after and terrorizing fish for the fun of it. It's been said that if an otter can't have fun doing something, it simply won't do it, making them the original "party animals," without a doubt.

It's good to see river otters once again playing in the rivers and lakes we drove them from decades ago. We can hope that, by continuing to clean up our waterways and allowing some undeveloped areas in which they can live, these friendly, curious fur-bearers will continue to be part of Wisconsin's wildlife heritage for years to come.

LAKE STURGEON
KING OF THE FISHES

"On the white sand bottom
Lay the monster, Miske-Nahma
Lay the sturgeon, King of Fishes"

—*Song of Hiawatha,* Longfellow, 1855

They look like something right out of a Hollywood "Jaws" movie, a monster fish that can grow to a fantastic size, with a sleek, torpedo-shaped body and a shark-like tail. The ancient-looking lake sturgeon has no scales but a leathery hide covered with bony plates of "armor," making them look even more menacing.

Despite their fearsome appearance, sturgeon are all bulk and no bite, since they don't have any teeth. Sturgeons spend most of their time feeling and tasting the bottom of lakes and streams with their mustache-like barbels or feelers that hang down from their mouth. When they find a tasty snack such as a snail, insect larvae, worm, or leech, they lower their tubular mouth and suck it up and swallow it after expelling the mud and gravel.

Sturgeon are found throughout the Northern Hemisphere, with more than two dozen species worldwide. The largest is the Russian sturgeon of the Caspian and Black seas, which can grow to more than 28 feet in length and weigh 3,200 pounds. Here in Wisconsin, a smaller lake sturgeon is found in the drainage basins of the Mississippi River, Lake Superior, and Lake Michigan. The Lake Winnebago system alone has the single largest concentration of sturgeon in the world. Although not as big as its Russian cousin, lake sturgeon are not small fry, either. A sturgeon caught in 1953 weighed 168 pounds, was more than seven feet long, and estimated to be 82 years old.

Lake sturgeon are ancient fish with an impressive evolutionary history. Fossil records show the sturgeon to be swimming the earth's waters almost a hundred million years ago, just about the time the last dinosaurs roamed the landscape. Early Native Americans, including the Winnebago and Potawatomi, speared them through the ice much the same as today's fishermen do.

Commercial fisherman in the 1860s considered sturgeons a nuisance because they broke their nets intended for smaller fish. If caught, sturgeons were killed in large numbers and stacked on the shore like firewood to rot. But by the mid-1870s, fish processors had discovered the value of sturgeon eggs as caviar. They also extracted a high-quality gelatin from the fish's swim bladder, called isinglass. From then on, the sturgeon was considered to be a valuable catch, and by 1900 the species was nearly exterminated due to over-harvesting.

Thanks to modern fish management, the lake sturgeon is making a slow comeback, especially in the Winnebago system where a short spearing season is allowed each February. In many other waters, however, the lake sturgeon is still considered rare and is on the watch-list of threatened species in Wisconsin. Sturgeon have had a difficult road to recovery since the early 1900s, partially because of polluted spawning streams, but also due to its own s-l-o-w reproduction system. Female sturgeons are not mature enough to lay eggs until they are 25-years old. Even then, they spawn only every four or five years.

Slowly, but surely, Wisconsin's own living fossil, the lake sturgeon, is making a comeback. With a little help from us, the sturgeon may one day again reign as "King of the Fishes."

SHREWS
NATURE'S SMALLEST MAMMAL

In the story of *Gulliver's Travels*, when Gulliver was marooned on the island of Brobdingnag, he found himself the tinniest living being in a land filled with giants. Such is the fate of the world's smallest mammal—the common shrew. Many shrews are no bigger than the tip of your thumb, and tip the scales at only a fraction of an ounce—about the weight of a thin dime. Like Gulliver, shrews really do find themselves living in a land of giants.

At first glance, shrews look a lot like mice, with their long, pointed snouts, but are actually members of an order of mammals called Insectivora, so named because they eat insects and other animal matter. Like moles, shrews spend a lot of time underground and have the same kind of velvety fur that allows them to go forward or backward easily in their tunnels. Because they spend so much of their lives in darkness, the shrew's vision is very poor. Their tiny, beady eyes are almost useless except to help them distinguish light from dark.

Pound for pound, or rather ounce for ounce, shrews are probably the fiercest little animals on earth. Unlike mice and most other rodents that eat mostly seeds, grain, and vegetable material, shrews are meat-eaters. They prefer to eat insects, earthworms, snails, spiders, salamanders, and other small creatures. Shrews, with their sharp, pointed teeth, are aggressive hunters. They don't hesitate to attack and kill mice and voles that are often more than twice their own size. Some species, such as the common short-tailed shrew, produce a poisonous saliva from a gland in their mouths. When they bite small mammals, the poison causes paralysis of the heart and lungs, eventually causing death similar to that caused by the venom of poisonous snakes.

Shrews are extremely high-strung, super-active animals that are in nearly constant motion, searching for food both night and day. Since they don't hibernate or even sleep much, even in the dead of winter, they must remain active, tunneling under the snow looking for dormant insects or mice to eat. To fuel their high metabolism and keep from freezing or starving to death, shrews must eat nearly their own weight in food every day. This would be like a fifty-pound youngster eating two hundred hamburgers a day. When food is in short supply, shrews will even eat their own droppings to get every last nutrient out of their meals.

Shrews are very abundant in Wisconsin, found in nearly every forest, field, and backyard in the state. We rarely get a chance to see them, however, since they spend most of the day in their underground tunnels or under the leaf litter, coming to the surface only to hunt under the cover of darkness. Shrews are solitary animals, preferring to live alone except occasionally during the breeding season which begins in January and February and continues through the spring and summer. Females build nests under woodpiles or logs and might have two or three litters of up to ten young each. In addition to helping aerate the soil with their constant digging, and eating harmful insects such as grubs and other pests, shrews are important to the survival of many other creatures. They are eaten in large numbers by owls, hawks, weasels, snakes, and skunks.

Other predators such as fox and coyote also kill shrews, but often do not eat them because of their foul, musky odor. Domestic cats and dogs won't eat them either, although, as most pet owners can attest, they like to catch them and deposit them on their owner's doorstep, for some reason.

Even if a shrew is lucky enough to survive all its predators, the bone-chilling cold of winter, and the constant threat of starvation, this nervous little animal still wears itself out quickly. Most shrews live for only a few months, and those which reach the ripe old age of fifteen months usually perish anyway. The shrew's teeth, unlike those of rodents which continue to grow throughout their lives, simply wear out, making it impossible for the shrew to catch and eat its prey, eventually leading to starvation.

Despite their short life-span, shrews are believed to be some of the oldest living animal species in the world, probably among the first true mammals to walk on the earth. Fossils of shrews at least 54 million years old have been found in North America. These tiniest of all mammals have survived the test of time in the land of giants, be they dinosaurs, woolly mammoths, or modern man. ▲

February

February is usually the snowiest month of the year in Wisconsin, and the full moon is aptly called the "snow moon." Although winter's cold and ice still grip the landscape, the sun shines a little brighter and longer with each passing day, causing icicles to grow as the snow melts and refreezes, over and over.

Groundhog Day is celebrated on February 2nd. However, you're not likely to find any Wisconsin groundhogs, better known as wood-chucks, up and about this early in the season, since they are still in deep hibernation in their underground burrows. Occasionally, however, the warm winter sun is enough to awaken raccoons, skunks, and other light sleepers who leave their dens in search of a late-winter snack.

Backyard bird-feeders are exceptionally busy places in February, when most of the wild seeds and fruits have been either eaten or buried deep beneath the ice and snow. The familiar *fee-bee* calls of black-capped chickadees can be heard in the forests as they fly from tree to tree searching every branch and twig for insect larvae or eggs.

By the end of this shortest month of the year, spring could be just around the corner, unless of course the groundhog sees his shadow. If so, we must endure another six weeks of winter, according to legend.

CHICKADEES
BLACK AND WHITE COTTON BALLS

"Why, pardon me . . . my little chickadee."
—W.C. Fields

Remember this old one-liner that W.C. Fields used in his classic movie of the 1930s in an attempt to woo his lady friend? The cute chickadee has always been associated with beauty, and is possibly the most universally liked bird of all our feathered friends. Their cheerful chicka-dee-dee call and friendly disposition can melt the heart of even the most diehard grouch.

Few can resist watching the antics of these energetic little birds as they hop, jump, and flit through the woods or ply the backyard feeder

24

in their relentless search for food.

Chickadees are one of our smallest birds, a fully-grown adult tipping the scales at a mere third of an ounce, about the weight of three pennies. They are so tiny that you could mail three chickadees for the price of single postage stamp—if you could figure out how to get them into an envelope.

Chickadees are common throughout Wisconsin, especially in forested areas where they can find nesting holes in trees in which to raise their young. Chickadees are rarely seen alone, since they prefer to flock together for safety and feeding. When not at your feeder, gorging themselves on sunflower seeds and suet, chickadees roam the woodlands in search of insects, seeds, spiders, pupae, and other snacks. If you listen carefully, you can hear members of the flock keep in touch with each other with a regular, soft *tseet* locator call. If they get separated from the flock or want to attract another chickadee, they use the familiar, loud *fee-bee* call. You can easily imitate this call by whistling through your teeth and get them to answer. Chickadees seem almost fearless of people and are easily taught to feed out of your hand, if you are patient. A few years ago, while bow-hunting, I even had a chickadee perch on the shaft of my arrow and another land on my hat as I was sitting in my tree stand.

Unlike most other birds their size, most chickadees don't migrate in autumn, although some will move farther south from their northern range during a particularly cold winter. The ability of the tiny chickadee to survive the subzero temperatures and cold, biting winds of winter seems impossible, but their secret to survival is also what makes them so cute—lots of fluffy down and feathers to keep them warm. Like us, chickadees shiver when they get cold to help keep their bodies warm. In fact, their chest muscles start quivering as soon as the temperature drops below 65 degrees. In addition, chickadees spent almost all their daylight hours searching for food to fuel their high-speed metabolism. With a heartbeat of 650 per minute and a normal body temperature of 109 degrees, this is quite a feat. At night, chickadees flock together and roost in sheltered areas such as conifer branches or in the hollows of trees. They are also able to lower their body temperatures during the coldest periods of the night to conserve energy.

Thanks to the chickadees' visits to our backyard bird-feeders, Wisconsin winters seem less bleak. Nothing cheers us up in the dead of winter more than these black-and-white cotton balls that seem to bring the joy of life wherever they roam.

SNOW GEESE
WHITE TORNADOES FROM THE ARCTIC

You could see them miles away against the dark, overcast skyline of a cold autumn day near Horicon marsh. Out of the gray clouds they came like a blizzard of living, breathing snowflakes falling from the sky—snow geese. Not just a few dozen or a few hundred, but thousands of them, all descending on single corn-stubble field on a hillside far away. By the time I caught up with them, the birds were already circling above the field, wave after wave of geese breaking away from the flock and flying lower and tighter circles towards the earth, like a giant white tornado. Gradually, as they found an open spot on which to land, they set their wings and disappeared into the flock of geese already blanketing the field like snow drifts.

Snow geese are nearly all white except for the black tips of their wings and their pink bills and feet. As you might guess from their name and color, snow geese are birds of the Arctic tundra area of northern Canada and Alaska. They're often seen in mixed flocks along with blue geese, which have a white heads and necks, but bluish gray plumage over the rest of their bodies. Up until 1972, the blue goose was thought to be a separate species, but most biologists now believe they are merely a dark phase of the snow goose.

Because snow geese live and nest so far from civilization, not much was known about them until recently when information was gathered from Inuit tribes. Summers are short in the Arctic and snow geese must nest quickly to take advantage of the relatively warm weather. They build their nests by scratching out a slight depression on the cold ground of the tundra and lining it with grass and down from their bodies. Both parents take turns incubating the seven or eight eggs. They watch over the newly hatched goslings as they feed on the abundant insects that fill the skies during the brief tundra summer. By the middle of September, the young geese have switched over to their parents' almost completely vegetarian diet of bulrushes, cordgrass, cattails, and other plants. They have also grown their new flight feathers by then, and are ready to join the long migratory journey south for the winter.

Snow geese are strong fliers and can cruise at fifty miles per hour at very high altitudes, usually from two to five thousand feet. Most of the snow geese we see here in Wisconsin arrive in October. They come from the James Bay area following the Mississippi-Great Lakes flyway south to their wintering grounds along the Gulf Coast of Louisiana and Texas. In spring, they will return north, using the same migration routes, and can be seen here usually by late March. Although snow geese are considered the most abundant of all geese in North America, we really don't get a chance to see many of them. Unlike their familiar cousin, the Canada goose, snow geese are powerful, long distance fliers and many flocks simply fly nonstop right over Wisconsin on their way to warmer climates. Good places to watch for them in spring and fall would be along the Mississippi River, Lake Michigan shoreline, or around the Horicon area in Dodge and Fond du Lac counties.

The sight of thousands of bright white, honking, gabbling snow geese set against the dark gray sky that cold autumn day long ago at Horicon Marsh was one of those watchable wildlife moments I'll never forget. Although goose hunting season was open and I did have a hunting permit for the Horicon zone, I never did try to get close enough for a shot. Instead, I gave these long-distance travelers from the Arctic the opportunity to rest and feed while I merely enjoyed the natural spectacle unfolding around me. There would be other days and other geese to hunt.

On the drive home that night, with the sound of goose music still ringing in my ears, I contemplated my empty game bag with nothing to show for my efforts except the memory of my close encounter with the white tornado from the Arctic. It was a successful hunt, after all, in my book.

CROWS
BIRDS OF A FEATHER FLOCKING TOGETHER

"If human beings wore wings and feathers, very few would be clever enough to be crows."
—Henry Ward Beecher, 1813-1887

The common crow is probably the most recognized bird in Wisconsin, found everywhere from rural farm fields to urban parking lots. My association with crows started back in the 1960s when my brother and a friend snatched a young crow from its nest to raise as a pet on our farm in Manitowoc County. Like most such ventures started by young boys, Mom ended up doing most of the work, looking after the young nestling and keeping it warm and fed until it was able fend for itself.

We named our crow "Max" or "Maxie," depending on whether you thought it was a he or she (it's nearly impossible to tell with crows). The crow lived uncaged with our family for nearly three years, during which time it became sort of an avian celebrity in its own right. Maxie was featured regularly in the local newspaper and became a true town character in the city of Kiel back in the 1960s. The crow was featured twice in the Milwaukee Journal and was even filmed by a Green Bay television crew for an evening news story. Although all this fuss over a "common" crow seems a bit unlikely, I swear it's all true—or I'll eat crow!

Unlike most other birds, crows have the ability to mimic the sounds of birds, animals, and even humans. Like parrots, crows have a complete set of voice muscles and they're often heard imitating other birds in the wild. Our pet crow learned to say his name and dozens of other words. Unfortunately, Max seemed to learn and repeat profanity best, issuing phrases such as, "gosh darn it," "please be quiet," and "go to heck." Well, something like that, anyway.

Crows are birds of a feather and for most of the year they flock together. But in spring they begin to pair up for the breeding season. Both parents work on building a nest, which is made of large sticks and perched high in an evergreen tree. Both parents take turns incubating the eggs and helping to feed the young. As we found out with Max, baby crows have enormous appetites and, like human babies, are not shy about crying out loudly when they want to be fed.

In the wild, crows will eat just about anything, but are especially fond of insects and grains, which makes them both friends and foes of the farmer. Max pretty much fed himself and became our best mouse catcher around the farm, much to the disgrace of our lazy cats. Like hawks and owls, crows disgorge pellets of undigested food such as fur and bones.

When Max was fully feathered, he often left the farm to fly with other crows, but always came back home each evening to his favorite perch just outside our house. By the fall of his first year, Max decided to visit the nearby city of Kiel, about a mile away—as the crow flies, that is. During the next two years, Max probably visited every backyard in the city and became nearly a permanent fixture at the local elementary school, his favorite hangout. He seemed to enjoy playing with children on the playground, even allowing the smaller children to pick him up. When classes started again in fall, Max would alight on the windowsills and watch the kids through the glass. Although not allowed in the school building, Max would eventually find an open door and hop down the hallways, sneaking a peek into all the classrooms.

After school, Max would hop along with the children down the sidewalks back to their homes, sometimes perched on their shoulders as they went. The next morning he was back at school, sometimes arriving by flying over the school bus. Max never did figure out the school schedule, however, and seemed puzzled by the children's absence during holidays and weekends.

Max, like many of the kids on playground, had a mischievous streak, and was known for his pranks and tricks. Occasionally, he would snatch hats, scarves, or mittens from the children and drop them on the school roof. Back at the farm, the crow's antics provided a wealth of entertainment for all the neighborhood kids and more than a little aggravation for the adults. The crow learned to pluck clothespins off freshly laundered clothing or walk with his muddy feet along the wash line. Max also seemed to be attracted to flower beds and would regularly help "thin" them out—a habit not appreciated by everyone. He also enjoyed flying off with nuts and bolts, making the job of farm machinery repair a real adventure.

Despite all his pranks, Max was usually welcomed by everyone in town. In the wild, however, crows have few friends and many enemies. One of the most formidable of the latter is the great-horned owl. Crows can often be seen mobbing an owl during the daytime to drive it out of their territory. At night, the owls mount a counter-offensive and raid the crow's roost and nests. Crows are normally very wary of humans, and for good reason. For centuries, we've poisoned, shot, bombed, dynamited, and trapped crows because we considered them vermin to be destroyed. This all changed in 1972 when the Migratory Bird Treaty between Mexico and the U.S. was amended and the hunting, trapping, and killing of crows became illegal unless they were doing damage to agricultural crops. This was reversed again in 1996, when Wisconsin passed new laws to allow an annual crow-hunting season once again.

Our pet crow's demise came when he was about two and a half years old. It came from the blast of a shotgun, but not from that of a hunter. Apparently, a neighbor did not find Max's antics as entertaining as did the rest of the community. Following the death of the celebrated crow, school children, teachers, and school officials all over town mourned his passing with many letters written to the local newspaper. The sentiment was so high that the newspaper editor wrote a front page editorial headlined, "Kiel Mourns Death" and a reporter for the Milwaukee Journal wrote of Max's passing with a special feature article entitled, "Mischievous Crow Shot, Kiel Children Mourn."

Today, most of us would agree that wild birds should be left in the wild where they belong, not kept as pets. Yet, somehow, the presence of Max the crow touched many people's lives and perhaps helped many of them to appreciate the natural world around us and the animals with which we share the earth. It's a legacy that most of us could only hope to achieve in our lifetimes.

Not bad for a "common" crow.

BALD EAGLES
SOARING TO NEW HEIGHTS

*"I would rather capture that old eagle
than a whole Yankee brigade."*

—Gen. Sterling Price, Confederate Army, 1863

It was the height of the Civil War when Wisconsin's 8th Regiment marched into battle near Cornith, Mississippi. Little did the Union troops know that the Confederates had already singled them out for the first attack in an attempt to capture or kill their mascot, a Wisconsin bald eagle named "Old Abe."

As the battle began, the eagle regiment of Company C rallied around Old Abe and fought courageously to the end. Luckily, early in the skirmish, one of the Confederate rounds of fire severed the leather strap that held Old Abe to his perch and he was able to fly high above the battlefield. Confederate sharpshooters attempted to blast him out of the sky, but Old Abe not only survived the battle but the entire Civil war. On June 26, 1864, the bird returned to Wisconsin with full military honors after serving three years in the Union army and surviving 36 battles and skirmishes. For the next seventeen years, the eagle led the easy life of a celebrity and even had his own room in the basement of the State Capitol until his untimely death during a fire in 1881.

Not many birds, or people for that matter, have ever achieved as much fame and historical significance as Old Abe did. Ever since the bald eagle was adopted as our national emblem by Congress, in 1782, this beautiful bird of prey has symbolized both the power and grace of the United States. Who would have guessed that by the time our bicentennial celebration began in 1976, the bald eagle would be an endangered species in most every state in the union, including Wisconsin?

The reason for the decline of this majestic bird included years of unrestricted use of pesticides such as DDT, which caused the eagles to lay thin-shelled eggs that broke in the nest. Cities, towns, farms, and summer cottages on lakes crowded out eagles from their former homes, especially in southern and eastern Wisconsin. The last known pair of nesting eagles disappeared from the Lake Michigan shoreline in eastern Wisconsin by the mid-1950s, never to return again. Even though several bald eagles are now sighted occasionally in this part of the state, most are migrating birds in search of open water for fish or some other prey and won't stay to nest.

Unfortunately, some eagles continue to be lost to shooting, despite the threat of a $20,000 fine and up to five years in prison. Adult bald eagles have the white-feathered "bald" head, white tail, and yellow eyes, making them easy to identify. Eagles less than four years old are mostly brown in color with brown eyes, making them victims of misidentification and the unfortunate target of some uninformed shooters.

But things have changed. DDT and other harmful pesticides are now banned. Eagles are laying thick-shelled eggs once more, and their nesting sites are being given special attention. Many Wisconsin citizens and conservation organizations are helping the bald eagle recovery by sponsoring the state's Adopt-an-Eagle program. Funds are appropriated to monitor individual eagle nesting sites. Bald eagle nests, usually four feet in diameter, are spectacular structures made of large sticks. Since they build a new nest on top of the old one, year after year, these nests can often grow to enormous proportions. One record eagle nest that eventually broke its host tree weighed more than two tons.

Most of us remember vividly our first encounter with a bald eagle in the wild, perhaps perched on a tall pine along a northern Wisconsin lake. If you haven't had the opportunity to see an eagle for yourself, winter is a good time to spot them as they congregate in open water areas, such as below dams, on the Wisconsin and Mississippi rivers in search of their favorite food, fish.

One popular bald eagle viewing spot in winter is the Prairie du Sac-Mazomanie area along the Wisconsin River. Everyone should have the opportunity to see the bald eagle in the wild. As John Denver sang in his "Rocky Mountain High" ballad, "he knew he'd be a poorer man if he never saw an eagle fly."

Thanks to many years of protection, bald eagles have continued to recover, and since 1996 are no longer considered a threatened species in Wisconsin. Who knows, maybe someday a pair of bald eagles might decide to nest along the western shore of Lake Michigan once again.

Old Abe would be proud.

BLUE JAYS
BULLIES OF THE BIRD-FEEDER

Remember that big bully back in grade school? You know, the mean, oversized kid that nobody could beat at any rough-and-tumble game like king-of-the-mountain on the snow pile? The one whose mere presence caused all the smaller and weaker kids to scatter, lest they end up being pushed, tripped, or given an icy face-washing in the snow?

Nature has its own version of tough guys, and in the winter world of birds the blue jay seems to relish this top-dog position. These big, bold, and beautiful bullies are always the undisputed bosses of the backyard bird-feeders. Other winter birds—cardinals, chickadees, sparrows, and juncos—seem to be able to feed in harmony together at the bird-feeder, but as soon as the blue jays make their appearance, all the others scatter for safety. Unlike most other birds that politely take one seed at a time to eat, blue jays fill their gullet with dozens of seeds and then fly away to hide them in secret stashes to eat later. Although they prefer sunflower seeds, blue jays can eat just about anything to survive. Depending on the season, their diet is mostly vegetable matter such as berries, wild seeds, and acorns.

Because of its sharp, powerful bill, it's been said that there's no nut too hard to crack for the blue jay. About a quarter of the blue jay's food is animal matter—beetles, caterpillars, even mice. Blue jays are also known occasionally to raid other birds' nests and eat their eggs or nestlings.

Despite all their bad habits, blue jays are still one of the most welcome birds to our backyards, probably because they are one of the most strikingly handsome birds in Wisconsin. Although they're year-round residents, we seem to notice them more in winter when their bright blue, white, and black plumage stands out against the wintry landscape. Blue jays are listed as songbirds, but they really can't carry a tune very well. Like their close cousins, crows, ravens, and magpies, blue jays can make a variety of noisy and raucous calls. They can even mimic other birdcalls such as the cry of a hawk, which comes in handy to help scatter other birds away from the feeder. Probably their best known call, and their namesake as well, is the loud, piercing, "jay ... jay ... jay" call, which they use mostly to warn other blue jays of a predator or a disturbance in the forest. Naturalist Henry David Thoreau once described the jay's call as "an unrelenting steel-cold scream; a sort of wintry trumpet, hard, tense frozen music, like the winter sky itself."

In late winter, the blue jay's noisy disposition suddenly turns to quiet whispers as spring courtship begins. By the nesting season, both males and females become almost speechless as they share incubation duties of the four or five eggs in their well-hidden nest. Young blue jay chicks are hatched weak, blind, and, as you could guess, naked as a jay bird. Later in summer and into autumn, blue jays join forces and form small flocks that feed together and take up their position as watchmen of the forest. Like their human counterpart men and women in blue, these "birds in blue" police their territory under a watchful eye. They become a living, breathing alarm system wired into every woodlot in the state. As soon as an owl, hawk, cat, human, or some other predator is spotted, they use their jay call to bring in reinforcements and often mob or chase the predator away. Anyone who's ever tried to sneak quietly into the woods to a deer stand or to bird-watch has no doubt had the experience of being discovered by the local blue jays, who usually announce their arrival to every other living creature within earshot.

As winter approaches, some of our blue jays gather together in larger flocks and migrate thousands of miles to warmer climates, while others decide to spend the winter in Wisconsin. Biologists are not sure why some decide to stay and others leave, but past migrations have often been spectacular. One such migration was recorded at an ornithological research station in Sheboygan County, where more than 2,500 blue jays were counted on single day migrating south along the Lake Michigan shoreline.

Blue jays may be the bullies of the bird-feeder, and their raucous calls may not be music to our ears, but our Wisconsin winters would surely seem a bit longer and certainly more dreary without these colorful, aggressive birds in blue to brighten up our backyards, parks, and forests.

BOBCAT
GHOST OF THE NORTHWOODS

You probably have read about wildcat drilling in Texas or heard about wildcat strikes by union workers, or maybe even watched a little Northwestern Wildcat college football on television, but chances are you've never seen a real Wisconsin wildcat. Despite nearly a half-century of roaming the fields, forests, and wild areas of the state, I have to admit that I've never actually seen a wildcat, better known as the bobcat, in the wild, either. Every year, there are always a few hunters lucky enough to catch a glimpse of one of these elusive ghosts of the northwoods, usually while sitting quietly on their deer stands in November. Bobcat sightings are rare even for people who live their entire lives in northern Wisconsin, since these secretive cats are almost completely nocturnal and spend the daylight hours hiding and cat-napping in brushy thickets, inside hollow logs, or under fallen trees. Like all cats, they are most active in the evening. They roam their territory every night to hunt for prey, but even then they avoid getting too close to houses, farms, or anywhere else where people might spot them. Usually the only evidence that they're even around is the fairly large round two-inch paw tracks they leave behind in the snow or mud.

Bobcats live in heavy forest cover, especially second-growth timber with lots of brushy areas, clearings, and wooded swamps for hiding places. Bobcats are still fairly abundant in the northern part of the state, but they once were common throughout Wisconsin, as well as most of the United States and Canada. Bobcats usually don't travel very far from their remote northern forest territory, but occasionally one will show up in the southern counties. The very first bobcat I ever saw back in the late 1970s was one of these rare southern wildcats. It was shot by a deer hunter on private land in the Baraboo hills and brought to the Devil's Lake State Park registration station for tagging and examination. Today, hunters and trappers must first apply for a permit before they can harvest a bobcat.

Bobcats are often described as looking like an overgrown tabby or tiger house cat, but they are about twice the size of a domestic cat. They can weigh twenty pounds or more and can grow up to three feet long. Besides their distinctive short, stubby "bobbed" tail and bright yellow eyes, bobcats have very wide faces with a ruff or long fur on their cheeks and pointed tufted ears. Bobcats have been trapped and hunted for centuries for their soft and yellow-brown spotted fur, which is used in the garment industry for coat collars and other trim. Bobcats once had a price on their head and were often killed on sight because people believed they would deplete game animal populations. Although there are reports of bobcats ambushing deer by jumping on their back from a tree and biting the jugular vein near the throat, this would be a rare kill for a predator as small as a bobcat. They may feed on deer that are sick, injured, or have died from other causes—such as being shot or hit by a car. More often, however, bobcats consume prey more their own size, such as snowshoe hares, cottontail rabbits, squirrels, voles, and mice.

Bobcats are loners for most of the year, except during the mating season in February and March. Although they are usually very quiet animals, bobcats can produce some high-pitched screams and low growls, especially during this time of year when the males are out and about, "tom-catting" around their territory, looking for females. Males stay with their mates only long enough to breed, and then they disappear. Females are left to find a suitable den site such as an abandoned fox hole or a depression under a fallen tree to give birth to her two or three kittens. Bobcat kittens are born complete with spotted fur, sharp claws, and ferocious appetites. Mother bobcat has her work cut out for her, suckling her young and later finding enough small game to feed her family. Young bobcats will stay with their mother until the fall season, but then leave to find their own territory.

Bobcats are one of the most beautiful and truly wild animals left in

Wisconsin. Thanks to their cunning and intelligence, they remain a part of our outdoor heritage. Who knows, maybe someday you'll be one of the lucky few who get a chance to catch a glimpse of these super-secretive wildcats. Until then, all we can do is keep watching and believing that these mysterious ghosts of the northwoods are out there somewhere.

WOODCHUCKS
THE SHADOW KNOWS

> *"How much wood would a woodchuck chuck,*
> *if a woodchuck could chuck wood?"*

This familiar tongue-twister is one of the many fanciful tales we've inherited down through the ages regarding the woodchuck, also known as the groundhog. Not only can a woodchuck not chuck (throw) wood, but it's probably misnamed as well. Early colonists were the first to call this animal a woodchuck, probably mispronouncing its Indian name, *wejack*.

The woodchuck is probably best known for its legendary, annual prediction of the arrival of spring. Every year on the morning of February 2nd, people throughout the nation—especially in Wisconsin and Pennsylvania—wait in anticipation to see whether or not the groundhog sees its shadow. According to folklore, if the groundhog casts a shadow, we will have to endure another six weeks of winter. If the morning sky is cloudy and the groundhog doesn't see his shadow, spring is nearly upon us. Of course, professional weather forecasters point out that the groundhog's predictions are correct only about fifty percent of the time. On the other hand, statistics show that meteorologists have about the same average.

Despite the groundhog's questionable reputation as a weather forecaster, hundreds of newspaper and television reporters from around the country flock to Pennsylvania to see Punxsutawney Phil, or to Sun Prairie, Wisconsin, to see Jimmy the Groundhog, and their predictions always make the local and national news on February 2nd. Not to disappoint the viewing audience, the groundhog makes his appearance right on schedule—with a little help from his owner and trainer, of course.

In the wild, woodchucks are rarely seen above ground in early

February, except during an unusually warm winter. Woodchucks in most parts of the country, including Wisconsin, would still be fast asleep in hibernation, deep inside their underground burrows. They wouldn't interrupt their slumber until a month or more after Groundhog Day, in late March.

The woodchuck is one of those animals to prove that fact is often stranger than fiction. Its mysterious, deep hibernation begins about the middle of November. After months of eating and packing on a half-inch of body fat (sort of like the holiday season for us), the woodchuck blocks the entrance to its burrow, coils into a ball, and goes into hibernation. As winter sets in and the soil begins to freeze around him, the woodchuck's body temperature drops from a normal of 90 degrees to a near-freezing 38. Even more unbelievable is the drop in the animal's heartbeat, which goes from 75 beats a minute to as low as four. During the winter hibernation, the woodchuck will lose thirty to forty percent of its weight—definitely one of the best overall weight-loss programs around. By spring, when the woodchuck finally emerges from its burrow, it has only two things on its mind—eating and finding a mate, not necessarily in that order.

Woodchucks are members of the squirrel family. They are strictly vegetarians and will eat just about any plant available. Because of its enormous appetite, the woodchuck often finds itself at odds with vegetable gardeners and farmers, making it a prime target for trapping, poisoning, and shooting. In addition, woodchucks are expert diggers, creating holes and tunnels throughout their territory, but they rarely do any permanent damage. Although guilty of eating garden and agricultural crops on occasion, woodchucks also eat thousands of weeds. In addition, their exceptional digging ability creates underground burrows for many other animals to use, especially cottontail rabbits. Woodchucks are protected in Wisconsin and cannot be hunted or killed, except by the owner of the land if they are doing damage.

Most of us rarely get to see woodchucks, since they spend nearly all their time digging underground tunnels or sleeping. The best time to see them is during the early morning or late afternoon when they come out to eat or sun themselves in open areas such as the edges of woodlots or the tops of rock and wood piles. Woodchucks may often be seen standing upright on their hind legs, similar to prairie dogs out west, to survey their territory or to get a better look at you. Although woodchucks prefer to be alone most of time, you might be lucky enough to see a mother with her four to six youngsters, called kits, playing around the burrow entrance in late April or May. As autumn approaches, the young will be forced to find their own home and dig in for the long sleep ahead.

Groundhogs may not be expert weather forecasters, and they can't chuck wood, either. But this unusual creature that sleeps for more than a quarter of the year is still one our most interesting animals in Wisconsin.

COYOTES
SONG OF THE WILDERNESS

I remember the first time I heard a coyote in the wild. It was late December and I had just reached the crest of a hill overlooking a large cedar-tamarack swamp where I had been bowhunting. As I paused to admire the bright orange sunset over the blue snow covered forest, I heard the loud distinct, "yip-yip-yip-owoo" call of a coyote. Instinctively, the hair on my neck raised and my heartbeat increased, even though I knew that coyotes are deathly afraid of humans and posed no danger to me. Soon, other coyotes joined in the howl-fest and, as darkness fell over the cold winter night, I could hear them yipping and howling as they gave chase to something in the forest below. As I trudged through the snowdrifts back to my car, I remember feeling thankful to be heading to a nice warm house and not have to face the fate of whatever prey the coyotes were after in dark, winter woodlands.

Coyotes don't normally hunt in packs like wolves, but occasionally will work together chasing deer or rabbits in relays as they travel the well-tramped deer trails in the deep snow. Although they do prey on weak and dying deer and occasionally fawns in springtime, most of their diet is made up of smaller mammals such as mice, ground squirrels (gophers), and especially rabbits. They also eat wild fruits, insects, frogs, fish, carrion, and just about anything else they can find to help them survive. A study done on the stomach contents of coyotes in Yellowstone Park a few years ago revealed an amazing assortment of items they had ingested, including string, rags, leather gloves, cellophane, rubber bands, tinfoil, shoestrings, rope, and banana peels. It's been said that a coyote will pretty much eat anything that doesn't eat him first.

Coyotes are members of the dog family and, with their black-tipped bushy tails, long muzzles, and erect ears, look similar to some of our domestic dogs such as the German shepherd or Siberian husky. Although coyotes grow only to 25-40 pounds in size, they often look bigger in winter because of their thick gray and reddish-brown fur, and are often mistaken for wolves in northern Wisconsin, especially with their piercing yellow eyes.

Coyotes prefer areas where woodlands are mixed with farms and homes and lots of brushy areas in which they can hide and hunt, giving rise to their "brush wolf" nickname. Because of their secretive habits, most of us rarely get a chance to see a coyote in the wild, even though they live in every state of the union except Hawaii. Unfortunately for many of us, our knowledge of coyotes might be based on the antics of Wiley E. Coyote of the old Roadrunner cartoons, rather than real life. Although portrayed as dim-witted bumbling boobs in cartoons, coyotes are said to be the most intelligent of all wild or domestic dogs. The proof may be in their ability to survive despite mankind's best efforts to exterminate them by shooting, trapping, snaring, poisoning, and running them down by snowmobiles, trucks, and planes over the last two centuries. Not only have they survived this onslaught, but coyotes have gradually expanded their range since the early 1800s, especially in urban areas of the east. As recent as the late 1970s, coyotes had completed their eastward expansion all the way to the Atlantic coastline.

Here in Wisconsin, coyotes have always been abundant in the northern forest areas, but are also now living in the more populated southern regions of the state, even on the outskirts of Milwaukee and Madison. As is usually the case when we expand our residential areas into rural woodlands, game officials receive more and more complaints about coyotes, mostly concerning coyote confrontations with our unleashed house cats and dogs. Wisconsin now has a year-round hunting season on coyotes, except in the northern region of the state during the deer gun season, and that is to protect the wolves that may be mistaken for coyotes by hunters.

Coyotes travel freely in family groups in winter and may cover up to eight square miles in their home territory. By late January or early February, adult pairs begin to breed and the pups from the previous year begin to drift away to set up their own territories. New pups are born in April or May and are cared for by both parents until they start to fend for themselves in late summer or fall. Although coyotes usually have five or six pups in each litter, life can be tough on top of the food chain. Only about half of coyote pups will survive to adulthood, and even then about seventy percent perish each year because of starvation, disease, being shot, or being killed along our highways. Much has been written about the evolution of an extra-large, half breed "coy-dog" in recent years, but research has shown this concern to be unjustified. Although coyotes can interbreed with domestic dogs and wolves, resulting in a hybrid that looks like a coyote, this is very rare. Even if they do interbreed, their offspring are incapable of further breeding. Coyotes instinctively fear and avoid wolves and dogs as much as they do humans.

Native Americans have countless colorful legends about the coyote. Sometimes, he's portrayed as a scheming scoundrel who lies and cheats, but more often he is revered as a divine being held in high regard by most tribes. One ancient legend explains that all forms of life, including man, pass through many worlds on this earth, but predicts one final world in which all will perish except the coyote, who is doomed to roam the earth forever—the last animal on earth. Who knows, if there is a last creature to survive on earth, it may very well be the cunning, intelligent, adaptable, Wiley E. Coyote after all.

CRAPPIES
ICE-ANGLER'S FAVORITE FISH

What's the most popular game fish in Wisconsin? Walleye? Muskie? Well, maybe, but in terms of the sheer number that actually make it to the frying pan,  it's got to be the crappie. Other than bluegills, more crappies are caught than any other fish in the state, especially in winter when they make up about 75 percent of all fish taken through the ice. When the cold, Arctic winds arrive and ice and snow cover our lakes, bluegills and bass become sluggish and feed less, but not the crappie. The frigid weather actually seems to increase their activity and appetites.

Both black and white crappies are found in nearly every river, pond, and lake throughout the eastern United States, but the black crappie is much more abundant in its northern range, which includes

Wisconsin. Both species have silvery-green bodies, although the black crappie appears darker in color because of the black splotches on its sides. The white crappie usually has more defined black bands on its body and is lighter in color, but the two can often be difficult to tell apart. If you really want to tell them apart and impress your fishing buddies, you can count their dorsal or top spines. Black crappies usually have seven or eight spines, the white crappie only five or six.

Crappies can grow up to eighteen inches long and usually don't get heavier than two pounds, although a state-record black crappie caught in Iron county tipped the scales at a whopping four pounds, eight ounces. Even though they're small in size, crappies can be fun to catch, especially by jigging a small minnow on light tackle through the ice.

Despite their popularity as game fish, crappies have always had a love-hate relationship with anglers and fish biologists. Back in the early 1920s, before man-made locks and dams controlled the level of the Mississippi river, the state conservation commission thought so highly of the crappie that it spent several years rescuing large numbers of them from the receding backwaters of the river. The fish were made available to the public to restock in other waters of the state. Within a few years, nearly every pond, lake, and river had reproducing populations of crappies, even in areas where they were not originally found, such as the streams entering Lake Michigan and especially in the lakes of central and northern Wisconsin. But the honeymoon between anglers and crappie was short-lived. Only 25 years later, the burgeoning numbers of the aggressive crappie began to affect the populations of other game fish in the waters where they were introduced. By 1949, even the Wisconsin Conservation Commission called crappies the "carp of the north" in their biennial report, and the love-hate relationship has continued ever since.

Crappies are prolific spawners and can reproduce quickly. One good-size female may lay up to 140,000 eggs during the spawning season in May and June. Males prepare nests in sand, fine gravel, or mud, and are notorious defenders of both the eggs and the newly hatched fry. In waters with a healthy balance of good-size predators such as walleye, bass, or northern pike, most of the tiny crappies are eaten by the larger fish and the ones that do survive quickly grow into the large crappies everyone wants to catch.

Unfortunately, in many of our over-fished lakes where most of the larger game fish are lacking, crappie populations can go unchecked, resulting in an explosion of undersized, stunted fish that nobody wants to catch. Since crappies themselves are predator fish, they can make the problem even worse by feeding on the fry of larger and more desirable game fish that eventually would have helped control their own populations.

Whether you love them or hate them, everyone seems to agree on one thing about crappies—nothing tastes better than a freshly-caught crappie taken though the ice out of a cold Wisconsin lake in winter. Their white, flaky fillets rolled in flour or cornmeal and pan-fried to a golden brown are enough to make your mouth water—maybe even enough to get us out of our warm, cozy houses and try some hard-water fishing ourselves.

WALLEYED PIKE
OLE MARBLE EYES

There's an old saying among anglers that ninety percent of all fish caught are reeled in by only ten percent of the fishermen. Well, at least that's what most of us fishing-challenged anglers believe, anyway. But when it comes to catching Wisconsin's most popular game fish, the walleye, this old adage may be a bit closer to the truth. Walleyes are secretive, finicky fish that are often difficult to catch without a great deal of knowledge and skill, or at least an occasional spurt of plain blind luck. Researchers have found that only half of all anglers who pursue walleyes are successful, and even then, they average only one walleye per fishing trip. Surveys have also shown that while it takes only about 75 minutes of fishing time to catch a bass, it can take up to five hours or longer to land a single walleye. Few Wisconsin fish are as highly prized and sought after as the popular walleye. Not many fish can claim the almost religious following they create and the near explosive emotional, political, and cultural fervor they seem to conjure up among anglers, fish biologists, government agencies, and elected officials nearly everywhere.

Walleyed pike and its smaller cousin, the sand pike or sauger, look similar and are often found in the same body of water, but the walleye is usually larger and always has the distinctive white tip at the bottom of its tail. Neither fish is actually a pike at all, but members of the perch family. The walleye's common name refers to its large, opaque, "wall-eyed" eyes. These glassy-looking eyes have a reflective layer of pigment in the retina that help walleyes see in low light conditions, especially at twilight and into the evening hours. When spotlighted at night, they even glow like cat eyes. Biologists have found that walleye can't detect color nearly as well as daytime predator fish such as bass or northern pike. Although they are somewhat color-blind and see the world mostly in shades of red and green, they do have one important, built-in advantage over other fish—they have excellent night vision and can stalk their prey in the evening hours when their victims can't see them coming. Because of their nocturnal habits and sensitivity to daylight, walleye usually stay in deeper and darker water during the day, then move into the shallows at nightfall, where they feed on smaller prey such as perch, minnows, worms, leeches, and aquatic insects. They also feed on overcast days, especially right before an oncoming storm front when choppy waves on the surface break up the light penetration into the water.

Walleyes were originally found in most of the larger rivers and lakes of Wisconsin, including Lake Winnebago, Green Bay, and the Fox, Wolf, and Mississippi river systems. Today, because of decades of stocking walleye fry and fingerlings from public and private hatcheries, they are found in more than a thousand lakes and in most rivers throughout the state.

Walleyes begin to move to their spawning areas very early in spring, usually as soon as the ice goes out from mid-April to early May. Some walleye are able to spawn on gravel bars or rocky shoals in lakes, if there is enough wave action to create currents to aerate their eggs, but most prefer to migrate up shallow rivers and streams to spawn. In some waters, such as the Winnebago and Wolf River systems, walleyes may migrate up to seventy miles upstream to find spawning grounds. Mature males, two to three years old and twelve or thirteen inches in length, are the first to arrive, followed several days later by females which are four to six years old and much larger at fifteen to seventeen inches long. A single large female can lay more than 35,000 eggs which are scattered on the rocky shallows of lakes and streams or the hard clay floodwaters of the Wolf River system. When the hatchlings emerge, 26 days later, they are left to fend for themselves.

Nearly everyone who has ever fished eventually tries his luck in landing "ole marble eyes." Through persistence and perhaps the sympathetic advice of a seasoned walleye fisherman, most of the ninety percent of us fish-challenged anglers eventually get at least part of our ten percent share of the walleye catch. Of course, a little plain, dumb luck can't hurt, either.

GALL FLIES
NATURE'S GOLDEN FISHING BAIT

At first glance, the goldenrod gall fly looks pretty much like any other run-of-the-mill housefly. Although sometimes called the peacock fly, it's really not very colorful and has only two dull brown spots to adorn its wings. It seems to have been named after its habit of raising and lowering its wings when walking, like a peacock fanning its tail while strutting about.

Gall flies are responsible for making those familiar ping-pong size bulges, called galls, found on the stems of some goldenrod plants. The insect is a member of the fruit fly family, which includes the Mediterranean fruit fly and other insects that can do serious damage to citrus groves in Florida and California.

The life of a Wisconsin gall fly begins in early summer when the female lays one egg on the stem of a rapidly growing goldenrod plant. In a few days, the egg hatches into a white, legless maggot or larvae, which immediately burrows into the center of the goldenrod stem and hollows out a chamber in which to live. The bulge or gall is formed when the maggot begins to give off waste products that irritate the plant, causing it to grow extra plant cells around it. Unlike its fruit fly cousins in the sunbelt, our native northern gall fly does not harm the goldenrod in any way and the plant continues to grow, mature, and flower normally.

In the dead of winter, when temperatures plummet and subzero winds howl out of the Arctic north, the goldenrod gall fly maggot stays toasty-warm inside its protective, insulated home. The thick pith of the gall may protect the insect from the elements, but it can't save it from predators, including woodpeckers and chickadees. The downy woodpecker knows the secret of the bulging stems of the goldenrod plant and chisels out a cone-shaped hole into the center of the gall to get at the tasty maggot snack.

People search for the gall fly larvae as well, to use as fishing bait. Before the advent of easily available over-the-counter bait at sport shops, every old-time fisherman knew that the tiny larvae inside the goldenrod galls were a top-notch live bait for pan-fishing.

In spring, as the sun warms the goldenrod galls, the larvae make their transformation from white maggots into adult flies. They get out of the gall through a tunnel they had chewed almost to the outside before settling in for the winter. When the larvae finally turns into a fly in spring, it must push this tunnel free of debris, which it does with a unique balloon-like bladder on the front of its head that inflates and deflates to clear the exit tunnel. Once on the outside, the flies do an elaborate mating dance to attract their mates and the whole cycle starts once again.

So, next time you come across a goldenrod patch, in winter or spring, search for the plants that look like they swallowed a ping-pong ball. If you see a tiny, crisp-looking round hole in the gall, you'll know that the fly has already emerged. If you see a larger, rough, funnel-shaped hole, it's a sure bet that the woodpeckers have beat you to it. But if you find a gall without any holes at all in it, it's time to go get your fishing pole.

SNOW FLEAS
SPRINGING INTO SPRING

You've probably heard of snowy owls, snowshoe rabbits, snow buntings, and snow geese, but have you ever seen snow fleas? They might sound like the figment of someone's imagination, but snow fleas are very real. Not only do they exist, but they are probably just out-side your doorstep in the backyard—by the thousands. But not to worry. Unlike their pesky blood-sucking cousins that may torment the family dog or cat from time to time, snow fleas are harmless and have no interest in pets or people.

Snow fleas are tiny, primitive creatures that belong to the most abundant insect family in the world, called springtails. For most of the year, snow fleas spend their lives hidden in the grass or under leaf litter, quietly feeding on decaying plants and animals. They are so small that they can barely be seen even under a magnifying glass. The only time snow fleas are really visible is when they appear on the surface of the snow in late winter or early spring.

I once gathered some snow fleas near my home and put them under a microscope to observe them. Because of their constant hop-ping, it wasn't easy to keep them in focus, but eventually I could clear-ly see why they are called springtails. They have two prongs on their tail area that bend under their belly and are held in place with hooks. When they release these hooks the prongs snap out like a mousetrap and flip them through the air.

A good time to watch for snow fleas is on a mild winter day or in early spring, when the temperature rises above freezing. Snow fleas emerge from the leaf litter at the base of tree trunks or along side of buildings where the snow has melted away. Look for snow that appears dirty or gives you the impression that someone sprinkled it with pepper. The tiny insects can create an impressive display when they emerge by the millions, literally blackening the snow.

Why snow fleas come to the surface of the snow is still a mystery. Whatever the reason, snow fleas spend most of the warm winter day hopping, mingling, and mating, before crawling back under the leaf litter by nightfall to avoid the freezing temperatures. Like so many other riddles of nature, the snow fleas' secrets remain to be discovered. ▲

MARCH
March

Spring is derived from an ancient Anglo-Saxon word for "rising." As March begins, the days become longer and the sun rises higher in the sky each day. Eventually, the length of daylight and darkness are equal, on March 21st, when the spring equinox arrives.

The first true harbingers of spring in Wisconsin make their appearance during the windy and often snowy month of March. Sandhill cranes are often the first to return to the still-frozen river bottomlands, followed by the familiar backyard favorite, the American robin. By the time the pussy willows have budded out, noisy redwing blackbird males are already staking claim to their nesting territories in cattail marshes.

Although March often roars in like a lion with heavy snowstorms and sub-zero temperatures, it often goes out like a lamb with much milder weather. The warm days followed by freezing nights of late March create ideal conditions for the sugaring season. Sugar maples are ready to be tapped for their sweet sap, which is boiled down to make delicious maple syrup. It's not surprising then that the full moon of March is called the "sap" or "sugar" moon.

AMERICAN ROBIN
WISCONSIN'S OFFICIAL STATE BIRD

"When the red, red robin comes bob-bob-bobin'along, there'll be no more sobbing when he starts throbbing his old sweet song."

—Frank Howard, 1883

Even when this old song was written to celebrate the return of the robins, the bird was considered the true harbinger of spring and a welcome sight after the long, dark days of winter.

Robins do seem to lift the spirits of us winter-weary northerners with their familiar "cheer-up, cheer, cheer, cheer-up" call we hear in our backyard in spring. Only male robins sing during the breeding season, to attract and court females. They also use this call to warn other male robins to stay out of the territory they've chosen to nest in. Chances are, no matter where you

47

live, you probably get a robin or two right outside your window, singing away day after day in early spring. Since robins like to sing before sunrise and continue on all day until after sunset, their old sweet song can turn into noise pretty quickly, especially if you like to sleep late on occasion.

While male robins are busy singing, females begin the real work of selecting a site in which to build a nest, usually in the fork of a tree but occasionally on an outside lamp fixture or a windowsill of a house. Female robins do all the nest building as well, using grass, mud, string, hair, and whatever else is available. She also does all the incubating, once her eggs are laid, and stays on the nest night and day

In his defense, the male robin does his share of work, as well, having to feed both the incubating female and the young chicks. No doubt you've watched robins hopping over your lawn in search of earthworms. It was once thought that robins could hear the worms in the ground because of their habit of cocking their head toward the earth. In reality, robins can actually see the earthworms near the surface before they grab them and pull them out.

Although born featherless, blind, and helpless, baby robins grow at tremendous rates, increasing their weight by a thousand percent in their first ten days of life. Once feathered, robin chicks are one of nature's cutest youngsters and have voracious appetites. Robin nestlings demand to be fed every five to ten minutes—a scenario familiar to any human parents who ever had teenagers in the house.

Even after they have left their nest, young robins are fed for several weeks on the ground by the parents. This is the time of year that well-intentioned people pick up the young robins, thinking they have been abandoned or have fallen from their nests. Some young fledging robins doubtless fall victim to the neighborhood cat, but most will survive and should be left alone to be taken care of by their parents.

Every year, robin sightings are reported in the middle of winter, and many of us see this as an omen of an early spring. In reality, these are just our "winter robins," the normal two percent that, for whatever reason, decide not to migrate south for the winter. Most robins do migrate to warmer climates, however, and don't return to Wisconsin until March or April from their wintering grounds along the gulf coast of Texas, Florida, or even as far away as Mexico.

Robins were named by early European settlers because the birds reminded them of the European robin. As it turns out, however, the American robin is not even related to its European counterpart, and is really a member of the thrush family. Robins were once considered an important food source for early pioneers and Native Americans, who used to hunt them. As late as the 1840s, market hunters were still shooting millions of robins for shipment to city marketplaces. Even John James Audubon, a noted naturalist, wrote of the delicacy of roast robin, which he described as tasting like woodcock.

Today, the robin is protected by Federal and State laws and is the official state bird not only for Wisconsin but also for Connecticut and Michigan. The robin has rebounded so well from the days of market hunting that it is now probably the best known and most numerous of all our native birds.

In addition to their natural enemies such as birds of prey, raccoons, and other predators, robins have created new hazards for themselves. Their habit of nipping off garden seedlings and gorging themselves on cherries and strawberries have not exactly endeared them to gardeners or to people who park their cars under the robins' perching trees. Despite this, robins continue to be welcomed into our backyards each spring and will no doubt be "bob-bob-bobbin along" in search of the perfect earthworm for many years to come.

SANDHILL CRANE
THE ANCIENT DANCE RETURNS

The early morning skyline was just beginning to turn pink as we scrambled into our grass blind deep inside the Sandhill Wildlife area in Wood county. In the distance, we could hear them coming—the unforgettable, rattling, prehistoric-like "garooo-oo-ah-ah-ah"...the call of the sandhill crane, described by some as sounding like an iron wheel grinding on a dry axle. Before long, a small flock of sandhills dropped through the rising marsh fog and set their wings to land on the mudflats we had baited with corn. The trap was set. Never having been so close to sandhill cranes before, I was amazed at their size. Standing four feet high with a wingspan of over seven feet, sandhill cranes can be impressive birds. As they milled about, picking up kernels of corn with their long beaks, we got a good look at their slate-gray plumage and the distinctive, dark-red bald patch on the heads of the adults. Some of the crane's feathers seemed stained with a rusty color that I later learned was caused by the ferric oxide in the marshlands they nested in.

Suddenly, one of the older cranes cocked his head towards our blind and used his sharp, bright orange eyes to focus on us, blowing our cover. With the warning call and the birds exploding in flight, it was now or never. We fired. Actually, it was more like a detonation, since we were not using shotguns, but mortar-type cannons that are supposed to shoot a net up and over the cranes. They would then be banded and released as part of a research project of the University of Wisconsin-Stevens Point. Unfortunately, one of our cannons misfired, sending the net sideways. In the end, we caught mostly the wind and a few very surprised mallard ducks.

Sandhill cranes are one of the very few wild birds to make a real comeback in modern times. Only a half-century ago, the very survival of these birds was in question. In 1929, wildlife biologist Aldo Leopold reported only five known breeding pairs of sandhill cranes left in the state. Even as recent as the 1980s, sandhills were still listed as uncommon in most of Wisconsin. But things seem to have changed dramatically in the last several years, thanks to legal protection and organizations such as the International Crane Foundation. Not only are thousands of sandhill cranes again flocking together in the large wildlife areas of central Wisconsin, they are also expanding their range and reclaiming many shallow marshes in other parts of the state where they haven't been seen for a hundred years or more.

One such area I've been observing is a river marsh near my home in Sheboygan County. Some years ago, I noticed a pair of cranes using the marsh for the first time, but they didn't actually build a nest there until after four years. Later, I learned that this is normal, since young cranes begin to pair up and look for nesting territory when they're about two years old but may not actually begin to nest and lay eggs until a few years later. Part of this long dating period, demonstrated every spring, are the elaborate sandhill courtship dances. The birds extend their wings, leap in the air, bow their heads, and strut around stiff-legged, all to impress their mates. If no admirer happens to be available, sandhills will sometimes dance to their own shadows.

Sandhill cranes prefer to live in large, isolated marshes and spend much of the spring looking for just the right one. Although the American robin is usually thought of as the official harbinger of spring, I always watch for the sandhill cranes, instead. They almost always come back to Wisconsin in mid-March, even if the marshes are still frozen and there's snow on the ground. Once they select the perfect marsh to make their home, they begin to build huge, bulky nests out of dead vegetation heaped up above the water line. Two mottled green-and-brown eggs are laid and incubated by both the parents.

Young sandhills eat pretty much the same things their parents do, mostly worms, grubs, insects, and seeds. As they grow older, they begin to use their long beaks to go after bigger marsh game such as frogs and crayfish. By late summer, young sandhills have grown nearly as large as their parents and are able to fly along with them to nearby farm fields to feed on waste corn and other grains left by harvesting. In late August, sandhill crane families start to flock together in the larger marshes. They begin to migrate south throughout September and October to their winter homes in southern Georgia and Florida.

In the Orient, cranes have been revered as symbols of longevity and an emblem of joy for centuries. After being absent from our landscape for so long, it's a real joy just to hear the sandhill's call echoing across the sky once again and see these magnificent birds perform their ancient dances in our marshes, just as they have for thousands of generations.

RED-WINGED BLACKBIRDS
SHOWING THEIR TRUE COLORS

After a long, cold winter, it's like music to our ears. Suddenly, overnight, nearly every cattail marsh in the state rings with the melodious "conk-cor-ree" song of the red-winged blackbird. No doubt about it—when the blackbirds are back, spring is just around the corner.

Red-winged blackbirds are often the first birds to migrate north into Wisconsin, usually right on the heels of winter in early to mid-March. The first to arrive are always the males, who each lay claim to an eighth- or quarter-acre of cattail marsh for themselves. Even though the snow and ice in the marsh hasn't yet melted, and the breeding season is still several weeks away, the males vigorously defend their turf. Male redwings are attractive birds, especially when showing off their colors on their displaying perches, usually the highest tree, bush, or cattail in their territory. After fluffing up their jet-black plumage, they arch their back forward and spread their wings to expose their brilliant red epaulets or shoulder patches lined with bands of bright yellow. Later, when the females arrive, usually around the second week in April, these aggressive male displays and loud songs become even more important in attracting mates and defending their territory against other males. Unlike their colorful mates, the female's plumage is mostly brown with light streaks, providing excellent camouflage for them to hide in the cattails, reeds, and grasses of the marsh.

Blackbirds are polygamous; a single male may pair with three or more females at a time during the breeding season. In May, the females begin to build their nests, either in the thick marsh grass or low to the ground in small shrubs and cattails. The nest is woven from coarse grass and lined with fine grasses inside. After the eggs have hatched, both the male and female aggressively defend the nest by calling out loudly and swooping down out of the sky to attack any intruder (man or beast) that dares to come too close. The parents are kept busy feeding their chicks mayflies, caddisflies, and other insects which are abundant in the lush, green marsh of summer. Eventually, the young fledglings leave the nest and flock together with other juvenile birds from throughout the marsh.

In late July or early August, after months of noisy activity in the redwing marsh, it suddenly becomes quiet and the blackbirds seem to disappear. This is the time of year when blackbirds begin to molt; they gather together in secluded areas of the marsh, quietly waiting for their new feathers to grow in. Later, usually in September, the blackbirds reappear again, this time in huge flocks as they gather in preparation for migration. As autumn approaches, their numbers increase as more and more of them join together in flocks of hundreds or thousands and perch on power lines and trees, and feed in newly harvested grain fields. Although blackbirds eat insects and weed seeds for most of the year, they can also feed on corn in the soft or milk stage, causing serious damage to the crop.

Blackbirds are in no danger of being driven off the planet by mankind anytime soon. Unlike many other birds that continue to be displaced by man's activities, blackbird numbers have actually increased over the years, thanks to cropland development, cattle grazing, and urban development. They are now abundant from Alaska to Costa Rica and are found in every state. Few other birds in the world can compare to the success of the aggressive blackbird.

Take a hike near any cattail marsh in late March and watch the colorful display of red-winged blackbirds showing off their true colors. Remember to listen for their familiar song, "*conk-cor-ree*"—spring is back.

STARLINGS
A EUROPEAN INVASION

It was a cool, crisp March day in 1890 when a small group of people interested in fine literature gathered at Central Park in New York City. But the reason for their meeting was not to read classical works or recite poetry, but to release sixty starlings which they had just imported from Europe. The goal of this somewhat overzealous group was to introduce into the United States all the birds ever mentioned in the writings of William Shakespeare. Within weeks of their release, the first pair of starlings built a nest and raised the first brood of "American" starlings—ironically, under the eaves of the American Museum of Natural History.

Although it doubtless seemed like a good idea at the time, the release of the European starlings quickly turned sour. These are very aggressive birds, and almost always try to push native birds out of any new territory they claim. Highly adaptable, they quickly began to expand their range into urban and farming areas across the country. Starlings were first sighted in Wisconsin in 1923, in the city of Milwaukee, and quickly spread across the state after that. By the 1940s, they had completed their westward expansion all the way to the Pacific Ocean, and by 1960 were beginning to outnumber native birds such as crows, robins, and grackles on bird counts around the country. In only seventy years, European starlings had not only colonized an entire continent but had increased their population from only a few birds in New York City to uncounted millions found everywhere today.

Despite their nasty habits and bad reputation, starlings are actually quite attractive birds. In spring, right before the breeding season, the male's plumage turns a glossy jet-black with iridescent flashes of greens and purples, contrasted against a bright yellow bill. In late summer, after

53

their molt, starlings grow new feathers that are tipped in white or tan, giving them a speckled appearance throughout the fall and winter seasons. Females and juveniles are more brownish than the adult males and usually have darker bills as well. Starlings, which belong to the same family as the famous talking mynah bird, can be clever mimics themselves. They often produce harsh metallic shrieks or whistles, but can also create pleasant melodic notes like true songbirds.

In their native home throughout Europe and western Asia, most starlings migrate south for the winter to the warmer climates of Africa and India, but in America many starlings don't migrate at all. A few starlings banded in Wisconsin were known to migrate as far south as Kansas, but the majority of them seem content to stay put. Many starlings merely congregate in urban areas where they gather together into large roosts to spend the winter. In many larger cities, such as New York, there may be up to 125,000 starlings in a single roost, creating health concerns for city officials and spawning an entire industry of urban bird-control companies. Despite the millions of dollars spent to deter starlings with fancy supersonic sound recordings, fireworks, razor wire, plastic owls, and expensive chemical repellents, this defiant and intelligent bird remains an urban problem everywhere.

Starlings are often called the "least loved birds" in North America, especially during the nesting season in spring. Although they need tree or building cavities in which to construct their nests, starlings never bother to carve out their own. I remember years ago watching a pair of flickers spend a week or two every spring, excavating a nesting hole in a basswood tree outside my boyhood home. In some years they were successful in getting off a brood, but usually starlings would move in, chase them away, and build their own nest inside. They will also steal nesting boxes from bluebirds and even remove the eggs and toss out the baby birds to take over a nesting cavity.

Starlings lay four or five bluish robin-like eggs which both parents incubate. Young starlings, with voracious appetites, are fed mostly insects such as grasshoppers and cutworms by the parents throughout the day. Although starlings are helpful to farmers and gardeners in spring by feeding on agricultural pests, later in the season they turn into destructive pests, feeding on grains and ripening tree fruits.

Along with the English sparrow and rock pigeon, the European starling is now one of the three most numerous urban birds in North America, and probably in most of the major cities of the world. Starling populations continue to grow, and they are expanding their range year after year. Perhaps that small group of New Yorkers who imported and released the first group of starlings in Central Park, for the sake of literature, should have done more reading themselves. It seems to me there's a story in Greek literature warning against opening Pandora's box.

SUGAR MAPLE
SWEETEST TREE IN THE FOREST

By mid-March the long, cold Wisconsin winter begins to soften and the days become a little warmer, a little longer, but are followed by cold, frosty nights. Soon the "maple moon" will rise over the horizon. No doubt about it, it's "sugaring" time again in Wisconsin.

Wisconsin's official state tree is the sugar maple. Also called hard or rock maple, the tree is found throughout the northeastern United States and Canada. In our state the sugar maple is often found growing in dense stands called "sugarbushes."

Sugar maples can be impressive trees, growing to heights of sixty to a hundred feet with trunks four feet in diameter. Because they are so common, the tree's five lobed leaves are familiar to most people, as are their helicopter-like seeds that spin and twirl as they fall to the earth. Sugar maples can live to the ripe old age of four hundred years, with two-hundred-year-old "youngsters" common in much of the state.

Although places like Vermont, Maine, and Canada are best known for their beautiful sugar maple woodlands, there are more than a hundred species of maples worldwide. As unlikely as it may seem, China and Japan are believed to be the center of the origin of maples. Japan alone has more than forty native species of maple, while North America has only thirteen or so.

To early American Indians, March was known as the season of the "maple moon." It was a time of celebration marking the end of the long, harsh winter and the return of spring. It was also the time of year for tapping maple trees and making maple syrup and sugar. Eyewitness accounts of sugaring methods by these early Americans are amazing. Without the aid of metal containers or pots, Indians were able to boil down the sweet sap in wooden troughs. This was accomplished by repeatedly heating stones red hot and dumping them into the trough to keep the sap boiling, an amazing feat considering that it takes forty gallons of sap boiled down to make a single gallon of syrup. Despite this slow method of production, Native Americans usually had plenty of maple sugar for cooking and drinks. When the European settlers first arrived, maple sugar was an important barter item, trading for European goods such as iron cooking kettles.

Modern maple syrup producers use stainless steel evaporators fired with propane furnaces, and collect sap in plastic bags hung on the trees. Occasionally you can still see the old-time method of buckets and wood fired evaporators demonstrated at nature centers or outdoor museums, where they recreate this interesting part of our heritage each year.

Unfortunately, most of us do not use real maple syrup these days. The popular brands of "maple flavor" syrup you pour on your pancakes or waffles are made mostly from inexpensive corn syrup or a mixture of ingredients, with an actual maple syrup content of perhaps two percent, or none at all.

A fun way to taste real maple syrup is to make your own—and you don't have to own a forest of sugar maples to try it, either. For several years, I tapped a silver maple that was growing in my backyard. Although I had only one tree to work with, it produced all the sap I could handle in most years, especially after I learned how to keep the robins and squirrels from sitting on my tap buckets and helping themselves to sweet sips of dripping sap. After collecting the sap, I boiled it down in makeshift cement-block firebox in the garden and finished the sap down into syrup on top of the stove in the house. A suggestion here is to be sure you have an understanding spouse before you attempt this, since the indoor evaporation process can leave a sticky film on everything in the kitchen. If you don't have time to make your own maple syrup (or don't want to threaten your marriage), you can usually buy real maple syrup at the local grocery store or at farmers markets, but be prepared to pay top dollar for this delicacy.

Wisconsin's sugar maples are valuable for many other uses beside maple syrup production. The tree's wood, exceptionally hard and strong, is used for making fine furniture, flooring, bowling alleys and pins, and is prime firewood. Even more important is the beauty that these trees provide in our local woodlands, parks, forests, home grounds, and city streets. Its hard to imagine an autumn drive through Wisconsin without the brilliant red and yellow leaves of the sugar maples to enjoy.

So, celebrate the season when the "maple moon" is upon us and enjoy some real Wisconsin maple syrup. It's "sugaring" time again.

WOOD SORREL (SHAMROCK)
NATURE'S OWN LUCK OF THE IRISH

Saint Patrick's day, which honors the beloved patron saint of Ireland, is celebrated on March 17th, the last holiday of the winter season. It's the time of year when just about all of us, Irish or not, get "a bit o' the green" in our blood. Soon, the warm spring rains will melt the last of the snowdrifts and the dreary brown landscape will once again sprout a green blanket of new grasses and plants. In Ireland, Saint Patrick's day marked the traditional beginning of the potato-planting season and was the day that farmers let their cattle out to pasture for the first time. Ireland is often referred to as the "Emerald Isle" not because of any precious stones but because of the country's beautiful and lush green landscape. Much of this greenery is owed to one of the best-known and beloved plants in the world—the shamrock.

Wisconsin is also home to several species of shamrock that grow wild in our fields and forests. One of the most common is the yellow-flowered wood sorrel. This small plant is found growing not only in forests, fields, and pastures, but also in our gardens and lawns, where it is considered more of a weed than a wildflower. Like all shamrocks, the wood sorrel has the distinctive clover-like, heart-shaped leaflets and a bright yellow flower with five petals. Although the yellow-flowered wood sorrel is a small plant, other species of shamrock can grow up to a foot high and have white, rose, or violet flowers.

The three-leafed shamrock became associated with Saint Patrick's day centuries ago when it was adopted as a religious symbol of the Holy Trinity among Christians. The shamrock is considered an omen of good luck, similar to a four-leaf clover, and has come to represent the Irish holiday itself. Many people still wear a shamrock on Saint Patrick's day, or at least wear something green to bring good luck for the year ahead. An old tradition calls for anyone caught not wearing a shamrock or something green on Saint Patrick's day to get a pinch from anyone who passes by, their assailant calling out, "green, green" to the nonconformist.

Wood sorrel or shamrock has been used in folk medicine in Europe and Asia throughout recorded history for various ailments, but especially in the treatment of cancer. In America, the Algonquins used it not only as a medicine but also as a powerful aphrodisiac. The Potawatomi of the Great Lakes region didn't use it as a medicine at all, but instead for food. They cooked it first and then added maple sugar to make a refreshing woodland dessert. Although some people to this day use wood sorrel as a flavoring to add to tossed salads, stews, soups, desserts, and even beverages, too much of a good thing could make you sick. The plant contains oxalic acid, which is a fairly potent poison if ingested in large amounts. I've never tried wood sorrel as a food, but enjoy the taste of the plant as a refreshing nibble on a hike in the woods. The leaves and stems have a thirst-quenching, almost lemon–like flavor that seems to really perk me up on a warm day.

An old Irish blessing says, "May the road rise to meet you. May the wind be at your back." If you're not wearing a shamrock or a bit of the green next Saint Patrick's day, you may want to watch your back, as well, especially if you hear someone call out, "Green, green!" If so, your luck of the Irish has just run out.

PUSSY WILLOWS
THE TRUE PROPHETS OF SPRING

According to the calendar, the spring equinox officially arrives March 21st each year, but winter's gray skies and cold temperatures usually hang on for at least a few more weeks. In time, the gloomy brown landscape turns green and spring flowers bloom once more. But if you need reassurance that the real spring is just around the corner, bundle up, hike over the melting snowdrifts, and go to where the wild willows grow. Here you'll find the true prophet of spring already in bloom—the pussy willow.

Although Wisconsin is home to more than thirty different species of willows, the pussy willow is easy to spot in March, before the other trees or shrubs have started to bud out. Pussy willows have the large, inch-long catkins on their stems covered with thick, silky fuzz to protect them from the still-freezing temperatures of early spring. They grow throughout the state along marshes, riverbanks, and in wet roadside ditches, usually along with alder trees and other willow species.

Only the male pussy willows have the large, fuzzy catkins that eventually burst open into bright orange-and-yellow stamens. The female's flowers grow on a separate plant, are much smaller in size, and are light green in color. Both male and female catkins produce brightly colored pollen and sweet nectar to attract early spring insects, including the solitary bee, to help them pollinate their flowers. By late spring, the female catkins have already matured and dispersed their seeds into the wind. The tiny pussy willow seeds float through the spring breezes with the help of special cottony tufts, which act as miniature parachutes.

Willows grow throughout Wisconsin and some are impressive trees, such as the black willow, which can grow up to fifty feet in height. Another, the weeping willow, is not native to America but was brought over from Europe by early settlers and is now prized in many of our parks as a shade and ornamental tree.

For centuries, willows have been used by mankind. They have been planted for erosion control along stream banks, harvested for their soft and light wood used in making baskets, crates, and boxes, and used for making high grade charcoal. Willow bark has also been used for hundreds of years both by American Indians and Europeans as a pain reliever. In the 1800s, scientists discovered that willow bark contains salicylic acid, a chemical from which common aspirin was eventually developed.

By far the most popular and definitely the "people's choice" of willows has to be the pussy willow. A spring tradition in many homes is to bring a vase full of pussy willows inside to brighten up the decor. Although pussy willows are protected in public parks and forests and must not be cut there, you may be able to harvest some on private lands if you ask permission first. Remember to bring boots, since pussy willows are commonly found in wet marshes. Willows are extremely hardy, and cutting a few branches won't harm the tree and usually stimulates more growth next year. Be careful to leave plenty of branches and catkins uncut, to enable the tree to pollinate and develop seeds naturally. If you can't get pussy willows in the wild, most florists and even some grocery stores have them for sale in spring as well. If you want a real treat, keep pussy willows in water and you'll be rewarded in a few weeks by the large, golden-yellow stamens that burst out from the buds.

It's amazing how a few stems of pussy willows in our homes can cheer us up and remind us that spring, sunshine, warm breezes, and longer daylight hours are on the way; all as predicted by the little tree with the fuzzy catkins. They've never been wrong before.

SKUNK CABBAGE
A ROSE BY ANY OTHER NAME

We've all heard the old saying, "April showers bring May flowers," but one spring flower in Wisconsin often blooms even before the winter snows have melted away.

Skunk cabbage begins to send up its bright green shoots in marshy areas as early as the end of February or beginning of March. Like a few other rare early-bloomers, skunk cabbage has the amazing ability to create its own heat source. Once the plant emerges from the soil it will keep itself at an almost constant temperature of just over 70 degrees, despite bone-chilling nights and occasional late-winter snowstorms.

You can find skunk cabbage in nearly any wooded or marshy area, or along woodland streams, anywhere in Wisconsin. Usually, the leaf buds are the first to emerge from the mucky soil and develop into tall, tightly-curled leaves resembling cabbage. Nearby, you'll find the mottled purple, brown, and yellow flower bud that is covered by a green-and-purple-specked hood called a spathe. The spathe is made up of a thick, spongy material full of air pockets which help to insulate the plant and conserve heat. The flower is visited by bees and flies that help to pollinate the plant. Seeking heat during cold spells, these same insects seem to congregate near or even inside the plant—sort of an insect version of a winter warming house.

If you have any doubt in your ability to identify the skunk cabbage, all you need to do is squeeze a part of the plant and smell your hands. Whoa! One whiff of its stench and you will instantly know why it's called skunk cabbage. The repulsive smell is one of the plant's warnings to you and any other plant-chewing critter not to eat it. In the event the smell did not deter you, one bite would no doubt do the job, since the plant contains calcium oxalate crystals, which cause intense burning of the tongue and mouth.

Despite skunk cabbage's offensive odor and toxicity, the plant has been used as both food and medicine down through the ages. American Indians called the plant *skota*, and used its roots primarily to make bread flour, but also to aid in the treating of asthma and toothaches, and as a blood-clotting agent on surface wounds. Believe it or not, they also used skunk cabbage as a seasoning to cover up even worse-tasting foods and bad odors. In more recent times, skunk cabbage roots were used as a narcotic and as an emetic (to cause vomiting) in the medical profession under the name of *dracontium*. Although most animals don't eat skunk cabbage, once the plant's flower spadix turns into seeds they are eagerly eaten by grouse, pheasants, and other birds.

Skunk cabbage thrives throughout the summer season, their large, heavy-ribbed leaves growing as much as three feet in length. By late fall, the leaves curl up from the chilling frosts, but occasionally the plant sends up more shoots and even blooms again just as the winter snows start to fall. Individual skunk cabbage plants are believed to be among the longest living of wild perennials. Some biologists have suggested that an individual plant could live a thousand years or more. Of course, nobody knows for sure, but it's likely they could live for a few hundred years, as long as there's enough moisture to sustain them.

Take some time to get out to your local marsh and discover the first true sign of spring—the blooming skunk cabbage. Just as a rose by any other name would smell as sweet, so too the skunk cabbage by any other name would smell just as ... well ... putrid.

BEAVERS
DAMMED IF THEY DO, DAMMED IF THEY DON'T

He was big, real big. He was a menace to society and the government was secretly plotting to take him out. My orders read like a *"Mission Impossible"* script: "Your assignment, Jim, should you choose to accept it, is to capture the culprit alive and relocate him to another part of the county. This message will self-destruct ..."

Who was this bad guy? Just the biggest, baddest, boldest beaver in the state. Well, at least in Manitowoc county, maybe. What was his crime? Malicious destruction of property, including cutting trees and flooding out backyards of cottage owners along Sy Lake by damming up the only stream outlet.

OK, so maybe it wasn't exactly international espionage, but for my first summer job working for the Wisconsin Wildlife Department, many years ago, it seemed like a big deal. But, as I soon discovered, trying to catch America's largest rodent—beavers can grow more than three feet long and weigh sixty pounds—was not going to be easy. First, I tried baiting a large wire-mesh contraption called a bailey live trap, with the beaver's favorite food. Beavers are strictly vegetarian and eat almost any kind of woody plant, but have a sweet tooth for aspen, birch, maple, and willow. Contrary to popular belief, they don't eat the inner wood of trees, only the leaves, twigs, and bark. Beavers have large and sharp front teeth and can gnaw down a five-inch-diameter tree in less than thirty minutes. Once they drop a tree, they cut the branches into smaller lengths, either for food or for building their dams and lodges.

After failing to capture a single beaver in several days, I moved the trap closer to the beaver's dam, where I could see he had been hauling sticks and packing them with mud to block the flow of the creek. Beavers are the only animals in Wisconsin—other than ourselves—that can actually change their environment to suit themselves. The dams they build create new wetlands that are valuable to many other animals such as mink, muskrat, otter, and waterfowl. On the other hand, their engineering feats can also cause problems when they flood out homes, cropland, or when they block cold-running trout streams. Beavers also build large, cone-shaped lodges by packing mud and sticks in a pile, often about fifteen feet in diameter. They then chew out the interior of the pile to create a living chamber with at least two underwater openings for entrances and exits.

Beavers don't hibernate, so these lodges are important to their survival. They also store tree branches underwater next to their lodge to eat during the long winter season. The lodges are also important to shelter the tiny beaver kits born in April or May. In some areas, especially larger rivers or lakes, beavers burrow inside the shoreline banks instead of building lodges.

Beaver pelts were once a valuable commodity. Much of the early exploration of this north country was done by trappers in search of them. Their fur was in high demand in Europe for centuries for the manufacture of gentlemen's top hats, jackets, and coats. Before settlement, beavers were abundant throughout Wisconsin, but due to unregulated trapping and shooting, and extensive logging, they nearly became extinct by 1900. Thanks to careful management, beavers have made an impressive comeback and are again abundant in the northern and western part of the state where liberal trapping seasons are again allowed. In some areas, they have rebounded so successfully that special beaver damage-control programs have had to be set up to help landowners control their numbers.

Eventually, I did manage to trap that large problem beaver at Sy Lake, but only temporarily. Unfortunately, nobody told me how to move a forty-pound beaver inside a metal live trap with no handles on it. As I lifted the heavy trap and began carrying it downstream, the beaver became agitated, hissed at me, and then lunged to take a bite of my fingers. Aware that these were the same formidable teeth used to chew through large trees, I instinctively dropped the trap. This gave the beaver enough momentum to break out of its confinement and swim to safety. Feeling a bit foolish, and maybe a bit cowardly, I never did tell my supervisor of my failed assignment. With the help of a co-worker, we did finally catch and relocate two other beavers in the same area that summer, but never did take out the biggest, baddest beaver of Sy Lake. For all I know, he's still there.

MINK
ALWAYS IN STYLE

It was pretty much like any other Sunday morning in the 1950s, a time when nearly all rambunctious eight-year-old boys were rounded up, dressed in their Sunday best, and marched off to the local church. But one particular Sunday was a bit different for me. Oh, I was in church all right, but my buddy Larry and I weren't exactly contemplating our eternal salvation as we were supposed to be doing. Instead, we were totally engrossed by the sight of the dead, furry critters hanging around the shoulders of the fancy lady sitting in the pew ahead of us. I remember we were fascinated by the animals' bright blue glass eyes glaring at us, and their sleek, soft fur, and dangling legs and claws. But what really tickled our funny bone was the clip on the two mouths that seemed to bite each other from head to tail. So began my fascination with one of the largest members of the weasel family—the mink.

Mink are one of those animals that are probably seen more often dead than alive. Wearing mink coats and stoles has been an important status symbol for women for many centuries both in Europe and America, especially during the peak of mink coat fashion from the 1940s to the '60s. Few other animals have fur as thick, soft, luxurious (or as expensive to own) as mink. An average full-length mink coat can take up to seventy pelts to produce. Today, nearly all pelts used in the garment industry are raised on fur farms rather than by trapping wild mink. Raising domestic mink has an interesting history, starting way back during the Civil War days. Although they originally took mink stock from the wild, ranchers soon began to breed them selectively to produce a wide range of fur colors—black, white, platinum, and silver-blue to name just a few. Wisconsin has always been a leader in mink production and has some of the oldest fur farms in the country.

Wild mink are similar in appearance to their domestic cousins, except that they have dark, chocolate-brown fur with an occasional white patch under their chin, and have tiny, beady, black eyes. Mink are never found far from water, making their homes in cavities or under tree stumps along the banks of rivers, streams, lakeshores, ponds, and marsh-es. They're common nearly everywhere from the Arctic to Mexico, but are especially abundant in water-rich states such as Wisconsin. Mink are not social animals and live alone most of the year. Because they are so secretive and hunt mostly at night, we rarely get to see them, even though they frequently live near populated urban areas and farms.

Biologists refer to mink as being semi-aquatic animals because they hunt not only on land, like their weasel cousins, but also under the water, as otters do. They're able to swim after and catch fish, frogs, and crayfish in the water, but their favorite prey is muskrat, if they can catch them. On dry land, they eat small birds, mice, rabbits, snakes, and just about anything else they can run down or pounce on. Mink are aggres-sive predators, killing by biting their victim in the neck region. Like weasels, they often kill more than they can eat at one time, caching the surplus in their dens. Unfortunately, mink also have a taste for poultry and can eventually wipe out an entire flock if they can find a way into chicken coops. Years ago, I once set a trap to catch whatever was mak-ing a nightly raid and killing the chickens on our family farm. Even-tually, I caught the culprit, which turned out to be a pure black mink that probably escaped from a local fur farm, or one that might have been cross-bred with a wild mink.

Since mink do not hibernate, they actively search for food throughout the winter season. They're particularly energetic in February and March during their breeding season. Some males may travel five miles or more in search of mates—the one time of the year they seem to tolerate associating with each other. In April or May, the female builds a nesting chamber, fills it with soft grass, leaves, and fur, and gives birth to five or six young. Mink kits are born blind and naked, and are only about the size of your little finger. The tiny mink grow up quickly, however, and stay with their mother throughout the warm months, dispersing in fall to find their own hunting territories.

Although mink are protected from hunting in Wisconsin, there is usually a trapping season for them from October through December. Wild mink pelts are usually worth more than domestic "ranch mink," but market prices fluctuate with supply and demand. Because of the difficulty in trapping these clever, solitary animals, there seems to be little threat to mink populations, at least from trappers. Probably of more concern is the continuing loss of habitat, especially where wetlands are drained, pollutants enter the water, or developments arise along streams and lakeshores. With luck, Wisconsin's wild mink, with their luxurious fur coats, won't end up becoming a luxury themselves, and will continue to prowl the marshes and riverbanks long into the future.

SEA LAMPREYS
THE REAL ALIEN INVADERS

The aliens have arrived! No, not extraterrestrial beings from a distant galaxy invented for the latest blockbuster movie, but real-life aliens that have invaded our shores. What do they look like? Actually, pretty much the way a Hollywood special-effects artist might have designed them— ugly, slimy creatures with dark, blue-gray reptilian skin, an eel-like body with fins, large gill slots, tiny evil-looking eyes, and a large sucking disc mouth filled with several rows of sharp teeth.

Lucky for us this alien, the sea lamprey, grows only about two feet long and is a threat only to fish living in the Great Lakes. Adult lampreys feed on lake trout, whitefish, chubs, and other deep-water fish in a gruesome, parasitic method worthy of the best horror film. Once they attach themselves to their victim with their powerful, sucking disc mouth, they use their rough tongue to rasp a hole through the side of the fish. They then secrete an anticoagulant chemical to keep the victim's blood from clotting and they remain attached, feeding for days or even weeks, until the fish dies or the lamprey is gorged enough to let go.

Sea lampreys normally live in saltwater oceans and return to freshwater tributaries only to spawn. They entered the Great Lakes earlier in this century after the Erie and Welland canals were built, and soon after adapted to living in fresh water year-round. Sea lampreys were first seen off the shores of Wisconsin in 1934, in Lake Michigan, and only four years later had infested Lake Superior as well. Although we consider the sea lamprey as a relatively new alien invader to our shores, they are hardly newcomers to the world. These primitive-looking creatures and their close relatives, the hagfish, are the only living members of an ancient family of jawless fish that swam the earth's oceans some 450 million years ago.

Despite their ferocious reputation as predators, sea lampreys actually spend most of their lives as harmless vegetarians. Adult lampreys spawn only once in a lifetime. They enter streams and tributaries in spring, where they build crescent-shaped nests in the gravel, deposit some sixty thousand eggs, and then die. After hatching, the tiny lamprey larvae leave the cold streams and burrow into the mud in quiet pools and bays, where they live by filtering out plankton that drifts by. There they remain for at least three years, and sometimes as long as fourteen years, before they suddenly become adult lampreys, usually in July. They then leave their river homes and enter the Great Lakes to spend the remaining twelve to twenty months of their lives feeding on fish before returning to spawn.

Attempts to stop the sea lamprey invasion of the Great Lakes started soon after their devastation of our native fish populations had become apparent. Commercial harvest of lake trout in Lake Michigan was once two million pounds a year as recently as 1940, but only fifteen years later had plummeted to zero pounds harvested in 1955. Biologists have tried a wide array of control methods over the years in their battle against this alien, including mechanical barriers in lamprey-spawning streams, weirs, traps, electrical shocking devices, and dams, but with little success. Then, in the late 1950s, a chemical substance known as

TFM was discovered that could selectively kill lamprey larvae in their spawning streams without harming other aquatic life. Today, chemical treatment to control lamprey populations continues throughout the Great Lakes, both in the United States and Canadian waters, but at considerable cost.

Even though mankind's chemical warfare against this alien predator has had some success, the outcome is not certain. Some research biologists are beginning speculate that a new, poison-resistant strain of sea lamprey may already be evolving. Not surprising for a creature that witnessed the rise and fall of the dinosaurs, survived all the ice ages, and continues to thrive in all its horrific, parasitic glory despite what we throw at it from our arsenal of mechanical and chemical weapons. What more could a Hollywood director want in the "perfect" alien?

PINE SAWYER BEETLE
A BUG THAT PINES FOR WOOD

The longhorns have arrived in Wisconsin by the thousands. No need to saddle up the horse, strap on your spurs, or practice twirling your lariat for these longhorns, however. Unlike the big, wiry, longhorn cattle of the old Western frontier, these longhorns cannot be herded or roped. They may not measure up in size to their bovine namesake, either, but pound for pound they're pretty impressive critters— for insects that is. Longhorn beetles can grow to three inches or more in length and sprout "horns" or antennae that are often as long or longer than their bodies. They also come from an exceptionally large family of insects, with more than twelve hundred species of longhorn beetles here in North America, and thousands more in the tropics.

The pine sawyer beetle is probably the most common longhorn in Wisconsin. Like all its longhorn cousins, this beetle has long, graceful distinctive antennae. Male sawyers usually have much longer antennae than the females. Their attractive mottled brown, expertly camouflaged body, and large, powerful jaws help to protect them from predators.

Sawyer beetles are best known for their ferocious appetites when eating the insides of pine trees. They're probably the only insects that, while eating, are more often heard than seen. A few years back, an old-time logger told me that on a quiet day in the forest you can hear the sawyer beetles chewing inside trees if you listen closely. Intrigued, but more than a bit skeptical, I decided to give it a try one day, carefully avoiding any part of the woods where someone might hike by and see a grown man trying to listen to trees. Sure enough, after sitting close to a few dozen trees, I heard a loud, hollow, rasping, "*Zzt..zzt..zzt..*" coming from the inside of an old pine tree.

Pine sawyer beetles lead unusually long and bizarre lives. Adult beetles lay their eggs on the bark of evergreen trees such as pine, spruce, or fir. After hatching, the white grub-like larvae begin to tunnel into the tree with their sharp, powerful, chiseled jaws. For the next two to four years, the larvae live in complete darkness, literally eating their way through life deep inside the tree. As they chew through the solid wood, a buzzing or "sawing" sound is produced from which their common name is derived. Since solid wood is indigestible, even to pine sawyer beetles, they must get their nourishment from the proteins and carbohydrates in the vessels and cellulose of the tree. Normally, this doesn't kill the tree, but the tunneling can reduce the value of the timber. Most sawyer beetles prefer to live in dead or dying trees, but are known to infest piled saw logs, especially if they are not removed from the forest soon after cutting.

When the sawyer larvae are fully grown, they tunnel to near the outside of the tree, stop eating, and spin a cocoon. In spring or early summer, they transform into adult beetles, chew their way out of the tree, and fly away. In summer, you might find one resting on a wildflower, eating pollen or chewing on pine needles. Sometimes they can be seen in the evenings, since they, like moths, seem to be attracted to lights. People are often startled to find these large insects around buildings or on window screens in the morning.

After waiting so many years inside their cool, dark, solid wood chambers, they are allowed only a few weeks of freedom in the warm and sunny outdoors. By the middle of summer they mate and die, long before the first frosts of autumn. But before leaving, they will already have laid their eggs on the bark of pine trees, and the sound of the buzzing and sawing of the next generation of sawyer beetles already fills the woods. ▲

April

April showers eventually bring May flowers to Wisconsin's woodlands, but rarely before one or two spring snowstorms roar across the state. Despite the often snowy start to the month, spring bird migration peaks near the end of April. Ducks and geese return to their nesting marshes and ponds, while pure-white whistling swans move on to their arctic breeding grounds after a brief rest stop in the state.

Almost overnight, the woods seem to come alive with returning songbirds—thrushes, catbirds, thrashers, and colorful warblers. In open meadows near wooded swamps, you can hear the distinctive *peent-peent* call and witness the unique sky dance of displaying woodcock. In the uplands, white-tailed deer appear shaggy as they begin to shed their winter coats, and bucks start to grow antlers.

At night, if you listen carefully, you can hear the loud *peep-peep* chorus of spring peepers and other early spring frogs, especially on warm, quiet evenings when April's full "frog moon" rises in the eastern sky.

WHISTLING SWANS
THE SONG IS UPBEAT

They come out of the eastern skies, usually under the cover of darkness. Flying high over Lake Michigan in long V-shaped formations, whistling swans begin to descend as Wisconsin's  eastern shoreline comes into their view. Almost ghostlike in appearance against the black sky, the swan's pure white plumage is often illuminated by the bright lights of coastal cities as they fly overhead. After gliding a few miles inland, the flock begins to break ranks and call to one another in their own peculiar, high pitched whistle. As they begin to circle, one by one, they set their wings and drop down onto a flooded farm field to rest.

Whistling swans, now called tundra swans by most biologists, migrate through Wisconsin every spring, usually from the end of March to the first couple weeks in April. This is the time of year when surprised motorists slam on the brakes and pull off the road to watch these majestic and graceful birds in our rural farmlands and marshes. Whistling swans are pure white in color except for their black bill, legs, feet, and a small yellow spot at the base of their bill. They really can't be confused with any other bird except for the larger and still very rare trumpeter swan, a close cousin to the whistling swan.

Unlike most other waterfowl that migrate north up the Mississippi flyway in spring, whistling swans fly in a northwesterly direction from their wintering grounds on the Atlantic coast near the Chesapeake Bay and the Carolina Sounds area. Tens of thousands of swans cross Lake Michigan each spring and spend several days resting and feeding in our state's cold, muddy marshes and flooded farm fields. But just as quickly as they arrived, they disappear overnight, continuing the long journey to their nesting areas in the remote arctic regions of Canada and Alaska.

Whistling swans prefer to nest in shallow lakes and ponds far north of the Arctic Circle. There, they build large, raised nests of seaweed, grass, and moss, lay eggs, and raise their young throughout the brief arctic summer. Young swans, called cygnets, are grayish in color and won't take on the adult's pure white plumage until their second year. They are, however, able to fly as fast and high as their parents by early autumn. Swans have been clocked at speeds of up to fifty miles per hour and at altitudes of three thousand feet and higher. Because swans fly mostly at night, they are expert navigators, using the stars and moonlit landscape as guides in finding their way back during migration.

All swans are protected throughout their range, thanks to fairly recent international migratory bird treaties. Years ago, swans were slaughtered by the millions by market hunters for their meat and hides. In the 18th and 19th centuries, swan skins were sold in the fur trade, mostly to European markets where they were used to make ladies' powder puffs and to adorn fashionable women's hats of the day. Between the years 1820 and 1880 the Hudson's Bay Company alone sold 108,000 swan skins to the London market. Swans were shot on their breeding grounds by settlers and Eskimos, who not only took their eggs but rounded up the birds for butchering during their molting period when they couldn't fly away.

Because the relatively rare trumpeter swans nested in areas farther south, including the heavily populated northern states such as Wisconsin, their populations suffered more than those of the whistler swans. In addition, they suffered from rapidly disappearing habitat as marshes and swamps were drained for cropland. By 1932, trumpeter swans were all but extinct with only 69 known birds known to be alive anywhere in the lower states. Luckily, a few small wild flocks were discovered in Yellowstone National Park and remote parts of Canada. Since then, swan recovery efforts have taken root in many states, including Wisconsin. Current efforts involve gathering trumpeter swan eggs from the wilds of Alaska, hatching them, and rearing the young in captivity for two years. After they have paired with a mate, they are released into protected wetland areas. Biologists hope eventually to establish at least twenty pairs of trumpeter swans here in Wisconsin. Whistling swans seem to be making a slow but sure comeback on their own, thanks mostly to the protection they receive and because of their ability to nest in the far reaches of the Arctic Circle, far away from US.

Early explorers Lewis and Clark reported "tremendous numbers" of swans nearly everywhere they went during their expedition in 1802. It's hard to believe that we nearly exterminated this species only a century later. The last known pair of trumpeter swans that lived and nested in Wisconsin disappeared sometime in the late 1800s. Maybe it's fitting that now, in the early years of a new century, there are strong restoration efforts to bring the trumpeters back to our state once again. Perhaps we'll be able to preserve enough marshes and farmland to allow for the safe passage of the whistling swans through Wisconsin as well.

WOODCOCKS
SKY DANCERS OF SPRING

"I owned my farm for two years before learning that the sky dance is to be seen over my woods every evening in April and May. Since we discovered it, my family and I have been reluctant to miss even a single performance."
—Aldo Leopold, Sand County Almanac

They say spring is a time when every young man's fancy turns to love. This annual infatuation with courting seems to be an overwhelming driving force throughout the natural world at this time of year, especially for birds. Spring just wouldn't seem complete without the cheerful calls and displays of songbirds everywhere, but there's one whose performance tops them all—the American woodcock. After migrating back to Wisconsin in late March, male woodcocks begin to claim their singing and displaying grounds,

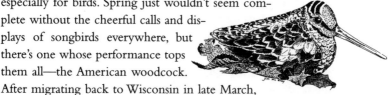

which are usually in wetland forest clearings, short grass fields, or sometimes even paved roads. Soon after selecting their territory, they begin their spectacular aerial courtship flights, which they perform during the twilight hours each morning and evening throughout the breeding season. Males strut on the ground, bobbing up and down and making a buzzy, nasal *peent, peent* sound. They then launch themselves into a spiral flight that takes them two hundred or more feet straight up in the air, while at the same time producing a musical twitter with the tips of their wings. On the way down they make a different musical note, then repeat the performance over and over, eventually attracting a female that joins in the courtship display, usually in the dark.

Woodcocks are sometimes called *timberdoodles* and have to be one of nature's most unusual-looking birds. They have small, stubby legs and a round, almost neckless body, covered in brown, dead-leaf colored plumage. They also have a long beak with a flexible tip, which they use like tweezers to probe into the mud for their favorite food, earthworms. Woodcocks actually have the unique ability to see behind themselves without turning their heads, due to the location of their large eyes set high in their skulls. Because of their peculiar head shape, woodcocks are the only birds with ears located in front of their eyes and a brain that is actually upside down in their skulls.

Woodcock can be found performing their sky dances near wetlands and wooded swamps and streams throughout the state in spring. After mating in April, females build ground nests in dense aspen or alder thickets and lay approximately four eggs. I once stumbled across a brooding woodcock by accident and got a chance to observe the unique distraction display hen woodcocks use to lure predators away from their nests. As I approached, she flew a short distance from the nest and landed on the ground, beating her wings and letting her legs dangle down as if she were injured. Had I been a predator, this tactic may have lured me away from the nest in an attempt to catch what looked like an injured adult.

Although actually a shorebird, the woodcock seems to have abandoned its former aquatic homes in favor of moist, wooded areas, and now is usually considered an "upland" game bird. Woodcock were once threatened with extinction due to over-harvesting by market hunters in the 1800s. They used "fire lightning" or burning torches to help them shoot hundreds of birds while they were on their feeding grounds at night. During the peak of market hunting, thousands of woodcock were sold weekly for about a $1.50 a pair in big city markets such as New York and Chicago. Because woodcock migrate south for the winter, like waterfowl, they were eventually protected under the Migratory Bird Treaty Act in 1918 and market hunting was stopped. Woodcock have enjoyed a comeback since then, but will probably never be as numerous as they once were, because of the loss of so much wetland over the years. Today, woodcock numbers are healthy enough to allow an annual fall hunting season, and *timberdoodles* remain a favorite game bird for many hunters throughout the state.

Woodcocks begin to migrate south to their wintering grounds along the Gulf Coast and southeastern states in October or whenever the ground begins to freeze and earthworms become hard to reach. Although they often travel together in large flocks, woodcock are rarely seen in migration because they fly at low altitudes and always under the cover of night. As quickly as they appear, woodcock seem to disappear magically, almost overnight, as fall approaches. But come next spring, they'll be back, and once again these odd-looking, little *timberdoodles* will treat us to their graceful sky dances.

PEREGRINE FALCON
NATURE'S FEATHERED MISSILES

The sparrow never knew what hit it. Like a deadly scud missile, the falcon came roaring out of the clear blue sky and struck with such a terrible blow that the bird was thrown into a spin and killed instantly. Before it could even tumble towards earth, the feathered missile made a breathtaking aerobatic turn and swooped down to catch the limp sparrow in midair with its sharp talons. With diving speeds of over two hundred miles an hour, it's no wonder that peregrine falcons are often nicknamed "bullet hawks."

The peregrine falcon's lightning speed and amazing flying agility have made it one of the world's best aerial hunters. Every part of the peregrine is built for speed, from its long, pointed wings and small, compact head, to its sleek, torpedo-shaped body. Even the color of its plumage aids in its hunting ability. The black stripes on its head help to reduce sunlight glare for sharper vision, much like the black grease a football or baseball player might apply under his eyes for the same reason. Peregrines primarily feed on small birds such as sparrows, starlings, and pigeons, but also have a taste for warblers, cardinals, flickers, blue jays, and other songbirds, much to the despair of backyard bird-watchers.

Female peregrines are called *falcons* and are about two pounds larger than males, which are referred to as *tiercels*, a Latin word meaning one-third smaller. Despite their small size, peregrines can take on much larger birds, including hawks, owls, herons, and game birds such as grouse, pheasants, and ducks.

Peregrine falcons have enjoyed a long and close relationship with man, serving as a trained hunting weapon for sport and to gather food. The sport of falconry is believed to have started about four thousand years ago in Persia or China, and spread westward into Europe where it reached its high point during the Middle Ages. Peregrines have always been considered birds of royalty, held in the highest esteem by generations of kings, emperors, and nobleman. Because of the aggressive aerial hunting techniques of falcons, the Mongolian ruler Genghis Khan recommended falconry to his army officers as the best school for warriors, reasoning that it demanded as much skill of men as of the birds. With the advent of gunpowder and firearms, people eventually found an easier way to take game birds, and falconry was largely abandoned except as the exotic hobby it remains today.

The word "peregrine" means to wander or travel, which was a good choice for a bird that once inhabited more land surface than any other bird in the world. Beginning in the late 1940s, however, peregrine falcon populations began to take a worldwide nosedive from which they have never fully recovered. By 1962, the last known breeding pair of peregrines reported in Wisconsin disappeared, and soon all the peregrines were gone from the eastern part of the United States. The loss of these beautiful birds of prey did not go unnoticed by biologists, who eventually proved that the birds were being killed by the pesticide DDT. Developed during the World War II era, DDT and its related pesticides were used as insecticides on croplands. The insects were eaten by small birds, and as peregrine falcons and other birds of prey ate these birds, they accumulated higher and higher concentrations of poison residue in their bodies, causing females to lay very thin-shelled eggs that often broke before the chicks could be incubated and hatched.

Eventually, safer pesticides were developed and DDT was banned in 1972. Biologists then attempted to reintroduce captive peregrines back to their former homes on the wooded bluffs and cliffs along the Mississippi. Unfortunately, these releases were not successful, since raccoons and great-horned owls raided the falcons' nests and destroyed the eggs and hatchlings. Surprisingly, success was eventually achieved by releasing peregrines right in the middle of some of the largest urban areas in the country—downtown New York City, Los Angeles, Milwaukee, and at electric power plants along Lake Michigan. As it turns out, the concrete ledges of tall skyscrapers make a fine substitute for a rocky cliff, and most cities have an abundance of pigeons, sparrows, and starlings for them to feed on. In a few short years more than seventy pairs of urban peregrines were living in some fifty cities around the country.

Although still rare, the slow but sure comeback of the peregrine falcon is truly a great environmental victory, both for the birds and for mankind. Perhaps eventually we'll learn to live side by side with the peregrine and someday the sight of these living, breathing, feathered missiles streaking across the blue sky will again become a common sight in the wilderness and urban landscape of Wisconsin.

TURKEY VULTURES
NATURE'S SANITATION CREW

Vultures. Just the name brings images of death, disease, and disaster. Maybe you have a Hollywood vision of vultures circling the skies of a hot western desert with some poor soul near death below them. Or maybe you think of the African plains with hordes of vultures picking apart the carcass of a fallen zebra. Most likely, you don't think of Wisconsin, but you might be surprised that vultures are common birds here as well.

Vultures that live in our state are called turkey vultures, so named by early colonists who thought the bird resembled the wild turkey. We can usually spot turkey vultures in much of the state in late March or early April, or whenever the weather turns warm enough to create the thermal "bubble" updrafts they like to soar in. I've seen turkey vultures circling near the lakeshore of Lake Michigan in the middle of March during unseasonably warm spells, but they disappeared as soon as cold weather returned.

Although several other birds, including hawks and eagles, also soar and circle high in the sky in spring, you can easily pick out the turkey vultures with their huge wingspan of over five feet, held at a v-shaped angle. Although vultures are awkward and clumsy on land, they are definitely not "turkeys" in the sky and can circle gracefully for hours on end with little effort. Another distinguishing feature of turkey vultures is their silence. While most hawks and eagles call out occasional shrieks and cries, turkey vultures are always silent. As it turns out, the birds don't even have vocal cords, and the most noise they can muster is a hiss or grunt.

Turkey vultures have been observed at heights of four miles or more into the atmosphere, but often they fly over fields and forests just above treetop level. If you look closely at these times, you may be able to see their beautiful, dark-brown feathers and the colorful, red, featherless head of the adult birds.

Though fierce-looking, turkey vultures are shy scavengers that rarely kill live animals, preferring to eat carrion such as road kills. In addition to their excellent vision at high altitudes, vultures also have a keen sense of smell, a useful tool for a bird looking for dead animals. Their menacing-looking beak is actually quite weak and the birds often have trouble breaking the skin of fresh carcasses. They either have to wait until the animal starts to decompose or rely on some other animal to break it open. Although the vulture's habit of eating dead and decomposing animals may seem disgusting to us, the birds fill an important niche in nature by cleaning up carcasses from the landscape.

Since meal times for vultures may be far and few between, the birds usually gorge themselves when they do find food. They even have a crop, an expandable pouch in their throat, to store extra meat for some future snack when pickings are slim. Because they must often reach deep inside the carcasses of dead animals to eat, vultures have evolved featherless heads. This helps them to keep clean and free of dirt and bacteria that could cause infection. After feasting, the birds wash themselves off in nearby rivers and streams or merely let their heads dry in the sun. Although turkey vultures keep themselves clean, they have little to fear from eating spoiled meat. Their powerful digestive systems break down germs, bacteria, or disease viruses that would poison most any other creature, into harmless, nutritious food for themselves.

Turkey vultures are found throughout the North America. Since they don't hunt and kill prey like hawks or owls, they don't really stake out a territory to defend. Because of this, vultures are free-roaming, covering hundreds of miles a day in their search for meals or just for the fun of riding the air currents. Vultures have been clocked at flying in excess of a hundred miles an hour, so they have no difficulty in crossing over several states in a day. An exception to their jet-set lifestyle is during the springtime when the vultures pair up to mate. They do not build a nest but merely lay their eggs on the ground, in a hollow of a tree or on a cliff ledge. Although most of the vultures we see are migrating to more remote areas of northern Wisconsin, a few remain closer to urban areas all summer, nesting in places such as the Kettle Moraine State Forest and other large tracts of wooded lands.

Vultures have always instilled a certain amount of fear in mankind through the ages. The bird has been seen as everything from a messenger from God to the ferocious gatekeeper of hell. Early American Indians believed the vulture to be a thunder god.

Neither a god nor a devil, turkey vultures are just another part of nature's tapestry, a species that happens to have been selected for cleanup duty. Although not as handsome or majestic as the bald eagle or as beautiful as a snowy owl, this gentle, useful bird proves that beauty is only skin (feather) deep. After all, it's a dirty job, but someone has to do it.

THIRTEEN-LINED GROUND SQUIRREL
NATURE'S LUCKY 13

They've been shot, trapped, poisoned, clubbed, drowned, fumigated, plowed up, and flattened by vehicles. They're eaten by fox, coyotes, cats, mink, weasels, badgers, hawks, owls, and snakes, just to name a few. How on earth could any animal survive this daily threat by man and beast? In the case of the thirteen-lined ground squirrel, very well thank you. In fact, not only is the ground squirrel surviving, but seems to be expanding its range in Wisconsin.

The thirteen-lined ground squirrel is often called a "gopher," even though it's not a true gopher at all, but rather a member of the squirrel family. Unlike its cousins that live high in the treetops, the ground squirrel prefers to keep its feet on the ground. This squirrel gets its name from the thirteen colorful lines, dots, and stripes on its back. Although striking in appearance and easily seen when out in the open, these markings help to conceal the squirrel, helping it to blend into shadow-flecked grasslands.

Ground squirrels are native to Wisconsin and have historically preferred to live in flat, well-drained, grassy areas of the state. Unfortunately, this same kind of land was in high demand for settlement and farming by early immigrants. Today, these are our backyards, crop fields, manicured lawns, parks, cemeteries, and golf courses we cherish so dearly. It's no wonder then that an animal that spends most of its time digging underground tunnels with multiple open holes to the surface would end up on a collision course with mankind. To make matters worse, a single ground squirrel can dig up to four tunnels a season, each twenty feet in length. Entrances to the underground system are often difficult to locate since the squirrels carry all the soil away from the hole in their cheek pouches and scatter it in the grass.

Despite their pesky digging habits, thirteen-lined ground squirrels can be beneficial, since they feed on native grasses, weeds, insects, and mice. On the other hand, they probably do just as much damage by eating cultivated crops, including sprouting corn. Although individual squirrels can't do much damage, the animals like to congregate together in groups of twenty or more per acre, forming colonies similar to prairie dog towns in the western states.

Ground squirrels spend most of their lives sleeping through Wisconsin's long, cold winters. Their ability to survive our frozen landscape is nothing less than a miracle of nature. By late October, they plug up all the entrances to their burrows with grass and begin to hibernate. As they slip into their deep sleep, their body temperature drops from a normal 86-106 degrees to a near-freezing 37 degrees. Breathing almost stops, with breaths normally at fifty per minute reduced to only four. Their heart rate also plummets from a hyperactive rate of 200-350 beats per minute to a near-death of 5 beats.

Usually by late March or early April, the ground has warmed up enough to awaken the ground squirrels, and they emerge from hibernation to mate, dig more burrows, and feast on the early spring greenery at their doorstep. Young ground squirrels, raised in underground nests, are born blind, toothless, and helpless at birth. By about July or so, the tiny young squirrels begin to emerge from their burrows to explore the landscape around them. The little ground squirrels seem almost unaware of danger and rely on their parents' long, high, trilling warning calls and whistles to know when to dive back into their holes.

Thirteen-lined ground squirrels are found throughout Wisconsin. If you are lucky enough *not* to have one in your backyard and want to see them in action, you can usually find them in mowed areas of local parks or vacant lots. Unlike bird-watching which requires you to get up at the crack of dawn, ground squirrels are late risers, rarely coming out until there's bright daylight, usually by 9 or 10 a.m. On cloudy days, they may not come out at all. At heavily used parks with picnic areas, young squirrels can be seen most any time of the day, especially if they know there are friendly kids with chips or popcorn to feed them. If you have the urge to do so, remember that junk food is not healthful for any wild animal, and that more than one squirrel has mistaken a finger for a cheese puff, peanut, or some other snack food, a mistake that can give a whole new meaning to "finger food."

Ground squirrels are not protected by either state or federal laws, and backyard gardeners and greens keepers continue their never-ending efforts to eradicate them from our manicured and orderly landscape. Despite all its vices, the ground squirrel plays an important role in the survival of other animals such as fox, badgers, and hawks that rely on it as a food source. In addition, ground squirrels are interesting and entertaining to watch—as long as they're not digging in your own backyard, that is.

COTTONTAIL RABBIT
HARE TODAY, GONE TOMORROW

"Here comes Peter cottontail,
Hopping down the bunny trail . . . "

This old, familiar song proclaims the arrival of the cottontail rabbit that delivers candy and brightly-colored eggs to children on Easter morning. But how did this otherwise common and insignificant animal become associated with the most important Christian holiday? The answer lies far back in the dim recesses of human memory, back to an ancient time when the Germanic people of northern Europe worshipped the pagan goddess of spring named "Eastre," an old Saxon word from which Easter was derived. The goddess Eastre's constant companion and sacred escort was a hare or rabbit, the symbol of fertility. Many centuries later, German immigrants to America brought along this curious combination of pagan and Christian Easter customs that celebrate both the rebirth of Christ and the renewal of nature.

The cottontail rabbit or hare certainly lives up to its reputation as a symbol of fertility. They start breeding in February and never really stop until late summer. The female's gestation period is only four weeks. When she is ready to give birth, she makes a round depression in the earth and pulls fur from her belly to make a warm nest for the young. Within an hour of giving birth, the female temporarily leaves her newborn to breed once again in preparation for the next batch of bunnies in four more weeks. A single female cottontail can produce up to six litters a year, each averaging about five to seven bunnies. If all her broods would survive and reproduce themselves, in only five years she would have a family of two and a half billion bunnies!

Fortunately for the planet, cottontails have many enemies. They are favorite prey for fox, coyotes, weasels, mink, hawks, owls, and just about every other meat-eating animal on earth. Many people also have rabbit on their menu. Rabbit meat is tender, delicious, and can be prepared in dozens of ways. As a game animal, cottontails are the second most hunted species in Wisconsin, with sportsmen harvesting more than 800,000 each year.

Cottontails live throughout Wisconsin, but are more common in the southern agricultural areas of the state. They prefer grassy, brushy field areas or forest borders, but seem equally at home around buildings, on farms or in cities. Although it seems at times that cottontail rabbits feed exclusively on our garden plants, they actually eat just about any kind of vegetation available, even poison ivy berries and stems. It's been said that it would actually be easier to list those plants they won't eat rather than all the ones they do eat.

Although cottontail rabbits have sharp claws on their feet, they normally do not dig into the ground, not even to get at carrots. They also don't dig underground tunnels and burrows, preferring to use woodchuck holes. Their burrows are used only to escape from predators or occasionally for protection from the cold in winter. Cottontails prefer to sit in their open-air resting areas called "forms," usually in grass or brushy thickets. There, they can watch for predators or listen for them with their large, sensitive ears that are constantly flicking forward and backward. The cottontail can also detect predators by using a keen sense of smell provided by its perpetually wriggling nose. Surprised by a predator, the cottontail can leap five feet or more into the air and run up to twenty miles an hour.

Despite their speed and extra-sensitive hearing, sight, and smell, most cottontail rabbits do not survive beyond their first year of life, but enough do survive to continue the delicate balance of nature's life and death cycle. Without cottontails, an important link would be lost in the predator-prey food chain, threatening not only meat-eaters but the cottontail rabbits themselves, since they would suffer because of overpopulation. Although they are cute and cuddly and fun to watch, I doubt that anybody wants 2,300,000,000 billion bunnies in the backyard.

SPRING PEEPERS
JEEPERS, CREEPERS

" Jeepers, creepers ... where'd you get those peepers"
Jeepers, creepers ... where'd you get those eyes."

When the warmth of spring finally blankets Wisconsin in April, we all feel a bit happier, healthier, and maybe even get the urge to sing along to old familiar songs such as this one. Nature has plenty of its own spring songsters, of course, and one of them actually is a peeper. They're the tiny frogs you may have heard as early in the season as late March, since a few of them emerge and sing even before the ice has melted on their ponds.

Spring peepers are one of our smallest frogs, adult males measuring a mere three-quarters of an inch from nose to tail. Despite their small size, spring peepers can belt out their songs with such bravado that on a quiet, spring evening you can hear them more than a mile away. Their call is a single, high-pitched *peep-peep*, which they repeat about once a second. Another common frog you might hear calling in the same pond at this time of year is the western chorus frog, which begins to sing even a few days earlier than the peeper. The chorus frogs' call is similar to that of the spring peeper, but is broken into four or five ascending, *it-it-it-it* staccato notes. Probably the best description I've heard is that it sounds like running your fingers slowly across the teeth of a hard plastic comb.

Only the male peeper "peeps" by inflating his throat into a large bubble almost as large as himself and calling over and over throughout the night hours. During the height of their breeding season, which can last for two months or more, they often call during the daylight hours as well.

Together with chorus frogs, spring peepers can produce an almost deafening noise with their loud, shrill songs, but apparently don't like to give public performances. I've tried to sneak up to one of their breeding ponds to get a look at the little crooners in action, but their bug-eyed peepers offer them excellent vision and the entire pond usually turns dead-silent as soon as they see a potential predator approaching. If you hold very still for a while, they may start singing again in a few minutes, but it requires patience.

Spring peepers, the most widespread tree frogs in America, can be found in nearly every marsh, meadow, pond, and wet ditch in the state. Despite being so common, peepers are difficult to observe in the wild and are more often heard than seen. After mating and laying their eggs on underwater plants, the adults leave their watery homes and spend the summer foraging for insects in drier woodland areas. They're light tan to dark brown in color and are most easily identified by the X-shaped mark on their backs. Like other tree frogs, spring peepers have suction cup tips on each of their toes and are excellent climbers. They also have the ability to change the color of their skin in only a few minutes, allowing them to blend right into the forest around them and avoid being seen by predators.

Unlike most other frogs that burrow into the mud under the water to keep from freezing in winter, spring peepers spend the cold months on dry land merely covered in leaf litter. How these tiny, cold-blooded animals can survive Wisconsin's coldest winters is truly a miracle of nature. Biologists believe the frogs use their bodies' own glucose or some other inner substance as natural antifreeze. This prevents their cells from being damaged by the freezing temperatures, even though ice crystals do form inside them. In late March, after the first few days of warm sunshine, spring peepers are aroused from their icy sleep and migrate back to their breeding ponds and marshes. Soon, they once again join in the never-ending chorus just as countless generations of peepers have done before them .

Stop by nearly any pond or marsh on a warm, calm evening in spring and listen for one of earth's most ancient music festivals now playing everywhere. Jeepers, creepers, it's a peep show you won't soon forget.

WHITE BIRCH
QUEEN OF THE FOREST

When I see birches bend to left and right
Across the lines of straighter trees,
I like to think some boy's been swinging them.
Some boy too far from town to learn baseball,
Whose only play was what he found himself,
Summer or winter, and could play alone.

—"Birches" by Robert Frost

Wisconsin is home to more than fifty different native trees, but few have ever been as revered and honored in literature, or steeped in our culture and history, as the white or paper birch. At the turn of the last century, author and naturalist Ernest Thompson Seton called the birch "the white queen of the woods" and it remains today almost everyone's favorite tree.

White birch is typically a northern forest tree, but can be found scattered in woodlands throughout the state and is planted as an ornamental shade tree in urban backyards, as well. The tree seems to grow well in nearly any type of soil throughout the state. No matter where it grows, birches love sunlight and are often the first trees to sprout up after a forest fire or some other disturbance, including clearcut logging. Similar to other "pioneering" trees such as aspen, white birch grows quickly and can reach heights of fifty to seventy feet, but does not live long—usually less than eighty years. Many birches die much sooner than this because they are susceptible to many diseases and insects. One of the more common of these pests is the birch leaf miner, a tiny larva of the sawfly which eats out the succulent leaf material between the upper and lower surfaces. The leaf remains whole but you can see through it in areas that were "mined," and usually the leaves turn yellow and die. Another threat to birches is the bronze birch borer, which is a larval form of a beetle that feeds on the woody tissue of the birch, often killing the tree in the process.

Although most of us think of birches as just attractive landscape trees in our parks and backyards, they are important timber trees in the northern forests as pulpwood for the paper industry and for the fine, hard veneer used for home paneling and cabinet work. White birch lumber is used for everything from clothes pins to toothpicks, and birch logs produce hot, long-lasting coals in our fireplaces. From the day it's cut in the forest until it shows up in your house as a finished product (it could be part of your daily newspaper) white birch provides thousands of jobs for Wisconsin citizens in a variety of industries.

To Native Americans centuries ago, white birch was a vital link to their survival. They utilized the tree's tough, naturally waterproof bark for dozens of purposes, from building the roofs of their wigwams to making cooking pots. White birch pots were created by sewing the bark together with fine spruce rootlets and sealing the seams with pine pitch. They could cook meats and make stews in them by dropping red-hot stones from a campfire in the pots, which brought the water to a rapid boil. In times of famine, the bark itself was nourishment, since the inner bark could be dried and ground into flour. The tree could also be tapped for its sap, which was boiled down into a sweet syrup similar to that from maple trees.

Probably the best known and most ingenious use of the tree by Native Americans was in using the leathery sheets of white birch bark to cover the cedar wood frames of their canoes. These strong, lightweight watercraft were used for centuries not only by the tribes of the northern states but also by the early European voyageurs and explorers. Even though modern canoes are now covered with aluminum, fiberglass, or plastic, the basic, graceful shape of the birch-bark canoe has remained virtually unchanged over the centuries.

White birch trees remain a vital link to our everyday lives. We enjoy these attractive "queens of the woods" in our backyards, while we make use of the many paper and wood products they provide. With proper forest management, the white birch will always be a familiar sight in

Wisconsin's woodlands, waiting for a new generation of children to go "swinging" on their branches.

LEOPARD FROGS
ENVIRONMENTAL CANARIES FOR THE 21ST CENTURY

"The river will teem with frogs. They will come up into your house and into your bedroom and onto your bed . . . even into your ovens and kneading bowls. The frogs will swarm all over you and your subjects."

—Exodus 7, The Bible

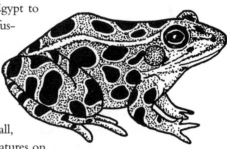

No doubt being knee-deep in the frogs that God sent onto Egypt to punish the Pharaoh for refusing to free the Israelites must have been unnerving and a bit messy. But it certainly wouldn't have been life-threatening—except to the frogs, I suppose. After all, frogs are one of the few creatures on earth that really don't harm or threaten us in any way. Most have no teeth, no claws, don't bite, and are gentle even when captured and held by small children. They don't even eat anything, plant or animal, of value to us. To the contrary, as every farmer and gardener knows, frogs have ferocious appetites for most things we don't want, such as slugs, flies, mosquitoes, beetles, grasshoppers, and other insect pests.

Wisconsin is home to a dozen different species of frogs, ranging in size from the tiny spring peepers to the largest bullfrogs. One of the most common is the northern leopard frog, which may be identified by the distinctive chocolate-brown spots outlined in cream color all over its bright green body.

Spring is the best time to see or hear leopard frogs in action. Soon after the first warm rains, they leave their wintering areas in deeper waters and travel to shallow breeding ponds and marshes. There the males begin to sing their low-pitched croaks that sound to us like someone rubbing a finger over a wet balloon. To female frogs, of course, this croaking noise is an irresistible love song. In late April, females lay jelly-like masses of up to six thousand black eggs that stick to underwater vegetation and hatch into tadpoles about two weeks later. By early June, the adult leopard frogs leave the breeding ponds and move inland in search of insects, sometimes more than a mile from standing water. They hunt for food by merely picking out a spot to sit and wait for their prey to fly or crawl by and lap them up with their long, sticky tongues. They don't even need to take a drink since they can absorb water directly from the air through their moist skin.

From the day they hatch into tadpoles until they are fully-grown adults, frogs face dangers and enemies at every turn. Just about everything likes to eat frogs, from the fish, water bugs, turtles, and herons in their water homes to raccoons, mink, and snakes on dry land. Many people still consider frog legs a delicacy. And what would freshman biology class be without the traditional frog to dissect?

Leopard frogs were once the most common frog species in Wisconsin, but their populations have dropped dramatically during the last fifteen years or so. Unfortunately, there is also a steady drop in frog populations worldwide, causing biologists to sound the alarm in the early 1990s that something may be seriously wrong with the environment. Although scientists around the globe have been working on an explanation for this phenomenon, no single reason has yet to be found, even though several combinations of man-made causes are suspected. We now know that habitat destruction, acid rain from our coal-burning power plants and factories, nitrates and phosphates from our fertilizers, and of course some of the one billion pounds of pesticides we Americans spray on our fields and gardens each year can all be lethal to frogs. In addition, the thinning of the ozone layer has increased ultraviolet radiation from the sun, which has been found to kill frog eggs and weaken their natural immune systems.

Some may wonder why we should we care if frogs disappear from the planet. After all, even God sent frogs down on Egypt as a plague on the earth. Besides the ethical and moral considerations, scientists believe these soft skinned, cold-blooded amphibians may be nature's modern version of the coal miner's canaries of the last century. Their demise may be a wakeup call that a man-made chemical disaster may be on the horizon, if we don't find ways of eliminating the pollutants and chemicals we dump into our environment every day.

Frogs have lived successfully on this planet for more than 350 million years. We can hope that the eternal spring chorus of frogs singing from our ponds will not fall silent because we unknowingly created our own environmental plague of biblical proportions. By studying the reasons for the drop in frog populations worldwide, we're also discovering how to better protect and preserve our favorite species—us.

FLYING SQUIRRELS
WORKING THE WOODLAND NIGHTSHIFT

Almost everyone has seen a flying squirrel—at least on television. Remember those old cartoon shows that starred Rocky the Flying Squirrel and his dim-witted but faithful sidekick, Bullwinkle Moose? After almost forty years of continuous reruns, Rocky is still seen on local network and cable programming featuring the heroic adventures of this animated flying squirrel. Wearing his trademark leather aviator's helmet, goggles, and scarf, Rocky, with a boost from Bullwinkle, could rocket into the sky in each episode to save the day.

Of course, real flying squirrels are a little more difficult to see in the wild, since they become active only well after nightfall and disappear into the darkness at the slightest hint of danger. They also can't fly nearly as well as their cartoon counterparts, and, truth be told, they really can't fly at all. Flying squirrels are expert gliders, however, and can sail through the dark night skies for two hundred feet or more in a single leap. They accomplish this by crawling up the sides of tall trees and launching themselves into the air with all four legs spread at right angles to their bodies. This stretches out their loosely folded skin or gliding membrane, which is attached to their wrists and ankles, creating a kind of square-shaped Frisbee. To avoid crashing into trees and branches they use their long furry tails held straight out behind them as a rudder to swerve and twist around obstacles.

Flying squirrels are small, attractive rodents with very large, sensitive eyes to help them see at night. Both the northern and southern flying squirrels live in Wisconsin. They are most common in wooded areas with oak and hickory trees, but are also abundant in the northern evergreen forests and in most urban areas. The northern flying squirrel is a little larger, has darker belly fur, and ranges from Wisconsin way up into Canada, while the smaller southern species lives from about central Wisconsin all the way to the southern states. Although flying squirrels are common throughout the state, few of us are aware of their presence because they rarely venture out to eat or play until well after sundown. Occasionally, they're discovered by accident, as I did several years ago while working as a ranger in the Northern Highland State Forest in Vilas County. One day we were assigned to cut down a dead tree hanging over a busy roadway. As the tree fell to the pavement, it split apart and out popped five very surprised and sleepy flying squirrels. Although dazed and sluggish as first, they quickly came to life and scampered off to find a new home in the forest—much farther away from forest rangers, no doubt.

Flying squirrels can often be spotted late at night raiding bird feeders. Since they're small enough to be able to squeeze through openings only one inch in diameter, they often take up residence in birdhouses, attics, or inside summer cottages. Most flying squirrels prefer to live in trees, especially older or dead ones with natural cavities in which they can build their nests of shredded bark, leaves, and moss. They need these hideouts as safe places to sleep during the daylight hours, to get shelter from the winter cold, and to raise their young .

Females give birth to two to six babies as early as April, with some late litters not arriving until August. Since male flying squirrels desert the family before their offspring are even born, it's up to the mothers to feed and care for their young alone. After they're weaned at about eight weeks old, young flying squirrels are ready for their first solo flight, and from then on glide through the night skies like their parents in search of food. Flying squirrels eat a variety of acorns, nuts, fruits, berries, and mushrooms, but hickory nuts are by far their favorite. They also eat quite a few night-flying insects such as large moths and winged beetles.

With their large eyes and excellent night vision, flying squirrels are well adapted to their twilight lives of working the graveyard shift of the forest. Because they are active only at night, they're able to avoid most of the daytime predators that endanger their sun-loving cousins, the gray squirrel and red squirrel. They still must keep a sharp lookout for nighttime predators such as the great-horned owl, which can pursue them on the wing, or free-roaming domestic cats that stalk the woodlands near farms and urban areas.

Although most of us are unaware of their presence, there's probably a real Rocky living somewhere close by in a local woodlot, park, or even in our own backyards. It's too bad we don't get a chance to see these gentle, attractive squirrels more often, but it's nice to know that they're out there each night, faithfully punching in on the night shift when the rest of us are just falling asleep.

BLOODROOTS
NATURE'S MAGIC MARKERS

There's nothing like a warm and sunny spring day in Wisconsin. After being cloaked in winter's snow and ice for so long, the fields and forests seem to come alive almost overnight, shedding their drab brown overcoats to reveal the fresh bright green of spring. Soon after, wildflowers add to the kaleidoscope of spring colors, and one of the first to appear is bloodroot. These attractive flowers, almost two inches across, have eight white petals. They can be found growing in rich soils in woods, brushy areas, and south-facing hillsides throughout the state and throughout the Eastern United States.

Since bloodroots appear so early in spring, usually April, they often fall victim to late frosts. To help them survive this hazard, their flower buds emerge on separate stalks with the leaves of the plant curled around them, which offers some protection from the cold weather. But even with this safeguard, many bloodroots are touched by a hard frost, anyway, causing their delicate petals to drop to the ground. Only the green seed pod on the flower stalk and its deeply lobed leaves remain and continue to grow throughout the season.

Although bloodroots are usually found in heavily shaded areas such as the borders of woods or along brushy fence lines, they take advantage of the warm spring sun by blooming early in the season before the trees and shrubs sprout leaves and shade the forest floor. Actually, bloodroots will bloom only in full sunlight and, like all members of the

Poppy family, have the ability to close their flower buds on cloudy days or when the weather turns colder, to protect their fragile petals.

Bloodroots got their name from the sticky reddish-orange sap that oozes from the end of the plant's stem when broken. I remember that, as kids, my brothers and I used to search out bloodroots in spring while playing in a woodlot on our family farm and dab red sticky spots on each other's faces and arms as a joke. We also discovered that the latex-like reddish juice from the bloodroot made a pretty good dye. Once dried on the skin, it could take days to wash off, although we probably didn't try too hard when we could get away with it. We also found that if the sticky sap got on clothing it would set in as a permanent stain, much to the chagrin of Mom on wash day.

Many years later, I learned that Native American Indians also made use of bloodroot centuries ago, and most likely picked it in the very same woods we used to play in as kids. No doubt Indian children also teased each other with these natural magic markers, but the adults had more serious uses for the plant. They used bloodroot juice as war paint or to paint their bodies for special ceremonies. They also used it as a dye for their clothing, basketwork, and even as an insect repellant. Bloodroot was also used by the Indians as a medicine to treat everything from rheumatism to ringworm. Later, early settlers used bloodroot as an ingredient in pioneer medicine to treat bronchitis and asthma. They even used it to treat colds, putting a drop of bloodroot juice on a lump of sugar to create an early American cough drop.

Although used as a medicine for centuries, bloodroot can also be poisonous. The plant contains protopine, an active ingredient also found in opium. If taken in small amounts this substance may cause only mild nausea, but if larger amounts are ingested it will eventually depress the blood circulation in the heart and result in death from overdose.

As a perennial, bloodroot blooms year after year. Individual patches can bloom probably for centuries, if left undisturbed. Whenever I come across these unique early spring wildflowers, I like to reflect on the possibility that a proud warrior may once have come to this same spot to gather bloodroots for war paint before going into battle, or I envision some pioneer farm kids teasing each other with its sticky sap while playing in the fresh spring woods. And yes, I still can't resist plucking a leaf myself here and there to watch the sticky reddish-orange juice ooze out of the stem just as countless others have done in the past—just for fun.

MOURNING CLOAK
BUTTERFLIES TOUGH AS NAILS

They're big, they're beautiful, and they're nearly always the first butterflies to appear in spring. Mourning cloak butterflies are easy to spot this time of year, with their attractive dark-brown velvety wings edged in yellow and sporting blue spots. Although they may appear fragile, these hearty insects are tough as nails. They survive the long, bone-chilling Wisconsin winter by hibernating in tree bark crevices, emerging again in early spring, long before other butterflies. Mourning cloaks can often be seen fluttering about the old snow piles of late March, and are usually out in full force by mid-April.

Most butterflies feed on the nectar of flowers to survive, but the mourning cloak emerges from hibernation long before the trees have sprouted leaves or spring flowers have bloomed. Luckily, Mother Nature always has a trick or two up her sleeve, and mourning cloaks can find all the nourishment they need by lapping up the sugary sap that drips from tree branches broken off from winter storms. Some people even attract mourning cloaks to their backyard feeders by putting out rotten apples or other fruit. I remember years ago seeing dozens of mourning cloaks and other butterflies in my grandfather's apple orchard, feasting on the fallen apples both in spring and again in fall.

Today, many people enjoy planting backyard butterfly gardens to attract and enjoy some of the more than one hundred different species of butterflies that live in Wisconsin. Recently, this hobby has expanded with the addition of butterfly houses, which serve both as safe shelters and as a place to hibernate for insects like the mourning cloak, tortoise shell, and angle-wing butterflies, all of which overwinter in the state. Plans for building butterfly houses are available at libraries and nature centers, and many birding and nature stores now sell completed butterfly houses as well.

Mourning cloaks got their common name long ago because they resembled the dark coats or cloaks worn by those mourning the death of a loved one. Despite their rather forlorn and distressing name, mourning cloaks can really brighten up the otherwise drab landscape of early spring everywhere they are found throughout North America, Europe, and Asia.

One of the first orders of business for a mourning cloak butterfly right out of hibernation is to keep flying until a mate is found. The female then lays clusters of fertilized eggs on some of her favorite food plants, such as willow and aspen trees. With their life cycle now complete, the early spring mourning cloaks soon die, leaving the future of their kind to the tiny, newly-hatched larvae or caterpillars. Because adult mourning cloaks perish so soon in spring, you rarely see them in summer when most other butterflies are abundant. By late summer and into fall, mourning cloak caterpillars stop eating, pupate, and re-emerge as a new generation of butterflies ready to hibernate through the winter, as countless generations of their kind have done before them. ▲

May

May ushers in a season of renewal and growth throughout Wisconsin. Farmers are busy working the earth and seeding their fields, sometimes late into the evening under May's full "planting moon."

Spring flowers such as trilliums, mayapples, and violets burst through the drab leaf litter to bloom and light up the woodlands. Trees and shrubs unfurl their newly sprouted leaves, as waves of warblers, wood thrushes, and brilliant orange-and-black orioles begin to build nests in their branches.

Bluebirds and tree swallows add a flash of color in the open fields and meadows as they stake claim to nesting boxes and search for early spring insects, often mayflies, to feed their hatchlings.

Every forest, meadow, marsh, and backyard garden seems to explode with activity in May, as nature's rebirth unfolds around us. But all too soon, the bright green of spring will fade as the days lengthen and the sun shines bolder and brighter each day in a march towards summer.

BLUEBIRD DAYS
BACK AGAIN IN WISCONSIN

Bluebirds have always been associated with the joy and happiness of life. Their cheerful song, colorful plumage, and friendliness towards people have inspired countless songs and verse. But, in recent times, bluebirds themselves have had little to be cheerful about. Their numbers had plummeted by ninety percent since the 1940s and their very survival into the next century was in question.

The reasons for the disappearance of our bluebirds were many. New agricultural pesticides killed and poisoned many of the birds' favorite foods, such as caterpillars, beetles, and grasshoppers. Many of the bluebird's traditional nesting sites were also destroyed. Farmstead orchards were cut down and plowed under while those that remained were cut clean of older trees or dead branches that once provided natural nesting holes for bluebirds. Another favorite nesting site in the tops of old-fashioned cedar fence posts also disappeared as wooden posts were replaced by modern steel posts.

Even more devastating to the bluebird population was another human blunder—the introduction of the European starling and house sparrow to America in the late 1800s. These aggressive, alien birds soon spread across the country, robbing bluebirds of the few natural nesting cavities available to them. By the early 1970s, seeing a bluebird anywhere in the countryside was a rare sight. Today, few people under the age of fifty have ever seen the bird in the wild.

But the whole bluebird story has yet to be written, and it may turn out to have a happy ending, after all. Thanks to the efforts of groups such as the Bluebird Restoration Association of Wisconsin and thousands of conservation-minded citizens across the country, the bluebird is making a comeback. The building of nesting boxes has helped bluebirds to repopulate areas they haven't inhabited for forty years or more. If you would like to help the bluebird recovery effort, you can start by erecting nesting boxes in your neighborhood or in the countryside, after getting permission from the landowner. Bluebird houses may be purchased at retail outlets or, if you prefer to build your own, detailed construction plans are available at most nature centers and libraries.

As with a good business, location is the key to success in attracting bluebirds to your birdhouses. Bluebirds are pretty fussy when it comes to nesting boxes, and won't use one if it's in the wrong location. Nesting boxes should be installed on a post four to five feet off the ground in areas of low vegetation such as open fields or large backyards in suburban and rural areas. They should be at least a hundred feet away from brushy or wooded areas to discourage wrens from moving in, and a quarter-mile away from farmyards to help keep out house sparrows. Tree swallows often compete with bluebirds for nesting boxes, as well, but you can accommodate both of them by placing two birdhouses in pairs about twenty feet apart. The swallows won't allow another pair of swallows to nest that close to them, but don't seem to mind if a bluebird pair should move in next door.

Bluebirds usually return to Wisconsin by the end of March or early April. The males arrive first to search for appropriate nesting areas to attract females when they arrive several weeks later. The female ultimately chooses which nesting box she will build her nest in, and she also does all the incubating of her five or so sky-blue eggs. The chicks are hatched and fledged in about eighteen days and then seem to disappear overnight, never to return to that nesting box again. Bluebird parents, however, do return again for a second nesting in June or even into July, but often select a different nesting box. By late August, bluebirds begin to flock together for their long migration south to the Gulf states. Some even fly as far as the Caribbean and northern Mexico.

Wisconsin has always been a favorite place for bluebirds and people here have always held a special place in their hearts for this bright, cheerful bird. It's seems fitting that the "bluebird of happiness" is again making a comeback in our area, with the help of average citizens.

WARBLERS
WHEN IN DOUBT, CALL THEM LBBS

Warblers are often described as the most beautiful and most abundant, yet least known, of all our wild birds. With more than fifty species of warblers in North America alone, identifying even a few dozen can take years of dedicated observation. Many have very southern-style names such as the Tennessee, Kentucky, Louisiana, Virginia, and Nashville warblers, while others have more self-descriptive names like the black-and-white, gold-cheeked, blue-winged, black-throated, orange-crowned, and yellow warblers, just to name a few.

Once on an early morning birding jaunt with a naturalist, I noticed that he pointed out almost all the more widely known birds—blue jays, cardinals, and chickadees—but seemed to be ignoring all the tiny, nondescript little birds flitting about in the bushes around us. When I asked him what these birds were called, he said, without hesitation, "Those are LBBs," and continued on with the hike. After a moment or two of hesitation, and trying not to sound too much like an amateur, I asked what exactly was an LBB? For all I knew, it was some sort of ornithological, scientific jargon.

"Oh," he responded sheepishly, "that means 'little brown birds'." In other words, he didn't know what they were, either.

One warbler that is easy to identify is the myrtle or yellow-rumped warbler. Unlike most other warblers, which are shy and elusive, the myrtle is a conspicuous, friendly little bird that tends to hang out around homes, gardens, and parks and doesn't seem to mind people. Its colorful plumage of blue-gray feathers with a black and white breast and head is easy to spot, but the real tip-off is the brilliant yellow spots on its rump, sides, and crown.

Myrtles are the most abundant of the warblers in Wisconsin. They're usually the first to appear in spring, sometimes arriving in the southern part of the state in late March. Unlike other warblers that must wait for the warmer weather to provide their insect food supply, myrtles can happily survive on old weed seeds and the berries of honeysuckle, Virginia creeper, or even poison ivy. In fact, these warblers got their original common name from their fondness of bayberry or wax myrtle berries, especially in the southern states. Like other warblers, myrtles are expert fly catchers and are responsible for the removal of millions of mosquitoes, deer flies, gnats, and other pesky insects during the summer.

You'd think all warblers could really "warble" out some pretty good melodies. In truth, most warblers are not very good singers at all. The myrtle warbler's normal call is a hoarse *tsip* sound, similar to that of a chickadee, although they can warble a bit during the breeding season in spring to attract mates.

Myrtle warblers are common in southern Wisconsin, mostly in spring and fall, but most prefer to nest in the large coniferous forests of northern Wisconsin and Canada. Like all warblers, they raise their families in the fast lane. After laying four or five eggs, hatching them in less than a dozen days, the parents feed the young for only two weeks or so before they're ready to leave the nest. By fall, they all flock together for the long migration to the southern states or on to the tropics of Mexico and Central America. Despite their speedy lifestyles, myrtles are in no hurry to migrate, and are always the last of the warblers to leave Wisconsin before the snow flies.

You can spend a lifetime getting to know warblers, either alone on quiet early-morning birding trips, or in the company of other birders. A good way to start is to tag along on a scheduled hike in a state park or forest, or with a local group such as your local chapter of the Audubon Society, which offer beginners a chance to mingle with seasoned, veteran bird-watchers. Or, if you prefer, you can get a pair of binoculars and one or two good bird identification books and go it alone. Before you know it, you will be able to tell your chestnut-sided warblers from the blackburnian warblers, and even be able to distinguish the Nashville from the Tennessee warblers. But even if you have a hard time telling one from the other, you can still enjoy the fresh morning air, good exercise, and wildlife watching. Remember that when all else fails, you can still call them LBBs and impress your friends with your birding expertise.

BALTIMORE ORIOLES
A SPLASH OF COLOR IN SPRING

They arrive in a splash of color each spring and light up our backyards, parks, and woodlands with their flashy, brilliant orange-and-black plumage. Few other birds catch our eye like Baltimore orioles (now often called northern orioles) do when they return to Wisconsin in early May. The handsome males are usually the first to arrive, followed by the much less colorful, dull-orange females a few days later. Somehow, these familiar backyard birds are able to find their way back to the same area of the state, and often even the same tree, year after year, after migrating thousands of miles from their tropical wintering grounds in Central and South America.

Orioles are probably one of the most conspicuous birds in our backyards. Not only do they stand out with their colorful plumage, but are noisy birds, as well. Both males and females sing a series of four to eight clear-whistled notes, often ending in melodious robin-like warble. They're especially vocal during the spring mating season when males sing from their highest perches, often singing together with other males. Even young nestlings sing from inside their nests, and once fledged, follow their parents while noisily begging for food day after day. Orioles are familiar to almost everyone, including city dwellers, since they prefer to live and nest in areas that have large, well spaced, broad-leafed trees such as those found along city streets, in parks, and in backyards and farmsteads.

Despite their common name, Baltimore orioles were not named after the city of Baltimore, nor are they even related to true orioles. They're actually members of the Icteridae family of birds, which includes blackbirds, grackles, and cowbirds. Early colonists to America

called them orioles because they had the same yellowish-orange coloration of the Old World orioles back home. They also named the bird
in honor of George Calvert or Lord Baltimore, founder of the Catholic
settlements in Maryland in 1632 , whose family coat of arms color was
black and orange.

There are 27 species of orioles in the Americas, most of which live
in tropical regions. Only three are found in the United States. The
familiar Baltimore oriole and the less common orchard oriole make
their home in Wisconsin and the eastern states, while the Bullock oriole is found in the western states. A few years ago, some biologists
believed that the Baltimore and Bullock orioles had actually hybridized
into one species in the Midwest, so some guidebooks began to refer to
them as American orioles. After further research, it appears the older
classification was sound, after all, and the familiar Baltimore oriole name
has returned once again. (Many guidebooks still include both the
Baltimore and the Bullock oriole under the northern oriole label.)

Baltimore orioles are probably best known for their unique and
attractive hanging nests. I remember watching orioles build these elaborate structures in large elm trees years ago on my family's farm. Male
orioles seem to pick out the mating and nesting sites, but after that,
females seem to do all the nest-building themselves. They select a forked
tip of a drooping branch, usually fifteen to thirty feet high, and start to
weave a long suspended sac out of grass, weeds, bark, and even string and
yarn if available. To discourage predators, they often build their nests
hanging over a stream, busy city street, or right over a dusty farm lane
where cows and machinery pass several times a day. Females lay four eggs
and do all the incubation themselves, but after that both parents become
busy feeding the hatchlings caterpillars, ants, weevils, and other insects.

Baltimore orioles are one of the most colorful and welcome birds
to return to our backyards each spring. You can encourage them to
spend more time in your neighborhood by offering them oranges cut
in half, or peanut butter, or you might want to purchase a special oriole nectar feeder available at most garden and birding centers.

Like spring itself, the splash of color provided by Baltimore orioles
fades all too quickly. By late summer, female and juvenile orioles start
to migrate south, followed by the males in late August or September.
By the time the orange and black colors of Halloween begin to appear
in autumn, most orioles are already basking in the warm, tropical sunshine of Central and South America. But come next spring, they'll

come back, just as they have for countless seasons, to brighten up our backyards with their flashy colors and familiar, cheery song.

FIDDLEHEADS
A FERN FOR THE BUTTER

They seem to pop up everywhere in spring. Some call them fiddleheads because they resemble the turned end of a violin, while others call them crosiers because they look like the curved end of a crosier or staff, carried by bishops. Whatever you call them, these familiar green plants sprouting in our spring woodlands are the uncurling fronds of our common ferns.

Ferns are found scattered here and there throughout our forests, but way back in prehistoric time they would have actually *been* the forest. Some 200 million years ago, long before the advent of flowering plants and seed-bearing trees, ferns and their relatives covered our hot, steamy planet from the equator to the poles. Most of these giants are now extinct and have long turned into coal beds, but a few tree-like ferns still survive in the tropics, capable of growing to fifty feet or more.

Wisconsin is home to dozens of kinds of ferns, most with colorful and descriptive names like cinnamon, interrupted, ostrich, maidenhair, sensitive, and royal ferns. Most prefer to grow in moist, shady lowland areas, but one of our best-known ferns, called pasture brake or bracken fern seems to thrive just about anywhere. They're found in swamps and marshes, but also in dry upland woods and even open fields, pastures, and burnt-over areas. In summer, this fern is easy to recognize with its tall, tri-forked stalks covered with delicate green leaflets. Like all ferns, brackens reproduce not using flowers and seeds, but millions of tiny spores which they cast into the wind.

Most ferns have tough, inedible stems when fully grown, and some are even mildly toxic to grazing cattle in summer pastures. But in early spring, when the fern's fiddleheads are uncurling, some people harvest them to eat as a wild vegetable. Cooked like asparagus and topped with a little butter and seasoning, they can be delicious. I tried a few over the years, with mixed results. Although most are edible, the best tasting fiddleheads come from the fronds of ferns that don't have many woolly fibers on them. Some species, like cinnamon fern, have so many down fibers that despite my efforts to remove the fuzz, it still felt like trying to swallow wet cotton balls.

Fiddleheads were once an important early spring food source for Native American Indians and early European settlers, especially after a long winter without green vegetables. Despite generations of use as food, recent studies warn that most ferns are slightly carcinogenic, so you may not want to eat too many of them. Fiddleheads may not replace your peas or green beans at the supper table, but they do have higher mineral and vitamin content than most cultivated garden vegetables. So, if you find yourself in a rustic, pioneering mood next spring, go on out and collect some of this ancient Jurassic junk food and prepare a wild, woolly (and free) vegetable dish for yourself.

COLLECTING AND COOKING INSTRUCTIONS

1. Break off fiddleheads in early spring when they are not more than 6 to 8 inches high.
2. Slide the stalks through your hands and fingers to rub off the woolly fibers.
3. Wash and boil them in salted water for few minutes, as you would for preparing asparagus.
4. Serve with melted butter and season with salt and pepper, or sprinkle with a mixture of grated cheddar and Parmesan cheese.

MAYAPPLES
NATURE'S DR. JEKYLL AND MR. HYDE

Mayapples are one of those woodland plants that seem to have a Dr. Jekyll and Mr. Hyde reputation. On one hand, the plant's large white blossom is one of our most beautiful spring flowers. Its attractive, flat-topped leaves give the appearance of small, green umbrellas shielding the forest floor from the spring rains. On the other hand, mayapple can be a menacing plant, since the stems, leaves, and especially the roots are laced with a powerful poison that can cause death in a few hours, if ingested. Yet, in smaller doses, this same chemical has been used for centuries in both home remedies and in many modern medicines for the treatment of everything from common stomach problems to cancer.

Another common name for the mayapple is *mandrake*, named by early colonists after an unrelated European plant of the same name. Since ancient times, the mandrake plant was believed to possess magical powers and was often used in sorcery and witchcraft. The plant's roots, like those of the mayapple, were thought to resemble the human form and believed to possess the power of the dark earth-spirits. In medieval times, many people believed that the plant uttered a shriek when pulled from the ground, which killed or made mad those who didn't cover their ears. Others believed the plant could be safely uprooted only by moonlight, and only after appropriate prayers and rituals were conducted.

Mayapples grow in rich woodland soils throughout Wisconsin from May to June. A few weeks after blooming, the large white flowers develop a green fruit, the size of a ping-pong ball, which is also poisonous. By late summer, however, yet another Jekyll-and-Hyde transformation will take place. As the fruit ripens and turns a yellow-amber color, it magically becomes safe to eat. I've picked and eaten many mayapples over the years and their peculiar sweet-sour taste and musty, fruity smell always remind me of the end of the summer season and the approach of autumn. Some people even make delicious jams and jellies out of the fruit.

Native Americans used mayapples for food and medicine, and also took advantage of the plant's powerful poison in magical rituals and used it as a weapon against their enemies. An early American explorer, Zeisberger, wrote in 1779 about the Delaware Indians: "In the use of poisonous roots, the Indians are well versed and there are many melancholy examples where they have by their use destroyed themselves or others. The roots of the may apple are a powerful poison which, who eats, dies in a few hours' time. The Indians enjoy eating the may apple fruit which has a sour but pleasant taste."

Mayapples, umbrella plants or mandrake—whatever you call them —are surely one of Wisconsin's most unusual wild plants. Pretty enough for an attractive floral bouquet right out of the ground, deadly enough to put you under it. An ancient and modern medicine used to save lives, or a powerful poison used to destroy them. Are they really the mysterious, magical ingredients for sorcerers and the likes of Mandrake the magician, or are they just another common woodland flower that bears delicious fruit in summer? Better ask Dr. Jekylll—or, better yet, Mr. Hyde.

MARSH MARIGOLDS
NOW SHOWING FOR A LIMITED SPRING ENGAGEMENT

According to the calendar, spring official-ly begins in March, but in Wisconsin the arrival of the real spring is usually delayed by several weeks. For me, a sure sign that spring is here to stay is when the local swamps become ablaze with the bright orange-yellow flowers of the blooming marsh marigolds.

Also called cowslips, marsh mari-golds can be seen in spring-time growing in wet meadows, marshes, and swamps, and along sluggish streams. The plant's flowers are easy to spot since they always bloom long before most other spring wildflowers and even before most trees and bushes have leafed out. Although most spring flowers are colorful, few can match the bright yellow blossoms that seem to light up the otherwise drab landscape of the marshes and swamps. Each individual plant may have a dozen or more flowering heads, as well. Despite the plant's common names, it is neither a marigold nor a cowslip, but rather a true member of the buttercup family.

Early European colonists found the marsh marigold a familiar and welcome sight when they arrived in the New World. The plant is native to both Europe and America. As they did for centuries in Europe, these early settlers used the marsh marigold for both food and as an important ingredient for medicines.

Marsh marigolds are considered to be poisonous and should never be eaten raw. When cooked, however, the leaves of the plant are safe to eat. They are rich in Vitamin A, Vitamin C, and iron. Although not a natural food junkie myself, I once decided to gather some marsh marigold leaves and give them a try. After boiling the spinach-like leaves for an hour with a change of water, as is suggested, I found the plant to be very tasty, especially with an added touch of butter and salt. In some areas of both America and Europe, people still make marsh marigold pickles from the plant's flower buds.

In years past, the marsh marigold has been used as a medicine to treat a variety of ailments, usually relating to chest or lung problems, and has long been a component of cough syrup. In addition, the plant has been the traditional medicine in the treatment of epilepsy, although modern drugs have now replaced it. An even more powerful drug derived from the plant was used as a strong heart and respiration depressant and as an insecticide. Probably a more familiar use of the plant was in the attempt to get rid of warts. People would squeeze the juice from the stem of the plant onto their warts to eliminate them. Whether this treatment actually worked is open to debate, but apparently enough people believed in it as a cure to hand it down as a home remedy from generation to generation.

Marsh marigolds are not rare or endangered plants, but in some areas they are threatened by the draining of marshes and swampy areas for farming or urban development. The plant often grows in areas that may not be classified as a true wetland, which is normally protected from destruction. Because of this, the marsh marigold may not be as easy to find as it once was. Good places to find this interesting plant are in low, swampy areas of local parks, along marshy streams, and in wooded drainage ditches. Remember, however, that all plants on state property and public parks are protected.

Marsh marigolds bloom for only a few weeks in the spring. But do take some time to discover this bright and cheery flower in a wetland near you. As they say at the movies, "Now showing, for a limited engagement."

JACK-IN-THE-PULPIT
BEAUTY AND THE BEAST

It was near the end of the 17th century and a small band of Meskwaki Indians was being pursued by their ancient enemies—the Sioux. When the Sioux warriors were closing in quickly and all seemed lost, the Meskwaki devised a brilliant and deceptive trap. They prepared several large pots of cooked meat and then abandoned them for their approaching enemies to find.

The Sioux warriors, thinking they had caused the Meskwaki to flee their camp in fear, boldly gorged themselves on the meat. A few hours later, the once proud warriors began to double up in pain and, one by one, most succumbed to death. Unknown to the Sioux, the Meskwaki had laced the meat with a finely chopped poisonous plant called *E-haw-sho-go*, better known to us as jack-in-the-pulpit.

How this delicate and beautiful spring flower could cause lethal poisoning remained a mystery for centuries until modern chemists discovered that the plant contains a deadly substance called calcium oxalate crystals. Luckily for us and any other creature that tries to eat jack-in-the-pulpit, this poison causes a stinging pain in the mouth, so a second bite is rarely attempted.

Despite the threat of poisoning, Native Americans used jack-in-the-pulpit as a medicine in small doses to treat a variety of illnesses, including coughs, fevers, and sore eyes. There are even accounts of Indians using the root tubers or corms as food, but only after months of drying or baking them to get rid of the poison. The plant's other common name, Indian turnip, suggests that it was once considered part of the menu for Native Americans.

Today, jack-in-the-pulpit is one of our favorite garden and woodland spring flowers. The plant is easily identified with its hooded flower cap and distinctive green, white, and purple stripes. The flower stalk is always accompanied by a separate three-leafed stem. The plant was named after its resemblance to the old-fashioned covered "pulpit" that clergymen used to preach from in churches. The term "jack" is just a general term for a man or boy, like jack-in-the-box, or a jack-of-all trades, but probably refers to the preacher or minister when this plant was first named.

If you take a look inside the "pulpit" by gently lifting the hood, you'll notice a ring of tiny flowers at the base of the spadix or "jack." These are the real flowers of the plant and are either all male or all female flowers on separate plants. Generally the healthier, stronger plants are female and the weaker plants are male. In an odd quirk of nature, a single jack-in-the-pulpit plant may change its sex from year to year depending on how much food supply it has stored up for reproduction. So the jack-in-the-pulpit you see this year might actually transform itself into a "Jill"-in-the-pulpit by next spring.

After blooming, the male flower withers away while the female flower matures and develops a large cluster of bright red, juicy-looking fruits perched on a lone stalk. Because of the high content of calcium oxalate crystals, these berries are very poisonous to most every creature except birds, which seem to gulp them down without any ill effect. In return, the birds benefit jack-in-the pulpits by distributing their seeds in their droppings throughout the woodlands.

Jack-in-the-pulpits grow in rich woodlands throughout the state and bloom from late May to June. Keep an eye out for these interesting plants on your next hike and contemplate their rich history, both as a beautiful spring flower and as a powerful weapon of war centuries ago.

PINK LADY SLIPPERS
NATURE'S PRECIOUS JEWELS

They sailed thousands of miles over treacherous seas to reach the hot, steamy, tropical jungles of places such as New Guinea, Madagascar, and the Amazon of South America. Like a scene right out of an Indiana Jones adventure film, they traveled by foot and dugout canoe, crossed piranha-infested streams, sidestepped venomous snakes, risked malaria and yellow fever, and dodged the poison-tipped arrows of hostile natives. What were these adventurers searching for? Not gold, silver, or precious jewels, as you might expect, but something more valuable—flowering orchids

In the late-1800s, wealthy Europeans were willing to pay thousands of dollars for a single new or rare orchid from exotic tropical lands to add to their collection. The orchid craze was so intense that an English import company once employed 140 full-time orchid hunters and sent them to the far reaches of the globe to gather new plants to feed this flower frenzy.

Today, orchids are still the most treasured plants on earth, but you don't have to travel halfway around the world to see one. One of the most beautiful and best known orchids grows right here in Wisconsin, as it does throughout North America and Europe. In Germany it was called *frauenschuh*, or lady shoes, while the Russians refer to it as *mariin bashnachock* or Mary's slippers. In Wisconsin, we call these beautiful native wildflowers either moccasin-flower or lady's slippers. All of the common names for this plant refer to the shoe or slipper-like shape of its flower. Its original name can be traced back to the 16th century, where it was first called "slipper of our Lady," in homage to Mary, the mother of Christ.

There are more species of orchids than are found in any other plant family, with more than 25,000 known species found everywhere from the arctic tundra to the tropics. We have 21 different species of orchids in North America, but the pink lady's slipper is by far the best known and probably the most common to grow in Wisconsin. Lady's slippers grow only in acidic soils such as those found in dry oak or pine forests, but also in wetlands, especially bogs. Lady's slippers are often unintentionally destroyed by people who attempt to transplant them into their backyard gardens. Because they can absorb nourishment only when there's a special fungus in the soil, these transplants almost always fail. Most greenhouses and gardening catalogs now have specially-bred orchids for home gardens, so there's no reason to attempt to take them from the wild.

Lady's slippers have an unusual way of getting insects to pollinate them. Their strange-looking flowers are made up of petals attached together, like an inflated sac. An entrance hole in the front and two exit holes on either side of the top of the blossom allow insects to enter and exit the flower. Insects, usually bumblebees, are attracted to the flower by its color and scent and enter the front of the flower to collect the sweet nectar inside. Since the petals are folded inward, they can't back out of the same hole they entered, and are forced to travel up through the flower sac in tunnels to find an exit. As they crawl through this insect funhouse maze, the bees touch and rub off pollen onto a bright green pad between the two exits, which is the female part of the flower. At the exit hole are the round projections of the male part of the flower, which dusts them with a gummy pollen to be deposited in the next flower they visit.

Not all lady's slipper orchids produce flowers, but the ones that do will eventually develop seedpods that release thousands of tiny seeds in fall and winter. Despite the large number of seeds produced, only a few will find the right conditions to sprout, since the seeds can't develop until they're joined by a special fungus, a situation that can take several years to occur, until conditions are just right.

Pink lady's slippers bloom in spring, usually in May and June. Because of the very special growing conditions they need to survive, and past abuses of uninformed wildflower collectors, they're not too common in most of our woodlands. If you're lucky enough to come across one this spring, please resist the temptation to take it home. Better to leave this beautiful orchid in the wild where it belongs for everyone to enjoy as one of nature's most precious jewels.

TRILLIUMS
LIGHTING UP THE SPRING WOODLANDS

Spring just wouldn't seem like spring in Wisconsin without the bright white glow of blooming trilliums illuminating our woodlands. These beautiful wildflowers stand out like white flags against the otherwise drab brown leaf litter of the forest floor, making them easy to spot. Later in spring, the bright white flowers of the trillium turn a pinkish color, eventually shriveling up as their seedpods begin to develop. Trilliums bloom from late April into June and can be found nearly anywhere in the state, but prefer the rich soils of mature hardwood forests.

Trilliums are members of the lily family, which include several other familiar plants, including Solomon's seal, lily-of-the-valley, and even wild asparagus. The most common trillium in Wisconsin is the large-flowered or white trillium, but other species, such as the attractive red trillium, nodding trillium, painted trillium, and the rare snow trillium, may also be found in the state. Learning to identify trilliums is literally as easy as one, two, three, since all of them have three leaves, three petals, three sepals, and three seedpods. Even the first part of their name, "tri," is Latin for three. Early Christian settlers in America called the trillium the "trinity flower" while others knew it as Indian shamrock. Later the plant was known as "birthroot," referring to its use for centuries by Native American and pioneer women as a medicine to ease childbirth or for menstrual problems.

Wild trilliums are one of those attractive native flowers that we nearly loved to death. Earlier in this century, trilliums were indiscriminately picked and dug out of nearly every woodlot in the state by unscrupulous greenhouse owners, florists, and backyard garden enthusiasts. Unfortunately, this unregulated harvest could not go on forever without hurting the native populations, especially since trilliums have such long and complicated reproduction cycles. Trillium seedlings need fully six years of growth before they can produce their first bloom and seed. In addition, they have evolved an unusual and interesting method of dispersing their seeds. In late August, the trillium's seedpods mature and begin to split open. At the same time, the plant's stem bends towards the earth and the seeds begin to fall out in clusters. The seeds are covered with a sticky, sweet goo that attracts ants, which then carry them back to their nests as food. The ants are able to eat the sticky outside of these seeds but not the hard seeds themselves, so they unwittingly plant trillium seeds throughout the forest, making them one of the earth's original flower gardeners.

Today, thanks to state legislation, wild trilliums are protected from harvest for commercial or personal sale. Trilliums, like all other flowering plants, have long been protected on state-owned land, including state parks, forests, and recreational and natural areas. Because of this, some of the most spectacular spring trillium displays may be seen in places such as the Kettle Moraine State Forest and other public lands.

It's said that good things usually come in threes. Thanks to the far-sighted efforts of ordinary Wisconsin citizens, this three-sided wildflower seems to have been saved from destruction. With continued protection, the future of the wild trillium looks as bright as the forest floors they illuminate across Wisconsin each spring.

GREAT BLUE HERON
GENTLE GIANT OF THE BIRD WORLD

"It was a grand sight to see them rise, so slow and stately, so long and limber, with an undulating motion from head to foot and looking so warily about them. It would affect our thoughts, deepen and perhaps darken our reflections, if so huge birds flew in numbers in the sky."

—Henry David Thoreau, April 19, 1852

Few birds are so impressive in flight as the great blue heron. With a wingspan of almost six feet, they seem to glide effortlessly through the sky, holding their long, thin necks bent backwards and outstretched legs trailing behind. Even on the ground, great blue herons are stately birds, and at four feet tall are the largest of all North American herons. Adult herons have attractive bluish-gray and rust-colored plumage, a white head, and a black stripe from their bright yellow eyes to the tip of their crown.

Great blue herons, common in Wisconsin, can be seen wading in the shallows of almost any wetland, lake, pond, or river. You may have to look closely, however, since a heron is often mistaken for just another piece of driftwood or a small dead tree in the water. Like any good fisherman, herons have almost unlimited patience and can stand nearly motionless for hours, waiting for just the right moment to snatch up a small fish, frog, or crayfish that wanders by. Herons have long, sharp beaks but don't actually use them to spear fish as was once thought. They clamp their beaks around their catch, flip it up in the air, and swallow it whole.

Years ago, great blue herons were despised and often killed by fishermen who thought these birds were harmful to game fish populations. Although they can do damage in fish hatcheries, biologists have found that herons eat mostly minnows, frogs, crayfish, and the smaller, stunted, surplus fish in lakes and rivers. In addition, herons feast on mice, rats, grasshoppers, and other agricultural pests, making them a valuable ally to farmers in rural areas.

Herons are largely solitary birds, usually seen alone except during the breeding season in spring and early summer. This is the time of year that herons pair up and gather in large numbers, sometimes several hundred, to nest together in large colonies called "rookeries." Most of us never get a chance to see these rookeries, since they are usually located in very isolated areas, often in stands of large, dead trees over standing water. A few years ago my wife and I had the unique opportunity to visit one of these rookeries when we inadvertently camped across from one at a canoe campsite in the Northern Highland State Forest, in Vilas County. Although we had seen a few adult herons during the day, and heard their familiar deep, croaking *kraak* voices booming over the lake, little did we know what the night might bring. All through our sleepless night at the campsite and into the morning, we heard the booming voices of hundreds of young herons incessantly croaking, *ak..ak..ak*, and flapping their wings. Young fledging herons have almost insatiable appetites, seemingly determined to let their overworked parents and the rest of the world know that they are hungry.

In the morning, we canoed across the lake to the heron rookery and found hundreds of nests, some of which were built in trees over dry ground. The nests were made of large sticks piled several feet thick and thirty to fifty feet up in the treetops. Almost immediately, we discovered a couple of dead baby herons lying on the ground. Heron parents won't feed their young if they topple out of the nest, so if the fall to the ground doesn't kill them, they soon die anyway. Only about half of young herons survive their first year. In addition to falling out of nests, some are snatched off their nests by predators such as eagles and raccoons, while others starve right in the nest if they hatch much later than their siblings. Although this may seem cruel to us, it's just nature's way of controlling the heron population and insuring that the strongest survive.

As we walked under the rookery, we noticed that all the vegetation under the nesting trees seemed to be whitewashed, and after a few near misses, decided to take a hasty retreat in order to avoid the bombardment from the sky. We later learned that in addition to their "poop-bombs," young blue herons also regurgitate undigested food down on intruders under their nests as a defensive reaction to predators (or people) that dare to visit their rookeries. Needless to say, it's best not to disturb a rookery at all.

Although great blue herons are still a familiar sight in wetlands everywhere, these gentle giants are not as numerous as they once were. Heron populations took a sharp decline in the 1960s, probably due to the same pesticides that harmed bald eagles, ospreys, and other fish-eating birds. But with protection status under the "blue crane" legislation passed in the 1960s in Wisconsin, and new wetland protection laws, great blue herons seem to be holding their own for now. With continuing efforts to protect heron rookery nesting sites and conserve wetland areas, perhaps future generations of humans will continue to experience Thoreau's "grand sight" of seeing these "huge birds flying in numbers in our sky."

SALAMANDERS
SLITHERING INTO SPRING

Spring is the time of year when every young person's fancy turns to love. It's the season for courtship, pairing, and bonding. But imagine how difficult it would be to find your true love if your vision was so poor that everyone you looked at was just a blur. And imagine not being able to whisper sweet nothings in your sweetheart's ear because you're mute, and even if you could, it wouldn't be heard because both of you are deaf, as well.

Such is the love life of a common Wisconsin amphibian called the salamander. But don't feel sorry for salamanders yet. It's true that they can't see very well up close and can't use their eyesight to find their mates. On the other hand, their farsightedness allows them to keep a sharp eye on approaching predators. It's also true that they can't hear very well and don't even have ear openings in their heads, yet they do have sensitive bones in their front legs that can detect vibrations similar to hearing. And yes, salamanders can't belt out love songs for their mates since they don't even have vocal cords.

Yet, somehow, despite all these handicaps, salamanders do manage to find each other as they gather near their breeding ponds each spring. But even then, they display some peculiar habits. After an elaborate mating ritual of thrashing and squirming together in the water for hours, the male drops one or two jelly-like blobs that contain the sperm. These sink to the bottom of the pond, where the female scoops them up and actually fertilizes herself internally. The eggs are laid in small clusters and hatch into tiny tadpoles with gills, just as other amphibians.

Salamanders look like tiny lizards, although they have no reptilian scales or claws. Instead, they have a smooth and slimy skin that prevents them from drying out and protects them from infection. Wisconsin is home to eight different species of salamanders. The smallest and most often seen in spring is the blue-spotted or Jefferson's salamander. It grows only four or five inches long and is mostly blue-black in color with turquoise flecks or spots on its sides. Another common salamander found here is the much larger black-and-yellowish tiger salamander.

All salamanders are harmless to people, but are ferocious predators to snails, earthworms, beetles, spiders, and anything else they can catch to eat. Not many other creatures are interested in eating salamanders, however. When a predator threatens the tiny blue-spotted salamander, it raises its tail, curls it over its back, and wriggles it from side to side in a warning. At the same time, it secretes a white, foul-tasting, sticky substance from the glands at the base of the tail—sort of a miniature version of a skunk.

Because salamanders are most active late at night or during rainy days in summer, most of us rarely get to see them unless we stumble across them in the garden or find them stranded in the window wells of our homes. For most of the year, they are secretive, remaining hidden under rocks, logs, and leaf litter. Biologists aren't even certain where most salamanders spend their winters, although they probably go underground or under the water to avoid freezing their tiny, moist bodies.

Less is know about salamanders than just about any other animal, and often what we do know is silly folklore. One of these is the old myth that salamanders can live in fire. In reality, salamanders simply like to hide under the bark of logs to keep cool and moist, but when a log is thrown in the fire, they scurry out to escape the heat, giving the false impression that they had been living in the flames.

New efforts to find out more about all amphibians is now underway worldwide, including surveys right here in Wisconsin. Frog and salamander populations have dropped dramatically everywhere, even in the most remote corners of the planet. Biologists hope to determine whether the long-term die-off is due to natural causes, a result of global warming, or some toxins we are releasing into the environment. Some have suggested that the soft, moist amphibian skin is simply unable to adapt to the increasing ultraviolet rays and the decreasing ozone layer of our atmosphere.

Nobody knows yet, but perhaps these seemingly insignificant, nearly blind, deaf and dumb salamanders may turn out to be an important factor in preserving our own health in the future. Time will tell.

TICKS
TINY TERRORS OF THE WOODLANDS

It was like a scene right out of one of those old Hollywood adventure movies. There I was, lying in bed on a hot, sweaty, sleepless night when suddenly I felt something squirm and slowly crawl up my chest. At first, all I could think of were those huge poisonous tarantula spiders like you see in the movies—but then I remembered that this was hardly the tropics of South America. I was inside a university summer camp barracks deep in the Chequamegon National Forest, in northern Wisconsin. As it turned out, the creature was no tarantula, but rather the giant spider's tiny cousin called a wood tick.

Ticks are small, brown, crab-like animals with very hard, flat bodies that are nearly impossible to squash by hand. Although they look like insects, they're really more closely related to the likes of scorpions, mites, and even king crabs. Wood ticks are common throughout most of the state and are most abundant in low, brushy woodland and grassy areas in early spring and summer. Wood ticks have the obnoxious habit of dropping onto and attaching themselves to any warm-blooded animal that happens to brush by them—mostly woodland creatures such as deer, mice, and squirrels, but occasionally people as well. Once attached, they seek out warm, moist spots on the skin, make an incision, and insert their sharp, sucking mouth parts to drink their meal of blood.

Since wood ticks were always part of our landscape, and are fairly harmless creatures, we've never paid much attention to them—until now. Starting in the late 1960s, a new member of the tick family suddenly appeared in our state for the very first time. Almost overnight, this smaller cousin of the wood tick, called the "deer" or "bear" tick, began making headlines all over the country and was dubbed by some as "one of the most serious pests known to man." The deer tick has the dubious distinction of carrying another dangerous critter, called a spirochaete (spy-ro-kete) which is the microscopic organism that causes the serious bacterial infection we now know as lyme disease.

Before the 1960s, deer or bear ticks were known to exist only on a small island near Cape Cod, but soon afterward were found in large concentrations near the small New England town of Old Lyme, Connecticut. Many of the town's children were coming down with a new illness characterized by severe headaches, fevers, chills, and stiff joints similar to those caused by arthritis. Eventually the connection between the deer ticks and the sick children was made and the newly discovered disease was named after the town, which probably did not thrill the local chamber of commerce.

Soon after that first encounter with lyme disease on the east coast, deer ticks expanded their range quickly. Outbreaks were reported in nearly every state in the union, including Wisconsin. In only fifteen years, lyme disease had become a household word and soon became the most diagnosed tick-borne illness in the country.

How these tiny deer ticks could have spread so quickly remains a mystery, but it's believed that most of new deer tick populations around the country were started when people brought ticks back from the east coast in camping equipment and RVs, or on pets.

Another reason for the amazing spread of deer ticks was the nearly explosive rise in deer populations since the 1960s. Adult female deer ticks feed almost exclusively on white-tail deer, gorging themselves with blood before leaving their host to lay some ten thousand eggs. Newly hatched larval ticks prefer to feed mostly on white-footed mice, but will take blood meals from dogs, cats, squirrels, chipmunks, and of course people. Once they mature, the females will once again search out deer blood to lay eggs, thus continuing the life cycle.

None of us can completely escape the possibility of being bitten by a wood or deer tick, but we can improve our odds of escape by using insect repellents that contain Deet, wearing long-sleeved shirts, and tucking pants legs into socks when going through brushy or grassy areas. It's also wise to check out your body after a hike in the woods, since it takes several hours for a tick to imbed it's mouth parts into your skin, and merely taking a shower won't always wash ticks off.

Not all ticks are carriers of lyme disease. The common wood tick, which is larger than the deer tick and has white markings on its body, is one that does not carry the disease. The deer or bear tick, which does carry the disease, is smaller than a wood tick, about the size of a poppy seed, and is plain brown in color. Deer ticks are also more commonly encountered throughout the summer and into autumn, when hunters often come in contact with them after harvesting a deer or bear.

If you find a tick imbedded in your skin, it is best not to pull it out with your fingers, since this might squeeze the tick's body fluids into the wound. Old-time methods such as touching the tick with a hot match, or trying to cut off its oxygen supply with Vaseline, usually don't work, either. The best way to remove a tick is to grab the head end of the tick with tweezers and pull it straight out. If, two or three weeks after the bite, a rash starts to develop in the area of the wound, you may be having the first symptoms of lyme disease and should see a doctor for testing and possible treatment.

The deer tick seems to be one of those remarkable, extremely hardy, alien creatures that we'll just have to live with from now on. Some people have promoted the idea of wiping out the entire white-tail deer population and trapping out white-footed deer mice in our woodlands as a possible solution to the lyme disease problem. At first glance this may seem like a good idea, until you consider that without the deer and mice to feed on, the tough, adaptable deer tick would no doubt merely move on to its other favorite warm-blooded animal—us. ▲

JUNE
June

Summer officially starts at the summer solstice, June 21st, the longest day and shortest night of the year. The warmer days and abundant food of the season are a welcome relief for all wildlife, but especially for the many newborn animals venturing out on their own for the first time. Many white-tail deer fawns are born this month. Although their spindly legs seem to wobble at first, they are able to outrun most of their predators within a few hours.

On warm, quiet evenings, whippoorwills return to serenade us through the night, while the awkward June bugs, attracted by house lights, can be heard bouncing off window screens. In the distance, the banjo-like *plonk-plonk* call of green frogs echoes in the marshes and ponds. Gentle warm rains induce delicious morel mushrooms to sprout overnight.

June's "strawberry moon" signals that the tiny, sweet wild strawberries will soon be ready for picking. Others call this month's full moon the "flower" or "rose" moon, because the showy wildflowers are at their peak, including the beautiful pink wild roses that bloom in old fields and along fencerows. Still others know June's full moon as the "honey moon" since honeybees are busy collecting sweet nectar in blooming apple orchards, flower-filled meadows, and backyard gardens.

RUBY-THROATED HUMMINGBIRDS
LITTLE DYNAMOS OF THE BACKYARD

If you blink your eyes you might miss them. Winging in at sixty miles per hour and not much bigger than a good-size moth, hummingbirds can be pretty hard to see. You might spot them as a small blur zipping past your kitchen window. If you have a flower garden or a nectar feeder, you may get a little clearer view of this speed demon—but not much.

Hummingbirds have the fastest wing beat of all birds, an amazing 75 beats per second. They also have the fastest heartbeat ever recorded—an unbelievable 1,200 beats per minute. No wonder these little dynamos are rarely seen sitting still. Despite the old belief that hummingbirds never stop beating their wings, the birds do rest throughout the day and at night, roosting in trees or their tiny nests.

To energize their hyperactive lifestyle, hummingbirds need high-energy, sugary food, such as the sweet nectar they collect from flowers. Because of their high metabolism, hummingbirds can eat up to fifty percent of their body weight in pure sugar each day—sort of like my kids used to do after trick-or-treating at Halloween.

Hummingbirds usually return to Wisconsin by early June, although in some years I've had them showing up at my window, begging me to put up the nectar feeder, in the middle of May. They migrate north each spring after spending the winter in such exotic places as Nicaragua, San Salvador, Panama, and Mexico. The tiny birds not only cross the length of the United States twice a year, but also fly nonstop some five hundred miles over the Gulf of Mexico.

Of the 230 species of hummingbirds worldwide, only 25 species make their home in the United States. Of these, usually only the ruby-throated hummingbird is found in Wisconsin, as it is in most states east of the Rocky Mountains. The bird got its name from the coloration of the male of the species, which has a beautiful, iridescent, red throat and vivid green plumage. Females and juveniles have more brownish feathers and white throats.

In early summer, hummingbirds are busy seeking mates and building nests. The nest they build is tiny, measuring only one inch wide by one inch deep, made out of spider webs, bits of lichens, and lined with thistle down. The female lays two pea-sized eggs, which hatch in a week or so. Males take no part in building the nest, incubating the eggs, or raising and feeding the young, leaving all the work to the females—a shiftless trait sometimes associated with certain human males, as well (or so I'm told).

Being the smallest and fastest bird on earth can have its advantages, but can also be dangerous. Hummingbirds have been known to become instant bite-sized meals for frogs and large fish, and have even been caught by dragonflies. Although they use spider webs to build their nests, they can also become entangled in the webs and can themselves become a meal for some of the larger spiders.

Hummingbirds seem to be a curious about us as we are about them. They are as likely to be found in urban backyards as they are out in the country, and are usually easy to attract and feed. All they really need is a good supply of nectar-producing flowers or a red-colored sugar water feeder you can make yourself or buy for a few dollars. You can purchase premixed nectar or mix your own by dissolving one part sugar in four parts of water. Some people add a red food coloring to attract humming birds, but it really isn't necessary if you are already feeding them. I like to buy dry hummingbird mix in packets that are added to water, since they include vitamins and minerals and are better for hummingbirds than just pure sugar. Hummingbirds usually plan a feeding route from backyard to backyard, so you'll probably be able to share your "hummer" with your neighbors once you get them established in your area. The birds seem to know a good thing and will return to the same area year after year and "beg" for their feeder to be put back up in spring—a welcome reminder that summer is on the way.

As spring approaches in your area, keep a sharp lookout for that fast-flying blur outside your window. Remember not to blink, or you might miss these interesting little dynamos of the backyard.

ROCK PIGEONS
UNLIKELY WAR HEROES

All seemed lost that cold, dreary October day in 1943. World War II was raging throughout Europe with no end in sight. In Italy, the British 56th Infantry had just called for massive air strikes against the Germans occupying the small town of Coloi Vecchia when the unexpected happened: The Germans withdrew from the city and a thousand British troops poured in, unaware of the bombardment just minutes away. With radio communications cut off, the British field commanders called on an American soldier by the name of G.I. Joe for help. His life-or-death mission was to reach the Allied headquarters in time to stop the scheduled bombing run on the village. Miraculously, he made the twenty-mile journey through enemy lines in only twenty minutes, just in time to shut down the bombers already warming up on the airstrip runways. G.I. Joe received several commendations for his heroic efforts when he returned to the United States, but was also considered a hero in England. He eventually became the only American to receive the coveted British Dikin Medal, in 1946. Not bad for an otherwise ordinary, lowly pigeon.

G.I. Joe was one of many homing pigeons trained for overseas duty by the U.S. Pigeon Corps, a military unit that once numbered more than 3,000 enlisted men, 150 officers, and more than 54,000 pigeons. Many of these feathered veterans gained considerable celebrity status over the years, including one of our state's own native sons called "Wisconsin Boy." At only twelve weeks of age, while serving in the U.S. 1st Infantry in Tunisia, this bird carried a vital message forty miles in forty minutes over enemy lines that helped pave the way for Allied victories. Other pigeons had the less glamorous but vital job of serving on the bomber squadrons. They were released with location information in the event the plane was shot down. Some pigeons were even trained to help reconnaissance and rescue teams find survivors of downed aircraft or sunken ships. Because of their excellent vision, they were able to locate the tiny orange specks (life jackets) on the vast waters of the ocean far better than human spotters could.

Pigeons have a long history of serving mankind. They were carrying our messages more than three thousand years ago in Greece, and even carried the news of the winners of the first Olympic games back home. Today, our sophisticated satellite communication networks have pretty much replaced the need for pigeons, but many people still train racing and homing pigeons and breed fancy varieties for sport and as a hobby.

In addition to their remarkable homing instincts, pigeons are prolific breeders, able to nest and raise their young nearly any time of year. This has made them an important food source throughout ages. The Egyptians had domesticated the birds for food almost five thousand years ago, as did the later Romans, who built special towers where pigeons were raised and fattened for slaughter. Even in modern times, pigeons were once raised in dozens of massive factories right here in the United States. The younger birds, called squabs, were sold to markets throughout the country years ago, but today they're usually found only on the menus of upscale restaurants. Occasionally, pigeons make up part of the hunter's game bag, as well. I've tried them myself, and have found that only the younger birds are worth eating. Older pigeons tend to cook up with texture of shoe leather, and taste that way, too.

Large flocks of pigeons in our cities and farmlands are now a common sight, but surprisingly is a relatively recent one. Pigeons are not native to America, and were believed to be first introduced into Canada by the French in the 1600s. They didn't appear on official published bird counts here in Wisconsin until 1942, but have been increasing in numbers ever since that time.

Because pigeons have been living with us for so long, it's hard to image them as ever being truly wild birds. Biologist believe they once lived on the rocky bluffs of the semi-arid deserts of the Middle East, and their official name as "rock" doves or pigeons reflect this. Because of their ancestral tie to high, rocky places, pigeons rarely roost in trees. Instead they prefer more cliff-like structures such as high-rise city buildings, church steeples, windowsills, barns, and silos. Unfortunately, their preference to roost and nest on these manmade structures often leads to conflicts with man, especially where their droppings on build-ings and city sidewalks make them a nuisance and a potential health concern. Many cities now have massive pigeon extermination and con-trol programs.

It may seem ironic that Americans now spend millions of dollars on an all-out war to eliminate the very birds that only few decades ago helped our country save lives and secure a victory during World War II. But I wouldn't worry too much about the survival of pigeons any time soon. The descendants and ancestors of the likes of G.I. Joe and Wisconsin Boy have been dodging the enemy for uncounted centuries, and no doubt will fly though the open skies victorious in the future as well.

STINGING NETTLE
A PLANT TO TEST YOUR METTLE

Whether you're a hiker, a hunter, or just like to take an occasional stroll through the woods, there are two wild plants you'd be wise to learn to identify. One of them is poison ivy, remembered by old rhyme, "leaves of three, let it be." The other plant is stinging net-tle. Unfortunately, there's no catchy jingle to help remind you to stay clear of this irritating plant. Even worse, stinging nettle is a nondescript green plant that seems to blend right in with all the more harmless woodland plants.

Stinging nettle grows just about everywhere, from empty city lots and roadsides to farm fields, gardens, forests, and swamps. The plant has coarsely-toothed leaves and a square-angled stem, but the real clue to identifying it is the thousands of tiny stinging bristles that cover every part of the plant. Unfortunately, many people "feel" the plant long before they actually see it. When touched, the hollow stinging hairs act as tiny hypodermic needles, injecting formic acid into our skin. The result is some pretty irritating itching and raised skin welts. As a young boy, I learned to recognize the plant from its very descriptive German name *brennen-netl*, or burn nettle. Unlike poison ivy rash, which can give you weeks of itching and scratching, the effects of stinging nettle usually last only a few minutes to an hour at the most.

Stinging nettle was imported from Europe and Africa by the early colonists, but the plant has many American lookalike relatives, including our own wood nettles, many of which are just as irritating to the touch. Despite its hellish reputation as a noxious weed here in America, to many Europeans stinging nettle is often described as a godsend. The late 18th century English poet, Thomas Campbell, wrote, "I have eaten nettles, I have slept in nettle-sheets, and I have dined off nettle-table-cloth. The young and tender nettle is an excellent pot herb. The stalks of the old nettle are as good as flax for making cloth."

Throughout history, nettles were an important source of food and fiber. Even the word nettle is derived from "net" plant, one of its common names which refers to using the fibers of the plant to make twine or weave cloth. Native American Indians spun and twisted nettle fibers between their hands to produce rope, cloth, fishing nets, and even bowstrings. As young plants, nettles can be eaten as greens, which are said to be similar to spinach in flavor and are rich in Vitamins A and C and high in protein. Nettles have also been harvested as cattle feed, especially in Europe. Although neither humans nor cows will eat nettles when green, the irritating stinging bristles and acid are neutralized when the plant is boiled or dried. Nettles were also used in various medicines over the years to treat everything from rheumatism to burns. Nettles are vital to the survival of the beautiful red admiral butterflies, since their larvae feed exclusively on this plant.

Like so many other interesting wild plants that grow around us, stinging nettle is one of those plants that you learn to hate or love. Your perception of it pretty much boils down to your experience with the plant. To some, it remains the heaven-sent miracle plant that helped our early ancestors survive, providing food, clothing, weapons, nets, ropes, and medicine. On the other hand, if you just took a stroll through a patch of stinging nettle in shorts, chances are you'd be convinced that it has to be a plant right out of hell.

POISON IVY
LEAVES OF THREE, LET IT BE

"Leaves of three, let it be;
leaves of five, let it thrive."

When summer is near, just about everyone is "itching" to get out and enjoy Wisconsin's great outdoors. Maybe a walk in the woods, a picnic at the beach, or a fishing trip to the lake is in your plans. But wherever you roam, take care you don't end up "itching" to come home again by stumbling into a poison ivy patch.

Poison ivy is a plant that everyone has heard of but few seem to actually recognize when they see it. The old rhyme "leaves of three, let it be" refers to the fact that poison ivy plants always have three leaflets. The problem is that many other plants in the woods and fields also have three leaves, including wild strawberries, raspberries, and jack-in-the pulpit, to name just a few. A better method of identifying poison ivy is to look for the shiny, oily-looking leaves in addition to the three leaflets. But color is also a poor indicator to use in trying to identify the plant, since the leaves turn from scarlet in spring to bright green in summer and then to either yellow or red by fall. In winter, when the leaves have dropped, look for the bare, crooked stems carrying waxy-looking white berries. You can get a poison ivy rash just as easily from these sticks and berries as you can in summer when the plant has green leaves. Unfortunately, there is no safe time to be in a poison ivy patch.

Poison ivy a is native plant that thrives in any open, sunny location, although it can also do quite well in moist, shaded areas such as woodlands and along streams and lakes. It can be a master of disguises, sometimes appearing as a short ground cover and other times as large individual plants. It can even grow as an upright shrub and often as a vine growing up the sides of trees. Even its leaves can change appearance from one plant to another, some leaves having smooth edges and others jagged, toothed edges, which some refer to as poison oak.

Anyone who has ever suffered a bad case of poison ivy rash can attest to the burning, painful itch caused by this plant. Despite what you've heard, you can't get poison ivy just by looking at it, although it may seem that way to some. You must actually touch the plant or get some of its poison oil called *urushiol* on your skin. All parts of the plant, including the leaves, flowers, fruit, even the roots and stems, can infect you. Usually it takes a day or two after contact with the plant before you start to itch and the white, shiny blisters appear on your skin.

Some people can be infected with poison ivy without leaving their home by touching the fur of a family pet that frolicked through a poison ivy patch. Luckily for your pet, animals do not get poison ivy rashes as we do. In fact, many birds and animals make their homes inside poison ivy patches and even eat the plants' poison berries with no ill effect. You can also get a bad case of poison ivy rash merely by touching or washing the clothes or shoes of someone else who walked through poison ivy, or touching garden tools used around the plant, or carrying in firewood from trees felled in poison ivy.

Probably the worst second-hand exposure to poison ivy can occur if you happen to stand in the smoke of burning poison ivy. The poison urushiol oil floats in tiny droplets within the smoke, covering exposed skin with infection, and can even be inhaled into your lungs. This can result in severe poisoning which will probably land you in the hospital; in severe cases it can result in death. I had first-hand experience with smoke-carried poison ivy as a young boy, as I helped to burn brush along fence lines on the family farm. Luckily, I didn't breathe the urushiol poison into my lungs, but I did get hundreds of large, watery, itching blisters from head to toe for many weeks after.

First-aid books usually advise that, to avoid getting the rash, you wash with a strong alkaline soap as soon as possible after contact with poison ivy. Unfortunately, it's usually too late by then, since urushiol oil enters your skin only ten minutes after you touch the plant. So, unless you have a poison ivy patch right outside your bathroom door, you're probably not going to stop the infection. It is a good idea to wash up, anyway, since the poison can be spread from one part of your body to another by the oil in your skin and certainly by the clothing you were wearing at the time.

Once you have the rash, there's not much you can do except to use over-the-counter remedies such as Rhuli-gel, Tecnu, and calamine lotion to reduce the itching. There is no magic cure. A few new products have been introduced that you apply before contact with poison ivy, if you must expose yourself to it. In severe cases of infection, you may need to see a doctor for a prescription to help ease the pain. Although the rash and watery blisters are not a pretty sight, doctors assure us that you cannot infect someone else from contact with you, although you may find few visitors who want to take the chance. I guess you can take some comfort in knowing that you are not alone in your itching, since doctors have estimated that more than one million Americans become infected by poison ivy each year.

The good news about poison ivy is that about thirty percent of people get none of the rashes, itching, and blisters from contact with the plant. They are the ones who like to grab a handful of poison ivy while bragging that they can roll in the stuff without any ill effect. But these lucky people may not want to be too smug and careless in handling the plant, since doctors warn that everyone's immune system changes as we age, and allergies we never had before can pop up at anytime—especially with poison ivy. So, like Clint Eastwood would say in one of his itchy trigger-finger movies, "Do you feel lucky, kid? Well, do ya ?"

WILD (PASTURE) ROSE
BY ANY OTHER NAME

What's in a name! That which we call a rose,
by any other name would smell as sweet.

—Shakespeare, Romeo and Juliet

Roses are by far the best known and most beloved flowering plant on earth. Some of our best literature is filled with references to roses, such as Juliet's famous "What's in a name" line in Shakespeare's *Romeo and Juliet*. Many well-known fairy tales also feature this popular plant, including the famous enchanted rose central to the story of Beauty and the Beast. Sleeping Beauty was known as the "Princess of Briar Rose" and her castle was surrounded by thick hedges of thorns that turned into roses as the hero prince cut through them to rescue her. Our history is filled with stories of armies marching off to war under the banner of roses and fantastic tales involving roses. It was well known that the enchantress of Nile, Egyptian Queen Cleopatra, seduced the Roman commander Mark Anthony by greeting him on her golden barge filled with roses and perfumed pillows stuffed with rose petals. Later, when he visited the queen in her palace, he found the floors, tables, courtyard, and even the surface of ornamental pools and entire lakes covered in rose petals. Even today, many important political announcements and historical meetings are held in the Rose Garden of the White House in Washington D.C.

Roses are now found almost everywhere on earth, with more than 10,000 cultured varieties grown worldwide. Despite their numbers, however, all of these cultured varieties have a common ancestor in one of the few dozen or so wild roses that still grow in our fields and forests. One of these, called the wild or "pasture" rose, grows throughout Wisconsin and can be seen blooming in early summer along roadsides, fence lines, open woods, stream banks, fields, and even in dry sand dunes along the Great Lakes. Wild rose grows as a shrub and has dark green, finely-toothed, leaves. In some areas, their branches form dense thickets that are nearly impenetrable because of their sharp thorns, providing excellent cover for wildlife. Wild rose blossoms are fairly large, with five flat petals that vary in color from pinkish white to almost red. These attractive and fragrant flowers always seem to bloom sometime in June and continue right into July and sometimes August. Later in summer, these flower heads transform themselves into small, round, edible fruits called "hips" which remain on the plant into the fall and often through the winter. These fruits are an important food source for wild birds and small mammals, especially during the colder months.

Native American Indians collected rose hips for a variety of uses. The Potawatomi used them as a treatment for lumbago and headaches, while several other tribes used wild rose to relieve heartburn and as a cure for stomach trouble. Almost all Native Americans and early pioneers used wild rose for food, however. Rose hips, with an apple-like flavor, not only taste good but are good for you. Researchers have found that they have 24 times more vitamin C per unit than orange juice. Rose hip vitamin supplements are widely available.

Even today, many people pick wild rose hips to eat fresh, or dry them for snacks. There are dozens of recipes for making rose jams and jellies, and there is even one for rose petal soup. I tried my hand at making wild rose jam, using a recipe that called for uncooked rose petals and lemon juice pulverized in a blender. Despite my reputation of being a bit culinary-challenged, even I had success creating a great-tasting rose jam—much to the amazement of friends and family members who hesitantly sampled it. Rose petal jam has a unique, sweet taste and an attractive pinkish-rose color, and will keep for several weeks in the refrigerator or for a year or more in the freezer.

Who knows, if Shakespeare's Juliet would have gone out with me and sampled my wild rose petal jam she might have uttered a different line, "What's in a name! That which we call a rose, by any other name would *taste* as sweet."

UNCOOKED ROSE PETAL JAM

After removing the white bases of the blossoms, put one cup of fresh rose petals (wild or cultivated) in a glass blender. Add ¾ cup water and the juice of one fresh lemon. Blend until smooth. Add 2½ cups of sugar and blend again.

In small saucepan, make a recipe of Sure-Jell pectin, following directions on package. Add the Sure-Jell pectin from the saucepan into the blender and blend again. Pour into small pre-sterilized (boiled) jars with screw caps that seal (like baby food jars). Allow to stand at room temperature for about six hours until nicely jelled

Store in refrigerator or freezer.

MOREL MUSHROOMS
A STORY WITH A DELICIOUS MOREL

Every spring, the annual hunt is repeated. Thousands of men, women, and children throughout the state comb the backwoods, scour the hillsides, and hike the riverbanks—not for deer or turkeys, but for the elusive and highly prized wild mushrooms called morels. Unlike other hunts, you won't need a state license or a federal stamp to go after this quarry. There's no closed season for morels, although most people hunt for about a three-week period in May or sometimes into June during a late spring. Also, there's no bag limit to worry about, except maybe how many you can carry in your bag, if you're really lucky. You also aren't required to get any special hunter training or certification, although a little knowledge goes a long way in mushroom hunting and can make the difference between enjoying a delicious wild mushroom meal or taking a trip to the local emergency clinic. A good photo I.D. book on mushrooms is a wise investment, but a better idea is to learn from an experienced mushroom hunter.

Luckily, morels are one of the best-known mushrooms in North America, and are safe to pick and eat even by amateur mushroom hunters. They really can't be mistaken for any other mushroom except maybe for one called the false morel or brain mushroom, which is rare in our woodlands and really doesn't look much like a real morel, anyway. Wisconsin is home to several different types of morels that come in a variety of colors and sizes, but all have the same honeycomb or sponge-like conical cap and hollow stems that break easily when handled. They also have the same nutty, earthy, mouthwatering flavor. Morels should not be eaten raw but they can be stewed, baked, or even stuffed with creamed steak or chicken. I like them best just sautéed in a little butter. Be sure to always wash them in salt water to remove the grit and dirt. I always cut them open lengthwise, as well, to check out the hollow interior for ants, slugs, or other critters you may not prefer as protein in your diet.

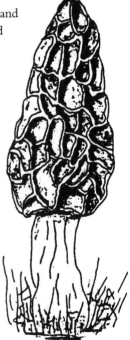

Because these tasty mushrooms are so prized and expensive to purchase at the grocer, if you can find them at all, morels have been called the "million dollar" crop. It's been estimated that if you could successfully grow only one acre of morels, you could sell them for a cool million. But, as thousands of farmers, gardeners, and agricultural experts have discovered, it's not that easy. Morels seem to have secret growth requirements known only to them. Dozens of morels may sprout in a particular area and then not repeat the performance for several years. Weather seems to play a big part in the abundance of morels, as well. Some springs are just too dry or too wet to produce a good morel crop.

So, where do you find these remarkable mushrooms? Well, you could ask other mushroom hunters, but good luck. I tried this when

I first started morel hunting in the forested hills and valleys of south-west Wisconsin, where some of the communities even sponsor morel festivals to attract tourists. After making a few inquiries, I soon learned from the blank stares and smug chuckles I got from the local mushroom hunters that to divulge a known morel hunting area is akin to telling someone where your secret fishing hole or big buck stand is located. A general rule for locating morels is that there really isn't any rule. They can grow most any place throughout Wisconsin, even on your own front lawn, but good places to check are old apple orchards, along rural ditches and stream banks, and around dead or dying elm trees. They pop up both in rich hardwood woodlands and in dryer, sandy, coniferous forest areas.

As with any other kind of hunting, timing is everything, especially in pursuit of wild mushrooms. An area may be devoid of mushrooms one day, but have several the next, the morels literally popping up overnight. Mushroom hunters who know their woodcraft look for nature's tradi-tional barometers to tell them when it's time to hunt morels. Some say it's when the bloodroot starts to bloom; others wait until the stinging nettle grows six inches high. An old favorite is when the oak leaves have unfurled to the size of a mouse's ear. One piece of advice I did manage to wrangle out of an old-timer was to watch for when the wild plum starts to bloom. I've used this guide wherever I searched for morels across the state, and it has always been pretty accurate.

If you haven't ever tried morel hunting or savored this delicacy, you might want to put on your hiking boots and head out to explore the springtime woodlands, fields, and stream banks soon. Where's the best place in Wisconsin to find morels? Sorry, I'm not telling.

WHITE-TAIL DEER FAWN
A PRINCE IS BORN

> "The prince is born, the prince is born, wake
> up everybody and see the new prince!' cried
> little rabbit as he spread the word of the new
> fawn to all the forest animals."

—*Bambi*, Walt Disney

So begins one of the most beloved and timeless of all Disney ani-mated feature films, *Bambi*, the story of a fawn born into a world of friendly forest animals and very evil men. Although this movie is now more than half a century old, it remains as popular today as it was in

1942 when first released. Unfortunately, it also remains often the sole source of information on deer for many people, despite decades of biological research on this animal.

Although Bambi's birth was the cause of much interest and celebration by the forest animals in the film, the birth of one more deer would probably go unnoticed in the real world of nature.

Fawns are born in Wisconsin anytime from late May to early June and sometimes even into July. A few years ago my youngest son, on one of his woodland romps, discovered two newborn fawns, still wet, near our home. The mother doe stayed with the fawns until they were able to struggle up onto their shaky legs and walk with her, which usually happens within ten minutes or so from birth. Later, the doe led the fawns away from the place they were born to avoid predators that might scent the birthing area. Not all woodland creatures are as kind as the cartoon characters appearing in the movie.

Later that same evening, we noticed the doe and one of her fawns near our house. Although the doe kept her distance from us, the fawn actually walked towards us and bedded down within a few feet of where we were standing. If it hadn't walked toward us, we never would have noticed it, since fawns have such excellent camouflage. The reddish-brown coat and white spots blended in perfectly with the brown leaves and light-speckled forest floor of spring. Fawns are also completely odorless in their first days of life, another advantage in a woods filled with predators. As we watched, the fawn curled up, lay as flat as it could, and remained motionless. Even its breathing could not be detected, which often fools people into believing that they've found a dead fawn. Although adult deer rarely use their vocal chords, fawns can be noisy, making bleating calls similar to those of lambs.

Most likely, these were not the first fawns the doe had given birth to. Typically, a doe will have a single fawn in its first year and thereafter will have twins each year, with triplets not uncommon. Deer live in a matriarchal society with does and fawns roaming together all year. Bucks live separately from the does and their offspring, except for a brief period during the breeding season in fall and part of the winter. Unlike the heroic stag in *Bambi*, real bucks take no part in raising the fawns. Throughout the first few weeks of its life, the doe stays near her fawns, ranging a few hundred yards away to feed. She returns to nurse them five to eight times a day.

Fawns weigh only six to eight pounds at birth, but grow rapidly throughout the summer. At one month of age, a fawn can already outrun a man, and by fall it will be able to jump eight feet from a standing position and travel at 35 miles per hour. Almost all fawns lose their spotted coats by September or so, and are then often difficult to distinguish from their mothers at a distance. Biologist believe that in some areas of the state, forty percent or more of the doe fawns will breed within their first year of life and will give birth to fawns of their own the following spring. Because of this, and the fact that most adult does give birth to twins, deer can easily double their population each year, especially if left unchecked.

Because the deer's natural enemies, such as mountain lions and wolves, no longer roam most of the state, deer must have their population controlled by hunting. Unfortunately, quite a few also fall victim to our automobiles and attacks from pets, as well. Although not the villains as portrayed in the movie, man, his machines, and his pets, have indeed become the top predator of deer.

Despite the many natural and man-made threats to fawns, most will survive and treat us to one of the most cherished sights in nature—a newborn fawn in the wild. Keep watch this spring. A new prince, or princess, is sure to be born in a field or forest near you.

GREEN FROGS
IT'S NOT EASY BEING GREEN

"It's not easy being green," according to a song sung by the popular television muppet, Kermit the Frog. Life isn't easy for real frogs, either, including one of Wisconsin's largest and most familiar amphibians, the green frog. In addition to the many man-made injuries to their aquatic homes, such as draining wetlands for development and pesticide contamination, green frogs face many natural dangers. Creatures such as mink, raccoon, sandhill cranes, snakes, and other predators find having a "frog in their throat" a tasty treat. The threat of being eaten is not much better for the tiny green frog tadpoles, either—some would say, even a "tad" worse. Many, if not most, young tadpoles disappear down the gullets of fish, herons, turtles, and kingfishers soon after they hatch.

Despite living on the verge of being something else's meal nearly every day, green frogs continue to thrive in suitable habitat, just as they have for thousands of years. One of the reasons for their success is their extremely cautious and wary nature. Even though they can't see very well, their large external eardrums allow them to hear even the slightest noise. If you attempt to sneak up and catch a green frog, it will usually allow you get just within a few feet and then use its powerful hind legs to jump three feet or more to safety in one split-second hop.

Most frogs spend much of their time on dry land, but green frogs feel safer close to the water, and may spend their entire life in a single pond or marsh. Occasionally, they do venture onto the edge of the pond to bask in the sun, but even then they always face the water so they can quickly dive back in to escape from a predator. When not disturbed, frogs usually slip quietly in and out of the water, but if they feel threatened they almost always make a big splash about it, perhaps to warn other frogs of the danger.

Another reason green frogs continue to thrive is because of their unusually long breeding season, which can last several months from late May through August here in Wisconsin, and even longer in the southern states. If you listen carefully near a pond or wetland in summer, you can hear the telltale *plonk-plonk-plonk* call of the male green frog that sounds like someone strumming a banjo or plucking a tight rubber band. During the day, males set up territories and defend them from rivals. Then, during the breeding season, it's girls' night out on the town for females as they move in and check out the male stud-muffin frogs for a potential mate during the evening hours. Males pump up their

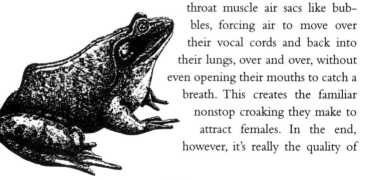

throat muscle air sacs like bubbles, forcing air to move over their vocal cords and back into their lungs, over and over, without even opening their mouths to catch a breath. This creates the familiar nonstop croaking they make to attract females. In the end, however, it's really the quality of the male's breeding territory rather than his singing ability that wins over a female.

Once a lucky male has been chosen, the female will lay floating masses of 1,500 to 4,000 eggs. Each egg is camouflaged a black color on top to blend with the dark bottom of the pond, and white underneath, to match the bright sky above. If the eggs hatch early in the season, the tadpoles will develop into adult frogs by late summer. But if they don't hatch until later in the season, green frog tadpoles have the unusual ability to remain frozen in time as immature tadpoles throughout the winter, and then are transformed into adults the following spring.

Studies have shown that frogs sing most frequently and loudly during the spring breeding season, and also seem to "talk weather" by getting noisy right before an approaching storm. I've always suspected that frogs sometimes like to sing for the same reason we like to whistle a tune, sing along to a favorite song on the radio, or play a tune on an instrument—just for the fun of it. Spring is a good time to visit a pond or marsh on a warm and quiet evening and enjoy the frog music. The performances go on every day, near where you live.

BARN SWALLOWS
NATURE'S DIVE-BOMBERS

"When the swallows come back to Capistrano" is a familiar old song about the annual return of the cliff swallows to the old San Juan Capistrano mission in California. Although not as well known, Wisconsin also has an impressive return of swallows each year, as thousands of tree swallows, bank swallows, cliff swallows, chimney swifts, and purple martins return in spring. Most swallows are similar in size and shape, making them difficult to tell apart at times, but there is one that's easy to identify—the barn swallow. This attractive bird has glossy, iridescent blue-black plumage with a yellow-orange underside and long, sharply pointed wings. It is also the only swallow that has a long, slender, deeply forked tail.

Barn swallows are very vocal, using their song not only to attract mates but also to defend their territory. This usually consists of a small area around their nest and over to their favorite perch, usually a nearby utility line. Barn swallows have a unique song that sounds like a high-pitched liquid twitter, interrupted every so often with a grating noise. They produce this "song" almost all the time, but especially in flight, and it increases in intensity when they fight among themselves or when they are driving off intruders such as cats, dogs, or people that get too close to their nest. Normally, these dive-bomb attacks are just bluffs, but I have seen barn swallows actually hit and roll farm cats onto their backs. Of course, sometimes the tables are turned, and occasionally a very lucky cat will manage to snatch a swallow out of the sky.

Barn swallows, as their name implies, often build their nests inside barns and sheds, although they will use pretty much any sheltered horizontal surface, such as under building eaves, inside car garages, under bridges, docks, and industrial buildings, or just about any other man-made structure. Nobody seems to know where barn swallows built their nests before people began building structures, but biologists speculate that they once built them in caves, rock ledges, or perhaps on the sides of tree trunks. Swallows will even build their nests inside buildings that are closed up at night. Years ago, I used to watch several pairs of barn swallows that nested inside a chicken coop on our family farm. Every night, they made sure they were back on the nest before we closed up the door to the chicken yard and each morning they were ready to fly out when we opened it up again for the day.

Barn swallows build their cup-like nests from tiny clumps of mud, which they set in rows, like bricklayers using mortar. They'll sometimes travel a half-mile or more to find just the right kind of sticky mud, which they carry back in their beaks to the nest building site. They also add grass and rootlets for support and later line the nest with soft down feathers of some kind—an easy task for the swallows in our chicken coop. Barn swallows often come back to use the same nest year after year, but each season they add a new layer of mud to the rim of the old one. Over time, some of these nests can tower a foot or two in height.

After laying about five eggs, white with brown speckles, both parents take turns incubating them. They always seem impatient on the nest, however, and switch every fifteen minutes or so, except at night when the female stays on the nest by herself. Baby barn swallows are one of the cutest birds in nature, especially when they've grown some feathers. They like to line up along the rim of the nest, looking down with their large black eyes and wide yellow mouths, which seem to have a perpetual smile. Feeding time for parent swallows can be an exhausting chore that begins at the crack of dawn and lasts until after dark. Biologists have found that each parent may fly as much as five hundred miles a day in search of insects to feed their eternally hungry hatchlings. They also must carry the hatchlings' fecal sacs away from the nest when they're very young. As they grow older, young swallows learn to back up over the rim of the nest to defecate—a good time not to stand under it for observation.

Once the fledgling barn swallows take flight, they may return for a few nights to the safety of the nest, but after that they leave for good and never return.

By mid-August most swallows are already getting the urge to migrate south for the winter, and by early September most have left our state for warmer climates. Barn swallows make one of the longest migrations of all birds, traveling through the southern states and on to Mexico, Central America, and to South America as far south as Argentina.

You'd think that, after spending the winter so warm and cozy in the tropics, swallows would just want to stay there permanently. But they, like other songbirds that travel so far south, need the longer days of spring and summer in the northern hemisphere to nest and gather enough food to raise their young. Eventually, like the eternally faithful swallows of Capistrano, they come north every year to announce yet another spring and summer season in Wisconsin.

BUMBLEBEES
BIG, BEAUTIFUL, AND BUMBLING

I saw it coming right for me—the biggest bumblebee I'd ever seen. Terrified, I froze, hoping it would go away. But instead, the menacing insect landed squarely on top of my head. Although I was only six years old at the time, I devised what seemed like an ingenious solution to my predicament. Slowly, I drew my trusty toy six-shooter from my holster, took careful

aim with butt of the gun, and clunked myself on the head. Needless to say, it was one of those childhood experiences that teach important lessons of life. I learned that bumblebees can inflict some pretty painful stings when they're angry, and also that the butt-end of a metal toy pistol makes a poor substitute for a fly swatter.

Unlike honeybees, which were imported to America from Europe, the large black and yellow bumblebees are native to our country. No doubt you've seen one bumbling around your backyard from time to time. If so, it probably was a queen bee in search of a nesting site. Bumblebees don't build the elaborate honeycomb hives that honeybees do. Instead they prefer to live in abandoned mouse nests, junk piles, straw bales, or in some other debris on the ground. Once a suitable nest is found, the queen begins to make wax brood cells and lays her eggs inside them.

The first bees to hatch are sterile female worker bees, which immediately begin to build more and more brood cells. The workers also take over all the food gathering so that the queen can concentrate on laying more eggs. After returning to the nest from foraging among the spring flowers, the workers deposit the pollen, which they had collected on their hind legs, into the egg cells for the developing larva to eat. They also regurgitate the nectar they sucked from the flowers into special honey pot cells. Eventually the water in the nectar evaporates and the "bee spit" gradually thickens into honey.

By the middle of summer, things are literally humming in the bumblebee nest. Besides the queen, hundreds of adult worker bees, and developing young, the colony has produced an entire army of female soldiers to defend the nest from enemies. Unlike the stinger of the honeybee, which is barbed and breaks off easily, the bumblebee's smooth stinger can sting and inject their venom over and over again.

As the daylight shortens in late summer, the queen begins to lay special eggs that hatch into fertile queens and, for the first time, into male bumblebees. At the same time, she stops producing worker bees and gradually the entire bee colony begins to fall apart. Bumblebees don't store huge of caches of honey, as honeybees do, so most of them don't survive our cold Wisconsin winters. By late autumn, all the workers, soldiers, male bees, and even the queen herself have died. The only survivors are the newly fertilized queens, who leave the nest in search of a shelter area to hibernate through the winter. Next spring, these newly crowned queens will take wing and single-handedly start their own colonies, just as countless generations of bumblebees have done before.

Despite their aggressive behavior, bumblebees play an important role in pollinating flowers of the garden, field, and especially agricultural crops such as clover. But, just like the black-and-yellow "warning" signs you see along the highway, it pays to give these black-and-yellow warriors the right-of-way, lest they make a beeline towards you.

HONEYBEES
LIFE'S A BUZZ

Native American Indians called them "white man's flies" and considered them a bad omen of things to come, and for good reason. The sight of honeybees in the wilderness could mean only one thing—European settlers were close by and had penetrated even more deeply into the wilderness. Soon, the advancing farmsteads and cities would drive their people from their traditional homes and force them to move even further west, as they had had to do so many times before.

Because honeybees are now so common everywhere, its hard to believe that they were not native to the American continent. After all, our own state legislature, many years ago, passed a proclamation making the honeybee Wisconsin's official state insect. But the familiar honeybee is actually an alien insect that was brought to America from Europe by early colonists. Exactly where and when they were introduced has never been recorded, but historians believe the first honeybees were introduced into Virginia in the early 1600s and spread over the entire American continent soon after.

Unlike so many other alien introductions that have eventually threatened our native species and altered our ecosystems, the honeybee became a welcome newcomer to America because of its important role in pollinating both wild and agricultural flowering plants. Today, more than a third of all the world's food supply depends on pollination from insects, most of which is accomplished by honeybees and their relatives. Of course, bees don't pollinate our crops and fruit trees out of the goodness of their hearts. They do it in the course of flying from flower to flower, gathering the yellow sticky pollen and sweet sugary nectar for their own use. Back in their hives, the bees regurgitate the nectar into wax storage cells, adding special enzymes in the process. Eventually, through evaporation, the nectar turns into honey, which they then store in vast quantities to help them survive the winter, and which we humans like to steal to satisfy our own sweet tooth. Honey is stored in hexagonal cells made from beeswax, a fat-like material the bees make from pollen and honey. Beeswax is another product we like to steal, using it to make everything from candles to lip balm.

Honeybees live in large colonies, usually in hollow trees in the wild. One good-size hive may have up to 50,000 members, nearly all of which are infertile female worker bees. There are perhaps a hundred or so males, called drones, and one fertile queen bee. The queen is the largest bee in the hive and her sole purpose in life is to lay eggs—lots of eggs. A queen may lay up to 1,500 eggs a day, one at a time in individual cells of the honeycomb. Over the course of her five-year life span, she may be responsible for producing more than a million bees.

Female worker bees are the hard-working housewives of the bee world. They build the honeycombs, feed and tend to the newly hatched bees, clean the hive, collect food and water, and defend the hive from predators. Worker bees wear out quickly during the spring and summer, especially when they begin to make the long trips back and forth transporting nectar and pollen from flowers to the hive. They usually live only about six weeks during the summer before dying of exhaustion from the 50,000 to 100,000 miles each flies in search of nectar and pollen.

In contrast to the busy female workers, male bees don't seem to have to work at all. They pretty much just hang around the hive and wait to be fed and groomed by the female workers—a scenario familiar to some human housewives, I'm told. The drone's only task seems to be to mate with the queen bee in the event that she stops laying eggs. Although the lifestyle of the drone might seem like a male utopia, all good things must end. As the summer draws to a close and the hive prepares to become semi-dormant for the winter, the male drones are no longer needed. At that time they are usually dragged out of the hive and either left to starve or are stung to death by the female worker bees. Since they are born without stingers, they can't even defend themselves. Next spring, the queen will lay unfertilized eggs and new drones will be hatched to take their place.

Honeybees have very gentle dispositions and rarely sting unless they feel threatened. Even so, many of us get at least one sample of their painful sting, usually by unintentionally stepping or sitting on one in our own backyards. Unlike hornets and bumblebees that can sting over and over again, honeybees can sting only once. Their stingers are barbed, like fish hooks, and tear off along with a muscular apparatus and venom sac from their body, causing them to die soon after they sting. Honeybee stings are so painful because of the live, flexing muscles attached to the stinger, which bores deeper into the skin even after the rest of the bee has left. Pulling the stinger out with your fingers or a tweezers can often make it worse, since the squeezing pressure helps inject even more venom into the skin. The correct way to remove the stinger is to carefully scrape it out sideways with a pocketknife.

Few other insects in the world are as important to our own lives as the honeybee. In addition to the uncounted billions of wild bees, there are more than 200,000 beekeepers in the United States alone, who raise almost four million colonies of domestic honeybees. Together, they pretty much cover the globe in a never-ending cycle that keeps our earth covered in lush, green, flowering plants and keeps us all alive and well-fed. The next time you take a bite out of a delicious, juicy apple, remember it was the honeybee that made it all happen.

JUNE BUGS
THINGS THAT GO BUMP IN THE NIGHT

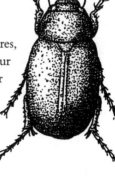

They're out there, those things that go "bump in the night." Although your mind can imagine all sorts of scary creatures, night stalkers, and bogeymen outside your window, more than likely the sound you hear is only one of our most common beetles, known as the June bug.

Like most night-flying insects, June bugs are attracted to outside security and house lights. You can hear them buzzing, crawling, and crashing against your window and door screens over and over again, as soon as darkness falls. By morning you'll usually find one or more of these reddish-brown, hard-shelled beetles still crawling around your doorstep or windowsill.

The fact that these large, awkward beetles can fly at all is nothing short of aviary magic. June bugs have heavy, square bodies with hard outer wing covers that they lift to unfold their papery wings. In order to fly, they must crawl to the top of a launch pad, such as a bush, spread their weak wings, and beat them like crazy to get and keep aloft in the night skies. The clumsy insect's landings are anything but graceful, usually resulting in a crash-landing at best.

Although we call them "June" bugs, a better name for them might be "May beetle," since that is when we first begin to see them in large numbers. Technically, June bugs are not really true bugs, either, but members of the beetle family.

Most people recognize June bugs when they are adult beetles crashing against our screen doors, but may not recognize them in their larvae form. They're the large, curled, semi-transparent white grubs you might find in the soil when you dig in your garden. They are also common pests under lawns, but are rarely detected unless you're unfortunate enough to have a skunk or raccoon visit you during the night to dig a few hundred holes in your lawn to get at these tasty grubs.

June bugs have a relatively long life compared to most insects, which live for only a few months. Their unusual three-year life cycle begins when a female lays her eggs in the soil. When hatched, the young white larvae or grubs spend the summer underground, feeding on plant roots. When fall approaches, they burrow down deep into the ground, where they spend the winter. The following spring, they return near the soil surface and again spend the summer feeding on plant roots. By the end of their second summer, the larvae turn into the familiar hard-shelled adult beetles. Even though they are fully mature beetles by then, June bugs remain underground and don't emerge until the following spring, in their third year.

As adults, June bugs take on a Dracula-like lifestyle, coming out to feed only at night. Lucky for us, they don't feed on blood but instead suck juices from plants. June bugs also mate and lay their eggs at night, making sure to burrow back into the dark cool earth before dawn breaks. The few you see around your house in the morning are probably coming to the end of their life cycle, too weak to return to the safety of their underground homes.

So the "bump in the night" turns out to be a pretty ordinary, harmless bug with a very extraordinary nightlife. Like your neighbor's teenage kids, these noisy bugs will continue to "party on" through the night and into the early morning hours, before literally "crashing" before the sun shines. But by nightfall, you can sure that the June bug will rise again. ▲

July

July is the warmest month of the year in Wisconsin. As the temperature rises, wildlife becomes less active and more difficult to observe. Thanks to the hot, dry weather, mosquito populations drop somewhat, but their numbers are quickly replaced by pesky deer flies. Goldfinches are busy in the summer sun collecting the soft down of thistle seed heads to line their nests. Butterflies flutter in the sunny, open meadows and roadside ditches now ablaze with summer flowers such as black-eyed susans, chicory, and ox-eye daisies.

In the country, farmers are busy baling hay and harvesting forage to fill their silos, sometimes working late into the evening as July's full "haying moon" rises over the fields. In the city, the nighthawks can be heard as they soar high above tall buildings feeding on moths and other night-flying insects. Their loud, nasal *peent ... peent* call is interrupted only by the sound and color of the annual Fourth of July fireworks display.

On hot, steamy days, thunderhead clouds build throughout the morning and afternoon, finally releasing their fury with thunder, lightning, high winds, and cool, refreshing rains. At night, beneath July's "rain" or "thunder" full moon, the marshes and fields twinkle like Christmas lights as fireflies light up the night with their summer dance.

NIGHTHAWKS
MASTERS OF THE DARK

It was a hot and steamy summer night in downtown Metropolis. Somewhere high above the concrete buildings and blinding streetlights you could hear a loud piercing *peent, peent, peent* cry echo in the night. Suddenly, someone shouted, "Look up in the sky! It's a bird. It's a plane. It's Super—." Oops, sorry, it was only a bird, after all. But not just any bird. This was a nighthawk-a sleek, fast-flying, aerial acrobat that's probably more often heard than seen by most of us.

Nighthawks, also called mosquito hawks, can be found sweeping the night skies in nearly every city and town in eastern America. Although they occasionally hunt during the daytime, it's during the evening hours when you're most apt to see nighthawks scooping up mosquitoes, moths, beetles, flies, and any other insect they can fit in their large frog-like mouths. When in flight, nighthawks look like real hawks, with their long, narrow falcon-like wings. But despite their name, they aren't at all related to hawks or any other raptor. Nighthawks are actually members of an oddly labeled family of birds called "goatsuckers," which were named after an old European myth that these birds secretly suck the teats of goats.

Nighthawks are usually one of the last birds to return to Wisconsin in spring, sometimes not showing up until well into June. The birds spend their winters in the tropics, some flying as far away as Argentina. After a brief courtship, nighthawk pairs begin to select nesting sites in which to lay their two eggs. Many years ago, they probably would have chosen the top of a gravely hill, sand dune, or beach area to nest, but today these sites are usually occupied by us humans. Instead of slipping towards extinction, nighthawks merely adapted to our urban encroachment, and now most of them nest on the flat gravel rooftops of tall office and industrial buildings, right in the heart of cities. As it turns out, in addition to being a fine substitute for their former nesting areas in the wild, these adopted man-made structures also provide protection from most of their natural predators. The only drawback is the intense heat that builds up on the open rooftops during the summer. While most mother birds brood their young to keep them warm, mother nighthawks cover their chicks to shade them from the blazing sun.

After only three weeks, young nighthawks have fledged and are ready to take to the sky with their parents. By early August, nighthawk families are already beginning to band together in large flocks for their early migration south again. Years ago, birdwatchers used to compare the huge migrations of nighthawks to those of the passenger pigeon. Although their numbers are not as strong as they once were, there are still some spectacular migrations today. Nearly every year in early August I've witnessed a natural wonder at Kohler-Andrae State Park, along the shores of Lake Michigan, in Sheboygan County—one that has probably been going on for hundreds of years. If the green darner dragonflies hatch out of the river marsh and take to the sky to mate at just the right moment, nighthawks numbering in the hundreds suddenly appear out of nowhere and sweep through the sky, diving and twisting, in pursuit of these apparently tasty insects. Even more impressive was a migration recorded at the Cedar Grove Ornithological Station, also in Sheboygan County, where researchers counted a total of 18,000 nighthawks flying south in a single day.

When resting during the heat of the day, nighthawks like to perch lengthwise on large tree limbs, making them nearly impossible to see due to their excellent camouflage. While flying at night, their dark bodies and swift aerial maneuvers as they chase insects through the dark skies make them appear to be shadows or large bats, if you can see them at all. Even though you probably won't be able to see one clearly, they can easily be heard. Just go downtown on a hot, quiet evening and listen to their unmistakable low-pitched, nasal *peent, peent* call. They might not be a superman, but they are certainly super birds, as they patrol the dark skies in their never-ending quest to search and destroy thousands of mosquitoes night after night.

PURPLE MARTINS
AMERICA'S MOST WANTED BIRDS

American Indians called them "the birds that never rest," and for good reason. When purple martins aren't performing their amazing aerial acrobatics to catch flying insects, they usually spend their time just gliding through the open sky for the sheer fun of it. Purple martins not only feed and play on the wing, they also dip to the surface of streams or lakes to catch a drink, and can even bathe while in flight. About the only time they seem to sit still is when they're in their nesting hole, sleeping at night, or incubating their eggs.

Purple martins are the largest of all the swallows. They are also one of our most attractive birds, with their sleek aerodynamic bodies and long knifelike wings. The adult males, when at least two years old, can be identified by their handsome and shiny blue-black feathers. Younger males and females are similar, but have somewhat duller plumage and light-colored breast feathers.

Purple martins probably have the unique distinction of being America's most desired bird. Every year, gardeners and bird enthusiasts spend considerable time and dollars attempting to attract these birds to their backyards. Because purple martins feed almost exclusively on flying insects and can drink on the wing, they can't be lured by birdfeeders or birdbaths. The only way to attract them is to erect multi-compartment nesting boxes, which can be as simple as a scrap wood structure set on pole, or as fancy as the expensive aluminum condominiums attached to telescoping poles that can be raised and lowered for cleaning. Maintaining martin houses can be a time-consuming hobby, since the houses have to be kept clean and guarded against more aggressive birds, such European starlings and house sparrows, that compete for the nest holes.

Although we think that putting martin houses in our backyards as a fairly recent hobby, early American Indians often hung hollowed-out gourds on poles around their villages to attract purple martins. No doubt, Native Americans enjoyed the beauty of these graceful birds as we do today, but they also knew that martins have an almost insatiable appetite for flies, mosquitoes, and other biting insects. A single martin can easily devour more than two thousand of the pesky insects in a day. Native Americans found uses for the purple martin other than being nature's original backyard bug zapper. Martins were encouraged to nest around Indian villages and pioneer settlements because their aggressive, defensive behavior drove away hawks, owls, crows, and blue jays which came too close to their nesting colonies. Thus they unwittingly prevented these scavengers from raiding chicken coops and stealing drying meat from outdoor racks.

Purple martins migrate back to Wisconsin each April and May. Older males are the first to arrive, to check out potential nesting houses. Some people call these first birds "scouts," but research has shown that they really don't go back and get the rest of the flock. Instead, they select a few empty nesting holes to defend from the other males and then wait for the females to find them when they arrive several days later. Once paired, martins seem very affectionate with each other as they feed, fly, and preen together. They even greet one another with a song after they've been apart for a short while.

Martins build their nests out of grass, twigs, and mud, as many other birds do, but in addition, the male has the unusual habit of bringing green leaves into the nest all the while the female is incubating her five white eggs. Although it's not certain why he does this, the leaves may help keep the eggs moist, or the gas released by the decomposing leaves may repel mites and other insects that might otherwise infest the nest.

By late summer and early fall, young purple martins are ready to take to the air with the adults for the long flight south for the winter. They gather together in large flocks and gradually migrate south to the Gulf of Mexico, from where they fly nonstop to Central America and on to their wintering grounds in the steamy tropical jungles of Brazil and Venezuela. But the winter holiday retreat to the tropics is brief, and by January purple martins are already beginning their spring migration north, moving about five degrees latitude every two weeks as they head back to their favorite nesting house here in Wisconsin.

Purple martins can be attracted to nearly any backyard. All they really need is a well-kept nesting house on a pole with at least 25 feet of open space around it. Because they need to drink, bathe, and catch lots of insects, houses within easy flying distance of ponds, streams, or lakes are usually more attractive to them. Martins can be shy about moving into a new birdhouse, but with a little patience and effort in keeping the starlings and sparrows out of nesting holes, eventually "the birds that never rest" may decide to move in with you.

AMERICAN ELM
GONE BUT NOT FORGOTTEN

Few trees are as All-American as the familiar American elm. These tall, graceful giants with their large, spreading canopies have provided shade and shelter for many historical events that helped shape our nation. According to legend, George Washington took command of the American Revolutionary forces under an elm tree in 1775, and after the war searched the bottomlands of the Potomac River for elms to transplant at his Mount Vernon home. Abraham Lincoln delivered some of his most eloquent speeches under the shade of these majestic trees and, as president, began the tradition of planting elms on the White House lawn. There's also the Daniel Boone elm tree in Kentucky, the Buffalo Bill elm in Iowa, the General Custer and Kit Carson elms in Kansas, and many more individual trees that played a unique part in historical events both big and small in every state east of the Rocky Mountains, including Wisconsin.

The American elm, the largest of our six native elms, can grow more than 160 feet tall and live for 600 years. You can spot them miles away because of their large size, straight trunks, and arching branches, together resembling the shape of a feather duster or giant champagne glass. Fifty years ago, the American elm was the most common shade tree in cities and villages throughout Wisconsin. Communities such as Milwaukee, Madison, and Sheboygan gained notoriety as "tree cities" because of the thousands of attractive elms that lined nearly every neighborhood street and boulevard. But then disaster struck. The ancient American elms of lore and legend began to die, not of old age, but of Dutch elm disease, a fatal tree fungus accidentally introduced from Europe.

Dutch elm disease was first discovered in the Netherlands in 1929. The new disease was of immediate concern to the Dutch, since elm trees were widely planted in Holland and their roots were responsible for holding many dikes from washing into the sea. Soon after the new disease was discovered, the United States quarantined all living trees from entering the country, but unfortunately it was already too late. Dutch elm disease had invaded America, probably hiding in beetle-infested English elm logs, which for decades had been imported from Holland for the furniture industry. Once released, the disease spread like wildfire, killing millions of elms as it spread from tree to tree, moving westward from the east coast.

Dutch elm disease arrived in Wisconsin in the 1950s and quickly spread throughout the state, infesting nearly all our American elms in only a few years. The city of Milwaukee lost more than 16,000 elms in a single year, and city foresters in every community struggled with try-ing to save the trees. The reason the disease spread so quickly was because of the European elm bark beetle. The insect attacks healthy trees and bores into the inner bark, eating out centipede-like tunnels through the sapwood. Although these borings weaken the trees, they usually are not fatal in themselves. Unfortunately, elm bark beetles also carry the fatal Dutch elm disease fungus on their bodies. After an elm is infected, the fungus spreads and kills the water-conducting sapwood, causing the leaves to turn brown and drop. Eventually, with the tree's lifeblood of water cut off, the elm literally dies of thirst.

Today, a few giant sentinel elms still dot our countryside, but more succumb to the disease each year. Researchers continue to search for solutions to combat Dutch elm disease and have had some limited success with injecting trees with antibiotic and chemical toxins.

Unfortunately, these methods are expensive and not always successful. City foresters now plant many different species of trees so that future diseases won't destroy the entire urban forest canopy. Communities all over the country still have their Elm streets, Elmwood avenues, and Elm Tree boulevards, but these are just ghostly reminders of the majestic, towering giants that once shaded these neighborhoods.

The American elm may never again be this country's favorite and most planted tree. After all, heads of state now discuss politics and war in air-conditioned concrete-and-steel buildings rather than under the cool shade of ancient elms. But the American elm's legacy and place in our history is secure as long as we care to remember them.

MULLEIN
MAGICAL, MYSTERIOUS, AND MEDICINAL

You can see them as you drive through the countryside, standing straight and tall, looking something like lone stalks of corn. Towering to heights of seven feet or more, these fuzzy-leafed plants are easy to spot throughout Wisconsin, especially in late summer. Sometimes, these familiar roadside plants grow branches near the top of their flowering spikes, making them appear to be a Wisconsin version of a saguaro cactus.

In reality, these large wild plants are neither cactus nor corn, but an interesting member of the snapdragon family called mullein (mull-in). Also called flannel-plant, Quaker rouge, big tobacco, candlewick, Aaron's rod, blanket leaf, and lungwort, to name just a few, the plant has a long association with people. In some rural areas the plant is often affectionately called "farmer's wipe," because of its large, soft fuzzy leaves—a handy natural convenience in the back forty far from the latrine.

Mullein is not native to America. It is believed to have been brought by early colonist to New England from Europe, where it had been used primarily as a medicine. Long before tuberculosis was controlled by better means, mullein was boiled in milk and used for bronchial disorders, coughs, and lung troubles.

Besides its medicinal uses, mullein also has a dark and magical history. In the sixteenth century, mullein torches were burned at funerals to drive away evil spirits. Mullein has been associated with witchcraft and superstitious beliefs since the middle ages, an association that continues today in some parts of the world.

Not all the plant's uses were associated with death and disease, however. In the days when no "proper" young ladies were allowed to wear makeup, girls would rub their cheeks with the fuzzy leaves of the mullein plant, which caused a mild but harmless reddening of the skin. Because it gave the appearance that the girls were wearing rouge, the plant was nicknamed "Quaker rouge."

Another use of mullein was for the bright yellow dye that could be made from its flowers. Years ago, old television commercials tried to convince American women that "blondes have more fun." Apparently, the ancient Romans believed this, as well, since they used mullein flowers not only to dye their clothing but also to tint their hair a golden color.

Although often labeled a weed in agricultural journals, mullein rarely interferes with crops, since it grows best in waste areas along roadsides, vacant fields, and empty city lots. The plant is a valuable source of nectar for a variety of insects and hummingbirds. In winter, the tall, dead stalks withstand the harsh winter winds and provide a handy pantry for woodpeckers and other birds that feed on the insect larvae that overwinter in the plant. Mullein is often used in floral arrangements, although many people just enjoy seeing this tall, attractive plant as part of the rural landscape.

Next time you see a mullein plant along the roadside, don't think of it as just a weed. Remember its long and interesting history, from its use as a torch during dark and spooky medieval funerals, to its role in adding blush to the cheeks of giggly Quaker girls. Growing side by side with man for thousands of years, mullein continues its long history as a magical and medicinal plant.

DANDELIONS
IF YOU CAN'T BEAT 'EM, EAT 'EM

Nobody knows for sure when dandelions were first introduced to America. Some believe they were brought into Canada by the Hudson's Bay Company to provide a green vegetable to augment their fur traders' mostly meat diet. Others believe dandelions were brought to the New World by early settlers and were later introduced to the west by homesick pioneer women who grew them in their gardens to remind them of home back east. Still others question whether dandelions were actually introduced at all, thinking that they may already have been growing here long before Europeans arrived on the scene.

The name "dandelion" has a European origin, derived from the French term *dent de lion*, or lion-toothed, referring to the serrated edges of its leaves.

Wherever they came from, dandelions are surely the most prolific and adaptable plant on earth, and probably the most despised, as well. The success of the dandelion has led to one of the longest-running battles between plant and man in modern times. Just the thought of this pesky plant can raise the blood pressure of many backyard gardeners and farmers who spend much time and money to prevent it from taking over their alfalfa fields and manicured lawns. But even with the best arsenal of powerful herbicides, mowing, pulling, and digging with special tools, the war has not been won. Not only has the dandelion not been exterminated, it continues to be expand its range around the globe wherever mankind settles to raise crops or mow lawns.

One reason for the dandelion's amazing success is its long taproot and tough rosette of leaves which have the ability to suck life-giving moisture from almost any location, even between the cracks of busy concrete highways. The hardy roots can continue to sprout new plants over and over again, despite heavy mowing and pulling. Unlike most other plants, dandelions have the unusual ability to flower and go to seed almost any time during the growing season. Their bright yellow flowers open on sunny days and close again at dusk or sometimes just before the approach of a rainstorm. After blooming, the flowers transform into the familiar fuzzy-winged seed heads, sometimes called puffballs or blowballs, that kids of all ages like to pick and blow into the wind. Legend has it that if you blow three times on the dandelion seed head, the number of seeds left on the stem will predict how many children you will have in the future. The tiny seeds have an incredible germination success rate of up to ninety percent, sprouting hundreds of new dandelion seedlings far from the single parent plant.

Dandelions are now considered a noxious weed and pest, but they once were a valuable food and medicinal plant. The sticky, milky juice of the dandelion was even listed as a major ingredient in several patent medicines. Naturalist and wild food expert Euell Gibbons once called them, "an herbal hero, [one of the] most healthful and genuinely useful plants in the world." Perhaps old Euell might have gone overboard in his enthusiasm for the plant, but he did recognize the importance of the dandelion through our history. Before the days when supermarkets were stocked year-round with fresh produce, many people became ill or died in winter from lack of vitamins supplied by fresh green plants. Many early pioneers, starved for greens through the long and cold winters, eagerly ate dandelion greens, rich in vitamins A and C, as soon as they emerged in spring. Even today, many people still enjoy the taste of young dandelion leaves in a salad, or boil them up like spinach. If you'd like to sample dandelions yourself, be sure to use only the young leaves, before the plant blooms, and avoid plants that might have been contaminated by pesticides in lawns or along roadsides.

In addition to its many uses in medicines and as food, dandelions have been used for centuries to make a delicious homemade wine from the plants' yellow flowers. Their long taproots, when roasted and ground, brew an excellent substitute for coffee or can be peeled and boiled to make a nutritious survival meal, one that has fed more than one lost outdoorsman.

Dandelions. Are they the most obnoxious, useless weed on the face of the earth, or, as Euell Gibbons would have us believe, the most healthful and useful of all wild plants? One thing is for certain—we will never totally exterminate this aggressive plant, no matter how hard we try. Maybe our ancestors had the best solution to the problem years ago. If you can't beat 'em—eat 'em.

CHICORY
SOMETHING'S BREWING WITH THIS PLANT

Chicory is one of those familiar roadside plants that everyone recognizes but few can name. They're the tall, ragged-looking plants with blue flowers. Although sometimes called cornflower or blue daisy, chicory is actually a close cousin to the dandelion and even has similar leaves and the same sticky white juice in its stems and leaves.

Unlike the dandelion, however, which starts to bloom in spring, chicory usually does not send up its tall two-to-five-foot flower stalk until mid-summer. A fascinating feature of the plant is that its flowers are open only in the morning and are usually closed by noon, unless it's a cloudy day. Another interesting chicory fact is that each flower lasts only one day, after which it closes and matures into a seed head. Without the advantage of a fluffy seed parachute, like the dandelion has, chicory must wait for the late fall or winter winds to shake and rattle its tall seed stalks and knock out the seeds onto the ground to reproduce itself. Many wild birds enjoy this natural bird feeder, especially goldfinches, which are often seen perched on the plants pecking at the seedpods.

Another common name for chicory is ragged sailor or blue sailor, which refers to an old legend in which a sailor said farewell to his sweetheart and then was lost at sea, never to return. The young maiden never gave up her vigil, waiting for him along the road near the sea. Because of her grief and devotion, the gods turned her into a chicory plant, forever more to wear the cheery bright blue color of the sailor's uniform in her blossoms along the roadside.

Since chicory is so abundant and seems to grow in nearly every ditch and vacant lot in the state, it's hard to believe that this plant was actually introduced into America from Holland in the late 1700s. It had been used since ancient times in the Middle East and Europe as a staple food and for medicine. Every spring, some people still enjoy gathering the young leaves of chicory for use in salads or for seasoning.

Another common name given to this plant is *coffeeweed*. The chicory root, when roasted and ground, can be used as a coffee substitute. Nobody knows for sure who brewed the first pot of this beverage, but it was used widely in the Southern states during the Civil War when real coffee was expensive and scarce. Even today, many Southern coffee drinkers prefer this naturally caffeine-free substitute, or at least like it added to their regular coffee.

Several years ago, I dug out several good-size chicory roots to try the coffeeweed's flavor for myself. After cleaning and roasting them in the oven, I found they did indeed smell like coffee, especially when broken open to reveal the dark inner core of the roots. Unfortunately, the beverage I brewed turned out to be mighty powerful and slightly bitter, so I mixed it with regular coffee to make an acceptable drink. Even then, I found chicory coffee to be one of those "acquired" tastes. You'll have try it and judge for yourself.

Like so many wild plants that were once considered important to mankind, chicory has been relegated to the history books, along with the blue-uniformed sailors who once sailed the high seas. Except for a few diehard chicory coffee drinkers, the plant is now of little importance to most of us, just another problem for the road crews that mow them down along our roadways. Yet, it's hard to imagine a summer in Wisconsin without the familiar bright blue flowers of the chicory plant to brighten up the otherwise dull, bland roadside ditches. Maybe in the end, this is the value and magic of the chicory plant—once a feast for the body, now a feast for the eyes.

PUFFBALLS
A NATURAL DELICACY

At first glance, they look like white volleyballs left in the woods by some forgetful kids. But when you take a closer look, you discover the soft, spongy balls are really common mushrooms called "puffballs." Often called the world's best known mushroom, puffballs are easy to identify and one of the safest to eat, as well.

Although there are at least sixteen species of puffballs, most of us recognize only the biggest one— the giant puffball. These mega-mushrooms usually grow from eight to twelve inches in diameter, but occasionally reach three feet and weigh a more than forty pounds. Puffballs grow best in rich, wet soils both in woodlands and in grassy fields. They can pop out of the ground any-time from spring to fall, but most of the larger ones seem to grow best in July and August here in Wisconsin.

Puffballs are delicious to eat, with a sweet, nutty, earthy flavor. If you'd like to try them, it's best to pick them while they're still solid and white both inside and out. Puffballs may be prepared in many different ways, but I like them best sliced and pan-fried in butter. They can also be deep-fried, sautéed, or just added to vegetable or meat dishes. Unfortunately, puffballs can't be dried or canned like other mushrooms, but can be preserved by freezing slices between wax paper. For the best flavor, however, it's best to eat them while they're fresh, right out of the woods.

North American Indians have always known puffballs were good eating and have gathered them for centuries for food, as early explorers and settlers soon learned to do. Native Americans also used the dry powdery puffball spores for medicine, especially to treat bleeding cuts and wounds. No wonder these unusual mushrooms were once considered a gift of the gods by our ancestors, since they could satisfy both hunger and healing.

Harvesting puffballs really doesn't hurt the population, since its underground root-like system, called mycelium, will produce more mushrooms next season.

All puffballs are safe to eat except when they begin to mature, usu-ally in late summer or early fall. At this time of year the puffball's outer skin begins to crack and split open, allowing the dry and dusty olive-colored spores to "puff" out into the wind, giving the mushroom its name. As kids, we used to tramp through the autumn woods, kicking ripe puffballs like footballs, sending up clouds of spores with each boot. Even now, I have trouble resisting the temptation to poof a puffball just for fun when nobody's looking. In the absence of such human puffers and place-kickers, nature has evolved its own method of distributing puffball spores. Once the mushroom has dried out, the wind tosses, turns, and rolls the puffball, sending clouds of smoky spores into the breeze. Even with the millions of spores released, however, only a few will find a suitable place to grow for next year's crop.

Watch for these unusual mushrooms to appear in a woodlot or field near you in summer. Perhaps you might want to savor a real out-door delicacy by picking a fresh, white puffball to eat, or maybe you'd rather wait until fall and help it scatter its smoky spores into the wind. Either way, you'll always get a kick out of puffballs.

SKUNKS
FEARLESS LITTLE STINKERS

The silly song of the 1970s, "Dead Skunk in the Middle of the Road," became a popular radio hit probably because it touched a universal chord within most of us. Everyone has experienced the nauseating odor of skunk being sucked into the car's ventilation system, or seen the familiar black-and-white furry blobs on the highways.

Although some animals seem to become pavement pancakes because of their own stupidity, the skunk is actually a fairly intelligent animal. The skunk's problem is that, genetically, it simply is not programmed to run away from anything that threatens it, even an automobile—a fatal mistake to make on a busy highway at night.

Other than man and a few natural predators such as great horned owls, the skunk has little to fear from most any other creature—and with good reason. Its ability to defend itself by discharging a repulsive scent or musk must be respected, if not admired. The skunk's ability to spray its foul musk at enemies is surely one of nature's most unique inventions. The skunk has two internal scent glands located at the base of its tail, connected to tiny spray nipples or nozzles located just within the anus. When the skunk raises its tail, these spray nozzles are exposed, a sure sign that it's time to retreat, if you haven't already. Like nature's version of a super soaker gun, these squirters can send a stream up to ten feet away with pinpoint accuracy, and as much as twenty feet away and still hit a target.

Most people are surprised to learn that skunks are very clean, quiet, and gentle animals that have very little odor themselves. As a young boy, my brothers and I captured a few young skunks we found along the roadside and cared for them for a while. They were very affectionate and easy to tame. Since they never attempted to spray us, we concluded that they were probably too young to be a threat. However, a visiting neighbor boy who was sprayed with a full load from our "tame" little skunks may have a different opinion. Later, we learned that

153

it's not a good idea to keep a skunk as a pet, since they cannot be immunized effectively against rabies.

Skunks release their scent only as a last resort when they feel their life is being threatened, and even then, they are careful not to get the substance on themselves. The foul odor is caused by an oily liquid in the scent glands, made from a sulfur compound that gives it a rotten-egg smell. Once sprayed, the liquid spreads out into a fine mist that can carry for more than a mile through the countryside, an odor that many of us have experienced on those quiet summer nights when a breeze drifts in through an open window.

Skunks live throughout the state in both rural and urban areas. They usually make their homes in old woodchuck holes along fence lines and forest borders, but also can live under sheds, barns, and porches. They are night hunters, spending the evening hours searching for bugs, grubs, mice, rats, and other pests. Despite the obvious services they perform for us, skunks still rank right up there with snakes and bats as unwelcome house guests. At times, skunks can cause some damage to our backyards, especially if they find their favorite snacks under the lawn. They're the ones that spend all night digging hundreds of little holes in your manicured lawn in search of June bug larvae and other grubs.

There are few worlds and few creatures that modern man has not conquered and tamed with his superior technology. Maybe that's why I still get a mischievous pleasure in seeing man, the ultimate warrior, turn tail and run as soon as the tail of the lowly, gentle skunk goes up in the air. Sometimes, nature has its own way of leveling the playing field.

SNAPPING TURTLES
REAL JURASSIC REPTILES

The ancient reptile crawled out of the muddy, primeval-looking swamp. Its huge plate-covered body was overgrown with green algae and its long tail had saw-toothed ridges. As it raised its huge head and long neck, you could see the massive jaws and sharp, hooked beak.

A scene describing a long extinct dinosaur from a Hollywood movie like "Jurassic Park?" Nope, just a fairly accurate description of a common Wisconsin reptile—the snapping turtle.

Actually, snapping turtles do have something in common with their distant dinosaur cousins. Scientists tell us that snappers shared their swampy homes with real dinosaurs some twenty million years ago, and have remained nearly unchanged since those ancient times. In fact, paleontologists have discovered fossils of turtles older than 200 million years, long before dinosaurs roamed the earth.

Snapping turtles are abundant in just about every lake, stream, pond, and marsh in the state. We rarely get to see them because they spend most of their time submerged in shallow water buried in mud, with only their eyes and nostrils exposed. At night, the large turtles become active, crawling along the bottoms of lakes and marshes in search of food such as leeches, worms, minnows, crayfish, algae, plants, and carrion. Some call them the "vultures" of our waterways, since they will eat just about anything, dead or alive.

In June and July, female snappers leave the safety of their marshes and swamps in search of dry land to lay their eggs. Turtles prefer dry sandy or gravely areas in full sunlight to dig their nests, and will travel great distances to find just the right site. Unfortunately, the gravel shoulders of our busy highways seem to be just the right place—from the viewpoint of a turtle, anyway. Motorists unwittingly kill many snappers as they slowly cross the highway or dig their nests along our roadways.

Mother snapping turtles lay 25 or so white, rubbery eggs, the size of ping-pong balls, cover them with soil, and then abandon them to hatch on their own. Occasionally, I've found turtle nests where not all the eggs got buried, and I snatched a few of them to watch them hatch. If you bury them in moist sand in an aquarium, they will almost always hatch out sometime after Labor Day. Newborn snappers are about the size of a silver dollar, with soft, flexible shells. I always return baby turtles back into the marsh or river as soon as they hatch, close to where their nest was found. In the wild, many nests are destroyed by predators such as skunks, opossums, fox, and herons, which eat the eggs or snatch up the young turtles as they hatch.

Adult snapping turtles can grow to more than 50 pounds and live for 25 years or more. Although harmless and docile in the water, the reptiles are transformed into hissing, snapping, formidable fighters when cornered on land. Their powerful jaws and sharp beaks can cause a painful bite. Because of this, snapping turtles have few natural enemies other than man's vehicles and sometimes man's appetite for turtle soup or stew. Trapping turtles for food, or "turtlin'," is still popular throughout the state, and legal harvest seasons are established for taking snapping turtles. I've tried snapper soup on several occasions and have found it to be delicious—if I don't think too much about the source of the main ingredient.

No, the sight of a snapping turtle won't cause the excitement of a Hollywood special effects creation, like a Tyrannosaurus Rex in a blockbuster film, but they do have one thing few other creatures can claim. They are true, living, breathing remnants of the Jurassic age of dinosaurs that you can see and touch. Well, maybe you should just see and not touch, if you want to keep all your appendages in place.

MOSQUITOES
YOU CAN RUN, BUT YOU CAN'T HIDE

They're called the world's deadliest animals, and they're out to get you. You can run, but you can't hide. Sooner or later, you'll hear the familiar "eee . . . eee" humming sound of their wings beating five hundred times a second as they hover above you like a miniature version of an Apache helicopter. Their eyesight is poor, but they know where you are. Using their super-sensitive antennae, mosquitoes can sense your body heat as well as the carbon dioxide and moisture your lungs expel as you breathe. Finally they zero in on their target and attack to get their blood meal. Ouch! Slap! Darn #@★ bugs.

Spanish explorers to America were the first to encounter these swarms of pesky, biting insects, which they named "mosquitoes," meaning little flies. Although mosquitoes may annoy us and ruin an occasional picnic or backyard barbecue here in Wisconsin, most are not a real threat to our health. In the tropics, however, mosquitoes are known to spread some of the deadliest diseases known to man, such as yellow fever, malaria, and a hundred other viruses.

The building of the Panama Canal by the French was nearly shut down because of these tiny insects. In 1882, France sent five hundred of its best and brightest engineers along with an army of workers to begin work on the canal. Unfortunately, none of the young engineers made it to their first payday. Mosquito-spread malaria and yellow fever

killed all of them and many other workers, almost as quickly as they could be recruited. Before the French gave up the project, seven years later, more than 22,000 workers had died. Eventually, the United States completed the Panama Canal, but not before learning a little about the mosquito first and how to control it.

The mosquito is probably the most successful creature on the planet, with more than three thousand species worldwide. It can live in virtually any habitat, from rain forests to deserts. Some of the thickest swarms of mosquitoes are found not in the tropics or in Wisconsin, but in the cold arctic regions.

As we all are painfully aware, mosquitoes like blood meals and aren't fussy about where they get them. Warm-blooded mammals such as deer, pets, and people are their favorites, but they also attack birds and even frogs. Only the female bites, sucking blood for the protein she needs to develop her eggs. Male mosquitoes are harmless insects that feed on plant nectar and are rarely even seen.

Mosquitoes have an impressive set of tools to collect their blood meals. Although it looks like a single tube to our naked eye, their stinging mouth part is actually made up of six needle-like parts. Four of these needles are like saw-tipped daggers that stab and cut your skin, while two others form a straw-shaped tube that sucks up the blood. Another drips a chemical into the wound to keep your blood from clotting. At the same time mosquitoes are sucking your blood, they inject saliva to numb your skin so you don't feel pain. Unfortunately, this same saliva is the cause of the itchy bump you get after they finish their meal, and also the source of transmittal of disease viruses in the tropics.

After the female mosquito has had her blood meal, she lays about four hundred eggs at a time in floating rafts, usually in stagnant water or even on wet soil. Once hatched, the larvae live near the surface of the water where they can breath air. After they've matured, their bodies split open and the adult mosquito crawls out and flies away. Luckily for us, mosquitoes have lots of enemies and only one or two of the original four hundred eggs will survive to become adults. Minnows and other fish eat mosquitoes in the water while frogs, birds, and bats eat them once they're air-bound.

Although we can help control mosquito populations ourselves by eliminating their breeding areas, such as stagnate water holes or old tires that collect water; we really can't control them entirely, especially during periods of wet weather, which creates thousands of mosquito breeding ponds everywhere. The best we can do is learn to live with them, use insect repellent, and take satisfaction in knowing that eventually the fall frosts will kill off the entire population.

Before then, however, many of the female mosquitoes with fertilized eggs will go into hibernation and many more will have laid their dormant eggs in the mud, getting ready for next season. By the following spring, like the two hundred million springs before, the mosquito will rise again.

DEER FLIES
INSECTS RIGHT OUT OF PANDORA'S BOX

According to Greek mythology, all the ills, evils, and pests that cause mankind to suffer flew out of Pandora's box when she opened it against the warnings of Zeus. Although not specifically mentioned in the legend, I'm convinced that first pest out of Pandora's box had to be the deer fly.

Even diehard nature lovers have a hard time finding something nice to say about a creature that makes its living by piercing your skin, sucking your blood, and leaving behind a mild poison that causes your wound to swell and itch. With mosquitoes, at least you can say that they feed many bird and bat species because of their sheer numbers. Deer flies, on the other hand, are not as plentiful and do not fly during the night hours, so their food value to other animals is not as important.

Deer flies are small, often colorful insects. They are part of the all-too-familiar family of biting flies that range in size from the little "no-see-ums" (about the size of a grain of pepper) to the much larger horse flies that have a wing span of two inches or more. Some people call deer flies horse flies, but the two are really separate species, each with its own characteristics.

You can always tell a deer fly by its brightly colored, iridescent green or gold eyes, usually striped in zigzag patterns. Deer flies also hold their wings at an angle, giving them a triangular appearance. To me, they look like miniature insect versions of stealth fighter jets, and they're just as deadly in their own irritating way. Deer flies have razor-sharp, beak-like mouth parts that they use to pierce and cut through skin, sort of like a scissors in reverse with the cutting edges to the outside. Then they both lick and suck blood from the wound.

If you are bitten by a deer fly, you may be sure it will be a female, since the females need blood to lay eggs and complete their reproduction cycle. Male deer flies are rarely seen and spend their days feeding on plant juices and flowers. Females are usually most active on hot, muggy days. They don't seem to like windy days or bright sunshine, so they tend to hide in wooded, shaded areas, especially near marshes, on those days.

Once deer flies find you, they'll follow you and keep buzzing around your head until they find a sleeve, collar, or hair landing spot, so they can crawl onto an exposed patch of skin to draw blood. Luckily, deer flies are not the quickest or brightest of insects and you can usually swat them before they bite. Most commercial insect repellents claim to repel deer flies, but I haven't found any that work for me, especially on those hot, quiet days when the flies are most active. In addition to biting humans, deer flies can be serious pests to horses, cattle, and other livestock. They also plague deer throughout the summer. You might have seen a deer bolt out of a woods or marsh along a road, shake its head, and run like crazy over a field trying to shake the pesky insects.

Deer flies usually appear in late May or June, but sometimes they don't make an appearance until July. The eggs that deer flies lay in swamps and ponds hatch into larvae that eat other aquatic insects. When the weather is hot enough, the larvae move to the shoreline and pupate into adult flies. Although they are more numerous near waterways, they can fly miles from their breeding places—to places like your backyard.

I guess deer flies are just one of those creatures we must learn to live with, even if we can't comprehend their role in nature. Maybe, like the early Greeks, we should just accept them as part of our world and blame it on the curiosity of Pandora.

FIREFLIES
NATURE'S MOST SPECTACULAR NIGHT SHOW

" Glow little glowworm, glimmer, glimmer. . ."

Ever wonder what exactly a "glowworm" is, in that old familiar song? To find the answer, take a drive on a quiet country road on a hot, muggy July night and park overlooking most any open grassy field or marshy area. There, if conditions are right, you'll be treated to one of nature's best summer spectacles. Hundreds, maybe thousands, of tiny greenish-yellow lights can be seen blinking on and off like some long-forgotten set of twinkle lights left over from Christmas. Most of us call these tiny, living light bulbs fireflies or lightning bugs. If you look closely, however, you'll find they're not really true bugs at all, and certainly aren't flies, but members of the largest family of insects in the world—beetles.

Fireflies overwinter as worm-like larvae buried in the soil, and emerge in spring to feed on other insects and small animals such as snails and slugs. Some species of firefly larvae and even their eggs can produce light and shine in the night, giving rise to their nickname. By early summer, these "glow worms" will pupate and transform into adult fireflies that light up the night skies of summer. Fireflies are found mostly east of the Rocky Mountains here in North America, but some of the most brilliant fireflies in the world are found in the tropics. One South American firefly called the "railroad worm" has eleven pairs of green lights along its body and is topped off with a red headlight.

Nearly all of the 136 different species of fireflies can produce light flashes in their abdomens. Biologists call this amazing natural phenomenon "bioluminescence" and have only recently been able to reproduce it in the laboratory. They found that the secret ingredient of the firefly's cool, chemical light is an organic compound called *luciferin*—named after the fires of old Lucifer himself, it seems. This unique compound mixed with oxygen and the enzyme luciferace creates the eerie yellow-green light of the firefly.

In the early 1970s, chemical companies started reproducing the firefly's lucerferin commercially. That eventually led to some useful consumer products such as light sticks, used as auto flares and other emergency lighting, and also to some popular light rings and sticks sold to kids at concerts, fireworks displays, and other nighttime programs. Scientists continue to explore the possible uses of the firefly light, since it's still the most efficient light source known to mankind. Most of the energy that comes from our power plants to our homes is lost; only about ten percent of the energy used by an incandescent light bulb goes to producing light, the other ninety percent producing heat. In contrast, the firefly turns more than ninety percent of its energy into light, with no heat produced at all.

Of course, fireflies don't illuminate the night skies of summer for our entertainment or for the scientists' academic research. They're out there flashing their little tails off night after night for one reason and one reason only—sex. Fireflies of different species have their own special flash patterns and signal each other for the purpose of mating. Almost all the airborne fireflies you see are males, while the females, some of which can't fly at all, are usually perched on the grass or ground. She will respond or flash only at males of her own species, luring one in closer and closer until they eventually meet up and mate. Most female fireflies will stop flashing after mating, but in some species the female will continue to signal males and capture them for a midnight snack when they are lured in.

Few things in the natural world are as awe-inspiring as the spectacular light show created by fireflies. Their strange, flashing green lights can somehow seem both eerie and comforting, as they light up the dark skies of a summer night. All too soon it seems the twinkle of the firefly dies down, her eggs are laid, and a whole new generation of "glow worms" waits patiently for their time in next summer's show. ▲

August

In August, the lazy, hazy days of summer often begin with warm and dry mornings. As the "dogs day" full moon sinks into the western horizon and dawn breaks, painted turtles crawl onto their favorite basking log in the pond to enjoy the morning sun. Nearby, in the open meadows, monarch butterflies alight on the delicate blossoms of Queen Anne's lace and other wildflowers, gathering nectar in preparation for their long migration ahead. By noon, when the day's heat and humidity hang heavy in the air, you can hear the familiar *zeeerr, zeeerr* call of cicadas high in the treetops as they sing summer's sweet song.

Despite the warm temperatures, hints of autumn are already beginning to show in northern Wisconsin. Red maple and staghorn sumac leaves begin to turn crimson, and blackbirds start to form flocks in anticipation of their flight south a few weeks hence. Nighthawks, shorebirds, swallows, and purple martins are already beginning to migrate by the end of the month.

Then, one evening, after a brilliant scarlet-orange sunset, August's full "red moon" rises to the gruff, low-pitched hoot of the great-horned owl and the monotonous chirps of field crickets proclaiming the approaching end of summer.

RED-TAILS
HAWKS IN A HOSTILE WORLD

*"The swoop of a hawk is perceived by one as
the drama of evolution. To another it is
only a threat to the full frying pan."*

—Aldo Leopold

Few Wisconsin birds of prey have been more persecuted throughout history than the red-tailed hawk. They've been shot, poisoned, trapped, and harassed ever since our forefathers came to this country to farm the land and hunt wild game. Even today, many people still call the red-tail a "chicken hawk," referring to the raptor's occasional appetite for free-roaming barnyard chickens.

But things have changed. Chickens are now mostly raised inside poultry factories, and hunters know they lose more rabbits and pheasants to urban sprawl than to hawks. Federal and state laws have also changed, providing complete protection for all birds of prey. Those who attempt to harm the birds in any way are faced with hefty fines and the threat of jail.

Probably more important than any law on the books, however, is the very real change in our attitude towards the hawk. The sight of a red-tailed hawk soaring above an open field or perched majestically on a dead snag brings out stirrings of power, grace, and wildness we often miss in our own lives. The sound of the red-tail's high-pitched scream as it soars in the thermals, high in the sky, can still send a primeval shiver up one's spine, reminding us that we still haven't tamed and conquered all of nature.

Despite our earlier attempts to exterminate the red-tailed hawk, this bird has survived and is now the largest and most abundant hawk in Wisconsin. Adult red-tails are easy to identify if you watch for the reddish-brown tail feathers as the bird banks into the sunlight while in flight. Immature red-tails are more difficult to identify, since they have the same brownish plumage and banded tail feathers common to many other species of hawks.

Red-tailed hawks are superb hunters. Their sharp, binocular vision allows them to sight a mouse in the grass hundreds of yards away. Incredibly, the red-tail's eyes are almost as large as our own, occupying more space than the bird's brain. Although the hawk has a large and formidable hooked beak, its real killing tools are the sharp, powerful talons it uses to stab and crush prey. The beak is used only for tearing meat into bite-sized pieces. Like all birds of prey, the red-tail does not drink water and must get the moisture it needs from mice, rabbits, squirrels, and other small game it feeds on.

Most red-tailed hawks migrate to warmer climates and more productive hunting grounds in winter. The shoreline of Lake Michigan acts as a migration route for many species of raptors, which sometimes move in impressive numbers. In 1960 a record one-day tally of 563 migrating red-tails were counted at the Cedar Grove Ornithological Station in Sheboygan County.

Red-tailed hawks return to Wisconsin in late February or March, to begin to nest. The birds, which pair up for life, perform some impressive courtship flights at this time. One bird will fly straight up into the air a thousand feet or more and then, with open talons, suddenly dive towards its mate. After mating, a large nest about three feet across is built with sticks and twigs. The female lays two eggs and incubates them while the male stands guard and feeds the female until the eggs hatch. The young red-tails are grown and ready to leave the nest by summer, but still have much to learn in order to survive.

Biologists estimate that more than eighty percent of the young hawks eventually starve to death in their first year of life. Even those that do make it through their first winter still have a difficult road ahead. They must find enough large tracts of land in which to hunt, and an appropriate nesting site when they're ready to pair up with a mate at two years of age.

The red-tail's ideal nesting site is in mature timber with a commanding view of the surrounding territory. Unfortunately, these are the same prime areas for humans' housing sites. With so many new homes being built in rural areas, the red-tails' hunting and nesting territories continue to be diminished.

In time, it's hoped that the red-tailed hawk will learn to adjust to the urbanization of the countryside—or perhaps someday we can learn to leave enough land undisturbed for birds of prey and other wildlife.

We've come a long way from the days of trying to destroy every last "chicken hawk." Today, more and more of us can appreciate the important role that birds of prey play in the ecosystem, without running home to get the shotgun.

GREAT-HORNED OWLS
TIGERS OF THE NIGHT SKY

Owls and man have lived side by side since the dawn of time. Unfortunately, throughout our long shared history, owls usually have been victims of our ignorance. From ancient times, owls have been associated with gloom and doom, often referred to as the "funeral bird" or the "bird of death.

In autumn, as Halloween approaches, every house seems to have a cardboard likeness of an owl displayed in the window along with the bats, spiders, witches, and goblins. Centuries ago, Europeans believed that owls carried witches through the night on their noiseless wings. Owls were also thought to be an important ingredient in any magical brew that witches stirred up in their cauldrons. Today, most of us don't think of the owl as being evil, although to hear the low, deep, "who's awake, me too!" call of the great-horned owl in a dark forest can still bring a chill and raise a few hairs on the back of our neck.

Because the great-horned owl is a night-hunter, few of us get a chance to see one during the daylight hours, except if we happen to spot it sitting motionless in its roosting tree. People used to think that owls were blind during the day, but they can actually see quite well and will fly away if disturbed. Great-horned owls shift into high gear as the sun sets, however, and spend almost the entire night searching for prey. Some call them the "tigers of the sky" because of their ferocious appetites and deadly hunting ability. They can attack and kill most anything small enough for them to carry off, including mice, rats, rabbits, squirrels, small birds, frogs, and snakes. They are also one of the few predators that don't mind eating skunks, porcupines, and even an occasional small house cat.

Because of their appetite for just about any living creature that walks, crawls, flies, or swims, the great-horned owl has many enemies. Crows, in particular, seem to hate great-horned owls and go out of their way to mob them and drive them out of their territory. A few years ago, while camping with my family in the Kettle Moraine State Forest, I discovered firsthand why crows hate owls so much. During the night, we heard a great-horned owl calling near the campground. Later, we were awakened by a noisy ruckus in the pine tree behind our tent and in the morning discovered a grisly scene of six fledgling crow heads neatly clipped off and lying at the base of their nesting tree—doubtless the work of the great-horned owl.

Despite all its enemies, very few are actually able to kill a great-horned owl, except man, of course. And owls, like other birds of prey, are protected by state and federal laws. Today, owls are probably threatened more by the grim realities of nature itself. Many birds die of starvation during the long, cold winters of Wisconsin, especially when rodent and rabbit populations are low. The birds also seem to be accident-prone; many are killed while night-hunting by flying into power lines, or being hit by trucks and cars.

Fall, just at dawn or dusk, is a good time

to get out and listen for the great-horned owl's call. The birds begin to pair up and establish their territories for mating in November, and tend to make a lot of noise about it, either to attract their mates or to warn other owls to stay away. Great-horned owls are not tolerant of other birds of prey in their territory, and have been known to attack and kill smaller owls. Because of this, barred or screech owls rarely inhabit the same area as a nesting great-horned owl. On the other hand, they will allow hawks to share the same territory, probably because hawks hunt by day and owls have the night shift all to themselves. Great-horned owls even nest in old hawk nests, since they do not build nests of their own. They also take over nests of herons, crows, and even squirrels, on occasion, usually with no quarrel from the evicted parties. In the natural world, might is right, especially when it involves a large predator bird with a four-foot wing-span and sharp, powerful talons such as those possessed by the great-horned owl. Nobody messes with the tiger of sky.

No longer the evil night-stalker, or superstitious death bird, the great-horned owl is now seen as what it is—an important natural predator that happens to hunt by night. I hope that this mysterious and majestic bird, with its loud chilling call, will continue to raise a few neck hairs for generations to come.

QUEEN ANNE'S LACE
A WILD AND CRAZY CARROT

It was the year 1603 when King James I brought his young bride Anne to his English castle. Like all royalty of the time, the king and queen had a passion for their royal gardens, which served as a welcome refuge from the daily pressures and problems of the monarchy.

Queen Anne was not only an excellent gardener but also an expert lace-maker of her time. As legend has it, one day she challenged her ladies-in-waiting to a contest to see who could make lace as beautiful as her favorite wildflower in the royal gardens. No doubt, the queen herself won the contest, and the lacy white flower would thereafter be called "Queen Anne's lace."

This same flower was brought to America by the early colonists and is now one of the most abundant roadside flower (or weed) in the country. Queen Anne's lace is the tall plant with the large, lacy-looking, flat-topped white flower heads you see along our roads and ditches.

Actually the flower is really made up of hundreds of tiny flowers, all bunched together into a flat cluster called an umbel.

In the center of flowering head of Queen Anne's lace you can often find a single dark purple flower. Biologists believe the purpose of this one purple flower in the middle of hundreds of pure white ones is to lure insects to the plant for pollination. But legend explains this oddity as representing a drop of royal (blue) blood of Queen Anne when she pricked her finger on a needle while sewing lace.

Queen Anne's lace is also commonly called "wild carrot." If you crush and smell the leaves of the plant, you'll notice an unmistakable carrot-like odor. The plant even has a long taproot similar to that of our garden carrot, although it is smaller and tougher, with a bitter taste. Despite this, Europeans and early Americans used it for food as well as for medicine. In the early 1900s, scientists discovered the importance of vitamin A and eventually developed our modern garden carrot—a direct subspecies of wild carrot or Queen Anne's lace. From then on, "eating your carrots" became mother's prescription for good health, good eyesight, and, of course, seeing better in the dark.

Once pollinated, the flower head closes in on itself in a circular ball that resembles a "birds nest," which is another common name for Queen Anne's lace. Late summer is good time of year to look closely at the plant, since many are still in full bloom while others are going to seed in the bird-nest stage. As fall progresses, these bird-nest seed heads open and close with the humidity in the air and drop their seeds to assure the next generation of plants.

Although a favorite in the royal gardens, Queen Anne's lace was not a native plant of England. It originated in the Mediterranean area and was spread around the world by explorers and colonists. The plant was mentioned in the writings of the Greeks and Romans as early as five hundred years before Christ. It was used even then as a food and herbal medicine. In early Greece the plant was called philon or "loving" root. Apparently, young lovers believed the plant to possess powers of exciting the passions and it was eaten prior to—well, you know.

Queen Anne's lace—wild carrot, bird's nest, love root, or whatever you call it. Are they just pesky roadside weeds, or are they beautiful, historical wildflowers? Or, as the Greeks believed, are they a powerful aphrodisiac? Any way, I'm sure the next time you see these white, flat-topped flowers along the road, or someone tells you to "eat your carrots," you'll think of them in a little different light. Who knows, maybe they really can improve more than your night vision.

PURPLE LOOSESTRIFE
PURPLE PLAGUE OF THE MARSH

They invaded our land more than a hundred years ago. A foreign intruder that marched into the wilds of America about the same time that the soldiers of the Union and Confederate armies marched against each other on the battlefields of the Civil War. At first, nobody really noticed this new, seemingly innocent looking European flower. All the finest Yankee flower gardens in the northeast states contained this hardy and long-lived new plant. Everyone admired its beautiful reddish-purple flowers that bloomed throughout the summer on stalks up to seven feet tall.

In Europe, the plant was called by a variety of names—red sally, purple grass, and willow-weed—but here in America, it became better known as purple loosestrife. Unfortunately, like many other plants brought to the New World, it left behind all its natural parasites and competitors and soon escaped cultivation. Ever since, it has spread like a plague, especially in marshlands, ponds, stream sides, vacant lots, and both wet and dry ditches. It first appeared in Wisconsin in the 1920s and has now spread to every county in the state, most heavily in southern areas.

Despite purple loosestrife's beauty, it has become a serious problem to the health of wetlands and river marshes because it is gradually displacing and killing native cattails and sedges. The end result is a solid mass of purple loosetrife plants which force out wildlife such as waterfowl, songbirds, and muskrats, sometimes causing them to disappear altogether.

To combat this intruder, federal, state, and local governments along with private citizens have waged an ongoing war against the plant for many years. A citizen task force was formed in Wisconsin in 1983 to address the purple loosestrife problem. Purple loosestrife hot spots were identified throughout the state, and efforts were made to pull, burn, spray herbicides, and mow them out of existence. Although some of these efforts proved successful against small patches, it was soon evident that, once established in large wetlands or streams, it was virtually impossible to eradicate the plant completely.

How could one foreign plant, in just a few decades, destroy a wetland that took hundreds of thousands of years to evolve? For one, almost nothing seems to eat purple loosestife, which means it has no natural predators to help control its spread. It is virtually useless as a food plant for wildlife. The plant also has amazing survival powers, stronger than those of any native species. When cut, it sends up shoots and blooms again in a few weeks. Even plant parts that are cut can sprout and grow new plants, and plants that are pulled up will send up new shoots if any of the tiny rootlets are left in the soil. Burning and aerial spraying of herbicides by the federal government in the eastern states also failed to stop this purple plague.

Even more amazing is purple loosestife's reproduction system. A single plant can grow more than three thousand individual flowers, each of which produces a seedpod packed with a hundred seeds—a total of thirty thousand seeds that are dispersed by wind, water, man, and animals to start new colonies—all from one plant. .

Biologist now feel that the best hope for control of the plant will be the introduction of an insect predator that we hope will munch the plant into control. Scientists have experimented with several dozen European insects and have narrowed down the list to two leaf chaffers and one root borer to help fight the plant. Controlled releases of these beetles have occurred around the state every year since 1995 in Wisconsin. So far these new insects have been shown to eat only purple loosestrife and no native plants.

Time will tell whether the purple invasion of our wetlands can be stopped biologically by another "friendly" alien from Europe. In the meantime, all we can do is fight our small skirmishes by pulling out new patches of loosestrife as they pop up and support the ongoing efforts of others to help save our wetlands. Despite the plant's nasty disposition, one can't help to stop and enjoy the brilliant purple color of the flowering loosestrife that lights up our marshes in summer. It's the kind of plant you can love to hate, I guess.

STAGHORN SUMAC
QUENCHING A THIRST FOR NATURE

It's the dog days of late summer. It's hot and you need a cool, refreshing drink. But what? You've already downed dozens of gallons of lemonade and iced tea to beat the heat this summer. Your tap water just doesn't seem to satisfy your thirst, and you've given up trying to convince yourself that your diet soda really does taste good. You drank the last of your Snapple and you're even out of brewskies. How can you quench your thirst now?

The answer might be growing right in your own backyard, or down the block in a vacant lot, or maybe in an abandoned farm field nearby. There you will find staghorn sumac, a small, crooked little tree with fuzzy branches and long palm-like leaf stalks. This familiar plant is also called the "Indian lemonade" tree, since it provides the ingredients to make a cool, refreshing natural beverage. In late July, thick cone-shaped clusters of flowers bloom at the end of the sumac branch stems. By late summer or early fall, these flowers turn into red berries, which are covered with tiny, sticky hairs that make them feel like velvet when touched. To some, the fuzz that covers the sumac branches reminds them of a buck's antlers in velvet, hence its common name of "staghorn" sumac.

A few years ago, I decided to make Indian lemonade from the sumac tree, despite my wife's skepticism. Her doubts dated back to the last time I tried this, when my concoction turned a bit moldy in her refrigerator. But, with a new recipe in hand, I went out and picked about a dozen ripe sumac berry clusters, stripped the berries from the stems, and washed them under cool water. I then took a handful of berries at a time and rubbed them between my hands, dropping them into a bowl filled with two quarts of water. This loosens the tiny hairs covering the berries and releases their flavor. Finally, I strained the liquid through a coffee filter to remove the pulp and fine hairs, and sweetened the liquid with sugar.

The end result was a delicious and refreshing pink-colored beverage with a fruity, almost raspberry or cherry flavor. Everyone who tasted it enjoyed it—even my wife, although I noticed she kept the poison center telephone number handy, just in case. I guess I shouldn't have told her that staghorn sumac is not only closely related, but in the same genus, as poison ivy. Or maybe I shouldn't have mentioned that the plant is packed with tannic acid that was once used to tan leather and to make a fine black ink.

Native American Indians used staghorn sumac as a medicinal herb and dried the berries for winter use. Until recent times, sumac was still listed as a drug in the United States, used as a gargle for sore throats. Indians also made flutes from the stems of the plant by pushing out the soft center. They also used these hollow branches to make spiles for tapping sugar maples in spring. Indians also dried the leaves to mix with tobacco to smoke.

Staghorn sumac, an attractive little tree that grows well in gravely soils, is used extensively in landscaping in urban areas. It seems to grow well even in cities, where other trees are damaged by air pollution. Sumac is one of the first trees to start to turn color in late summer. Its leaves, which turn several beautiful shades of crimson and orange, always remind me that the hot summer days are almost over and autumn is on the way. But, until then, it's time to enjoy a cool, refreshing (and free) summer beverage right from nature.

TIMBER RATTLESNAKES
DON'T TREAD ON ME

Few animals are so universally feared and despised as rattlesnakes. Even back in America's Revolutionary War days, the rattlesnake insignia on the "Don't Tread On Me" flag came to symbolize the fierce independence and dangerous fortitude of the colonists seeking freedom. Almost all American Indian tribes believed that rattlesnakes possessed supernatural powers. Hundreds of myths and legends about them were retold from generation to generation. Despite the danger that this creature posed to people living in the wilderness, almost all Native Americans had a strict taboo against harming or killing a rattlesnake.

There are dozens of species of rattlesnakes throughout the United States, but only two are found in Wisconsin. The massasauga, or swamp rattler, is an endangered species found in only a few isolated lowland

areas of the central and southwestern part of the state. The timber rattlesnake is more common, but is rarely seen, since it lives in remote,
rocky bluffs along the Wisconsin and Mississippi River valleys and in
the Baraboo hills. As a state park manager, I lived, worked, explored,
hunted, and hiked some of the better known rattlesnake areas in southwestern Wisconsin for many years, but still encountered these reptiles
on only three occasions in all that time. Only one incident, at Devils
Lake State Park, involved an actual rattlesnake bite to a hiker. The victim later told me he came across the rattler while hiking along a park
road and was trying to "save" it from being hit by a car by moving it
off the road with a stick when it struck out at him. Since not many people are worried about rattlesnakes being run over by cars, I suspect the
real scenario was a bit different from his version. More than likely, he
was trying to kill it with a stick for a rattlesnake skin souvenir, and got
too close. Although he survived the bite, the gentleman did spend several days in the Baraboo hospital and became quite ill when his white
blood cell count dropped dangerously low.

Larger rattlesnakes have enough venom to bring death to a human
within twelve hours, if the bite is left untreated. Doctors advise that, if
you are ever bitten by a rattlesnake, to stay calm (yeah, right) and seek
medical help at once. Although the thought of getting bitten by a rattlesnake is frightening, in reality you have a much better chance of getting struck by lightning in Wisconsin. Since 1981 there have been only
five rattlesnake bites reported in the entire state, and only one rat-
tlesnake-related fatality has been documented in the state since 1900.

The timber rattlesnake is a large, heavy-bodied snake that grows to
about four feet in length. It is usually yellowish-brown in color, with
black crossbar markings. But the best way to identify it is to look for
the distinctive rattle on the tip of its tail, which it always holds up in the
air when it's crawling. When cornered or frightened, rattlesnakes vibrate
their tails, creating a loud buzzing sound as a warning. The rattle itself
is actually made up of loose interlocking shells that are formed each
time the snake sheds it's skin. Older rattlers may have ten or more rattle segments, but since many of them break off, they really can't be used
to judge the age of the reptiles. Like most other snakes, rattlers have
poor eyesight, except at close range, and have no external ears or even
eardrums. They rely on their ever-flicking tongues to "smell" the air
and sense vibrations. Like all pit vipers, rattlesnakes have an open hole
or "pit" located between their eye and nostril. This unique organ acts as

a heat sensor in locating warm-blooded animals such as mice, rats, voles, chipmunks, and ground squirrels, which make up most of their diet. Since rattlesnakes don't have any teeth designed for chewing, they must use their long, hollow fangs to strike out and inject a powerful venom into their prey, so it can be swallowed and digested.

Timber rattlesnakes generally prefer to stay far away from people. They spend most of the year high in remote rock bluffs, or hibernating during the winter deep inside rock crevices. But in July and August, as the weather turns dry and prey becomes harder to find, some rattlers move to lower ground in search of food, and it is here where they may cross paths with people. Usually these are male or non-pregnant female rattlesnakes. Pregnant females, which don't feed at all, spend the summer high in the bluffs basking in the sunshine. In late August or September, they give live birth to six to fifteen baby rattlers. Rattlesnakes are not prolific reproducers. Females don't mature until they're over nine years old, and even after that they breed only once every three or four years.

Timber rattlesnake populations in Wisconsin have dropped dramatically in recent years. Even though bounties on them were stopped in 1973, uncontrolled harvest of rattlesnakes continued in areas outside wildlife refuges, such as state parks and natural areas. They were hunted both for sport and for commercial use of their hides in making hatbands, belts, and boots. Recently, Wisconsin joined Illinois and Minnesota in an effort to save the timber rattlesnake. It is now listed as a protected species.

The timber rattlesnake is one of Wisconsin's most impressive and probably most feared animals. Although most of us would not want one in our own backyard, it's comforting somehow to know that we still haven't destroyed every last dangerous creature in the wilds of Wisconsin. There's an old Cherokee legend about rattlesnakes that ends in a simple but profound statement: "Let them alone and they will let you alone." Maybe it's an ancient lesson we all need to re-learn.

The Badger
OFFICIAL WISCONSIN STATE MASCOT

"On Wisconsin, On Wisconsin
Grand Old Badger State. . . "

—W.T. Purdy, 1909

Almost everyone in Wisconsin has heard this familiar state song or has seen the University of Wisconsin's mascot, Bucky Badger, at sporting events. Even the great seal and official flag of Wisconsin sports the likeness of a badger. But how did the badger, an obscure and rarely seen relative of the skunk, rise to such to such prominence as to represent the state of Wisconsin?

It all started back in the early 1800s during the lead mining days. Some of the miners who entered the state from the south decided to stay through the winter months. They dug holes into the sides of hills for temporary shelter, similar to the dens that badgers live in. At the same time, other miners and Illinois farmers who hauled the lead ore to the markets in the summer returned home each year to harvest their crops. Because they appeared and disappeared like migrating suckers in the creeks, they were called suckers. Eventually, the Badger nickname stuck here in Wisconsin. For some reason, however, Illinois has never identified itself as the Sucker State.

At first glance, the badger would seem to be a poor choice as the symbol of our state. With its low-slung, chubby body and short, stubby legs, the badger would also seem like an odd mascot for a mighty football team. But looks can be deceiving and badgers are known as powerful fighters. Their two-inch claws and full set of sharp teeth can be formidable weapons when they are cornered. Even students at the UW–Madison campus gave up their live badger mascot back in 1948 in favor of a papier-mache Bucky Badger, when the real animal became too vicious. Badgers can also emit a foul spray from their anal glands, although it's not as potent as that of their skunk cousins.

The badger's reputation as a fighter has even entered the English language. The word "badger" is often used as a verb meaning to bother,

pester, or annoy someone. It comes from the old and cruel English custom of staging fights between dogs and badgers.

Despite their legendary toughness, badgers prefer to lead solitary, peaceful lives in the prairies, meadows, and woodlands of Wisconsin. They are mostly meat eaters and are in constant search of anything they can catch or dig out of the ground, such as mice and ground squirrels. Although not plentiful anywhere in the state, badgers occasionally show up in areas that have light or sandy soils in which they can dig. With their large claws and muscular legs, badgers are truly born to dig, and can easily out-dig a man using a shovel. Besides digging for their meals, badgers also excavate holes as dens to sleep in, often digging a new burrow every day. Females dig longer-lasting burrows in which to raise their young in April or May.

Badgers are strikingly handsome animals with attractive white markings on their face, long, colorful fur, and powerful bodies. Unfortunately, very few Badger State residents can claim ever to have seen one in the wild. Besides their secretive, nocturnal ways which make them difficult to observe, there just aren't many badgers around to see. Their populations first plummeted in the early part of the century when much of their favorite habitat was transformed into farms, factories, and cities, and many badgers were trapped and poisoned as vermin. Even though badgers where given complete protection in 1955, their numbers never really recovered, since most of their habitat had disappeared.

I hope that enough of our prairies, meadows, and woodlands can be left undeveloped to allow this unique and interesting animal to survive into the next century. It would be a shame to allow the official state animal of the great State of Wisconsin to disappear, except in costume at the Badger football games.

LUNA MOTHS
GHOSTS OF THE SUMMER NIGHT

Moths are one of nature's most mysterious and intriguing creatures. They're seen most often on hot summer nights as they gather by the hundreds at street lamps, outdoor house lights, and even the headlamps of moving automobiles. Why moths are attracted to our artificial lights is still not known, but biologists have discovered that moths are most active on moonlit nights while searching for mates. Perhaps they're merely confused by the thousands of "mini-moons" we've created to light up modern civilization. Centuries ago, our ancestors pondered this same question as they observed moths flying into their campfires and hearths, and dancing around their candles and lanterns. People back then often called moths "the souls," based on the superstitious belief that moths were actually the souls of the dead that flew through the dark night skies, seeking light.

It's easy to see why people once associated moths with the supernatural, especially if you've ever seen one of our largest and most hauntingly beautiful moths—the luna. This moth looks like a small pale-green ghost as it quickly appears and disappears out of the darkness. The luna is one of our largest silkworm moths, with a wingspan of more than 3 inches. It has long, delicate extensions or "swallowtails" on its rear wings. Luna moths are a beautiful lime-green in color, with purple-brown edging on their forewings. They also have unique see-through eyespots on all four wings. The advantage of these wing-windows is unclear, but they may aid in the moths' identifying each other in mating, or possibly in helping them to avoid predators such as owls and bats, by breaking up their outline in the moonlight.

Luna moths were named after the "Goddess of the Moon" from Roman mythology. Many people still call them "moon moths." They are native to North America and found throughout Wisconsin, especially in wooded areas. Luna moth larvae are large green caterpillars that feed on a variety of plants, especially the leaves of certain nut-bearing trees such as hickory, butternut, and walnut. When they grow large enough (about the size of your thumb) they begin to spin a cocoon by wrapping a leaf around themselves and winding silk around and around

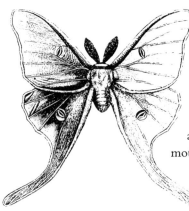

into an oval shape. The cocoon then falls to the ground and the larvae overwinter in the forest floor leaf litter, protected from the cold by its own natural anti-freeze. Adult luna moths don't emerge from their cocoons until the warmer weather returns, usually beginning in late June and going into August. Male luna moths have large antenna which are covered with scent organs used to locate females in the dark of night, sometimes as far away as a mile or more.

Luna moths can be difficult to observe, since they have such short life spans. After hatching from their cocoon they must rush to find a partner, then mate, lay eggs on food plants, and die, all within only about two weeks. Because of this rush to reproduce, they don't even stop to eat and must live off the fat reserves from their former larva state.

Luna moths are finely-tuned ecological barometers of our own environment. Unfortunately, their numbers have dwindled since the 1960s, most likely from the combination of pesticide use, pollution, and scarcity of their favorite food sources—butternut, hickory, and walnut trees. But despite being so rare, every now and then on hot summer nights we are treated to the sight of these pale-green ghosts of the forest, dancing in the moonlit skies of summer, just as they have for untold generations.

CRAYFISH
WISCONSIN'S OWN LITTLE LOBSTER

"You get a line, I'll get a pole,
I'll meet you down by the crawdad hole,
Honey, babe of mine."

—Early American Folksong

Spending a lazy summer day fishing for crawdads along a slow-moving river was once a favorite pastime for common folk in rural America, especially in the deep South. Here in Wisconsin, crawdads, better known as crayfish, are found in nearly every river, stream, lake, and pond. Despite their common name, crayfish are not fish at all, but rather crustaceans, like crabs and shrimp. With their hard exoskeleton, fan-like tail, stalked eyes, and large claws or pincers, they look pretty much like a miniature version of a lobster.

Crayfish are shy, solitary creatures by day, spending most of their time hiding under stones or plants in the water. Some even live on land by burrowing down into the soil and pushing it up and out of their burrow, until they reach water. But at night, crayfish become expert predators, hunting by scent for their favorite prey—water insects, worms, snails, tadpoles, and even small fish. They in turn are preyed upon by many other critters, including raccoons, mink, otter, turtles, herons, cranes, and larger fish. Often, a predator manages to bite off only part of the crayfish before it escapes. Luckily, crayfish have the amazing ability to regenerate a lost eye, leg, or claw by simply growing a new one the next time they molt their exoskeleton.

Crayfish were once sold as live fishing bait throughout the state, but this practice was banned in 1983 because of the invasion of its alien cousin from the South, the "rusty" crayfish. Once established in lakes and rivers, rusty crayfish harm the aquatic ecosystem by stripping away all the aquatic vegetation and consuming fish eggs. Because our harmless, native crayfish are difficult to tell apart from the rusty crayfish, it is now illegal to possess live crayfish of any kind while fishing inland waters in Wisconsin, with the exception of the Mississippi River.

Even though using crayfish for bait is a thing of the past, they may still be harvested for food in Wisconsin. Many people throughout the world consider crayfish a delicacy. Centuries ago, the Romans kept crayfish in special earthen pots to fatten them up for royal banquets or to feed to their slaves. Early settlers from Europe were thrilled to find crayfish in America, just like back home, and we have enjoyed eating hot, steaming plates of crawdads ever since.

Never having tasted crayfish before, I decided to give them a try recently when I saw them for sale at the local grocer. Despite some strong objections from my wife and daughter, and comments such as, "Oh yuck!" and "That's gross!," I prepared them anyway, and thoroughly enjoyed eating them.

If you would like to try this special dish yourself, you'll need about a dozen large crayfish per serving. Be sure to wash them well in water and eviscerate them by twisting and pulling back each middle tail fin to remove the stomach and intestinal vein. Then, just drop the crayfish into boiling water that has been seasoned with parsley, leek, and one chopped carrot. Cook for no longer than five to seven minutes. The crayfish will turn reddish in color, just like a lobster. Serve them in the shell with melted butter on the side, and use your fingers to separate the tail from the body and to crack open the shell against the curve of the tail.

Crayfish are plentiful in Wisconsin's waters and they provide a delicious special taste treat. Makes you want to go grab the ole fishin' pole and head on down to the crawdad hole, doesn't it?

PAINTED TURTLES
LIFE IN THE SLOW LANE

You can usually find them basking in the warm summer sun. What a carefree life they seem to lead. Nothing to do all day but eat, drink, sleep, swim, and sunbathe. No, this isn't a tourist at one of Wisconsin's famous resorts, but one of our most familiar reptiles—the painted turtle. As their name suggests, painted turtles are truly one of nature's most colorful works of art. Their shells are attractive olive-green on top, bright yellow underneath, and edged in patterns of red and orange. Even their head and legs seem to be carefully painted with brilliant red and yellow stripes.

Painted turtles are the most widespread of any species of turtle in North America, found in nearly every pond, lake, river, and marsh in our state. Despite being so common, they often go unnoticed, unless you know where and when to look for them. After spending the night resting and sleeping underwater, they crawl onto to a rock, log, stump, or other floating debris to bask in the warm morning sun. Turtles are fussy about their basking sites. Not just any old rock or log will do. It must be located in view of the shoreline, but not too close, and has to be in full sunlight. Once a good basking area has been found, several turtles will often use it at the same time, occasionally even stacking themselves up four to five deep, one on top of the other, to enjoy the sunshine. After basking for several hours, the turtles slide back into the water to feed on small aquatic animals such as tadpoles, snails, insects, and worms. They also eat plants—duckweed, cattail, and algae—and serve another important function in keeping the water clean by feeding on carrion. Later in the afternoon, the turtles return to their basking sites to catch a few more rays, and then feed again just before nightfall.

Other than crawling out of the water to sun themselves, painted turtles rarely leave their aquatic homes, except once a year when the females search for dry

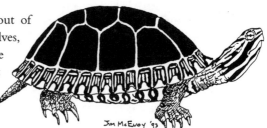

Jim McEvoy '93

179

land on which to lay their eggs. They begin to mate as early as March and continue well into late summer. Male turtles are smaller in size and have long front claws, which they use to hold the females during courtship. After one or two months, the female leaves the water to find a nesting spot, preferring sandy banks, gravel knolls, or mowed fields and lawns.

After digging out a nest hole, she lays about eight eggs, carefully buries them, and then walks away, never to return. Like millions of generations of turtles before her, she depends on the sun's heat to incubate the eggs until they hatch. Although most turtles hatch out by late summer, those eggs that were laid late in the season may stay in the nest and not hatch until the following spring. How these tiny, cold-blooded hatchlings can survive the subzero temperatures of winter remains a mystery of nature. But, somehow, many do survive and eventually the warm rains of spring signal them to dig themselves out and head for the water.

Painted turtles can live for up to forty years in the wild, and adults have little to fear from most predators because of their unique ability to draw their heads and legs into their hard, protective shells when threatened. Unfortunately, this armor doesn't help much when they cross a busy highway, especially at their normal slow pace. Newly hatched painted turtles can also become traffic victims as they attempt to reach water from their nesting sites. Even if they're lucky enough to make it to the water, many are eventually eaten by water snakes, game fish, and wading birds such as herons. Many more turtles never even get a chance to hatch out at all, since the eggs are routinely dug right out of the nest and eaten by skunks, raccoons, fox, and even ground squirrels.

Despite all the hardships and hazards they face, painted turtles continue to thrive in Wisconsin, even in the urban waterways of our largest cities. Because of this, these gentle creatures are probably the best known and beloved of all our reptiles. More than one kid or adult has discovered the joy of seeing a painted turtle up close, and maybe carefully handling one before releasing it back into the wild.

Turtles have held a fascination for people throughout the ages. In the Orient, the turtle is still revered as the symbol of a long life, one of the four benevolent spiritual animals. Next time you come across a painted turtle, take time to reflect on the fact that these colorful turtles and their relatives have been slow-w-w-w-ly walking the face of the earth for nearly 175 million years. Maybe there's something to all this sunbathing, eating, sleeping, and slow-paced vacation lifestyle, after all.

MONARCH BUTTERFLIES
MIGRATION IS NOT JUST FOR THE BIRDS

Late summer is time for the great migration to begin. No, not the wildebeest of the Serengeti, or the caribou of the northern tundra that you've seen on public television. This time, it's right in your own backyard—the great monarch butterfly migration.

Every year, starting in late August, some unknown natural cue tells the monarchs that it's time to head south before the fall frosts arrive. And south they go, by the millions, following familiar landmarks and natural barriers such as the shorelines of lakes and rivers. Although in most years we don't get to see large flocks of monarchs in the Midwest, a few years ago I came upon this natural spectacle at Kohler-Andrae State Park, along the shores of Lake Michigan, in Sheboygan County. There I found several hundred monarchs that had settled into a pine woods during the night to escape a windstorm off the lake. The butterflies covered nearly every evergreen bough, looking very much like black-and-orange Christmas tree ornaments. The monarchs were slowly fanning their wings and warming up in the morning sun, getting ready to head south on their migration route along the lake.

Monarchs are probably the best-known butterflies in Wisconsin. Many of us are familiar with their black, white, and yellow caterpillars that eventually transform into light green chrysalis with shiny gold dots, probably one of nature's most beautiful creations. A few weeks later, they emerge as fully-grown butterflies and take to the skies in search of mates. You can tell the sex of a monarch by the distinctive black dots, called alar glands, on the bottom wings of the males.

Until recently, scientists were baffled as to just where monarchs migrate each year. By using tiny wing tags and some topnotch detective work, they were able to trace the route of our Wisconsin monarchs all the way to a single mountain forest region in Mexico. This remote area is not the hot tropical rainforest as you might expect, but a cool mountain forest with spruce trees, and occasional frost and snow. There, along with sixty million other monarchs from throughout North America, they spend the winter covering the forest in a fantasy land of living orange drapery.

Another mystery was how the monarchs could get there to start with. After all, butterflies rarely live more than a few weeks before they mate, lay their eggs, and die. How could they fly thousands of miles in several months to a distant mountain range in Mexico? The answer turned out to a surprising yet ingenious quirk of nature. It seems the monarch butterflies that emerge early in summer are the non-migrants that live only thirty to forty days or so. The monarchs that emerge in late summer are able to live eight to ten months, and not only migrate to Mexico, but some even survive to return the following spring. These are the butterflies you see early in spring with the tattered and faded wings. Most monarchs that migrate in fall will not return, however, but will stop on the way back to lay eggs in the southern states, dying there before completing the migration. It may take up to three or four further generations before they return to the northern states by late spring or early summer.

Monarch caterpillars feed exclusively on milkweed. The plant's toxic milky juices seem to make both the caterpillar and the adult butterfly taste bad, making them unpalatable to birds and other predators. Monarchs face plenty of other hazards, however, such as violent rain and windstorms that can knock down entire flocks during migration. I've occasionally seen the Lake Michigan shoreline littered with hundreds of monarchs washed to shore after such a natural disaster.

Even more threatening, however, may be the continuing destruction of milkweed patches that the butterfly needs to eat and reproduce. Our passion to cut and spray herbicides along our roadsides, fields, and backyards may be contributing to the decline in monarch numbers in recent years. Unfortunately, the monarch's wintering grounds are also being threatened by logging and cattle grazing in the mountains of Mexico, and occasionally the monarch experiences weather-related disasters, as well. In 1996, freezing temperatures and heavy snowfalls killed millions of monarchs at their wintering grounds.

Ancient people once carved stone images of butterflies, believing them to be messengers from the gods. Maybe they were right, and perhaps the message has to do with our environment. I hope that the international conservation efforts now underway will halt the destruction of the Mexican forests so vital to the survival of the monarch. Maybe even we can learn to live with less manicured landscapes by not mowing and spraying every last milkweed patch out of existence. If not, one spring we might find ourselves left with only stone butterflies.

CICADA
SWEET SUMMER SONG

Everyone knows that robins herald the arrival of spring, and that migrating geese mark the start of autumn, but what cues us to the onset of summer? I mean the real summer, when the sun is hot, the air is still, and the days are muggy, the kind of weather when all living creatures have given way to the slow "dog days" of summer—all except one.

High in the treetops you can hear the loud, familiar *zeeerr, zeeerrr* breaking the silence of the day. People have mistaken this noise for everything from tree frogs and locusts to the whine of a power line. In reality, this familiar sound belongs to the call of an insect called a cicada (saw-kay-da).

The cicada looks something like a super-size fly and is about as big as the end joint of your thumb. It has a large, oblong head with funny-looking, wide-spaced, and bulbous eyes. The noise (song) of the cicada is made by special hollow body cavities that are covered on one side by a membrane similar to that of a drum. Only the male cicada sings. Sort of the "old blue eyes" of the insect world, the males croon away day after day in hopes of attracting that special female.

With more than 75 species of cicada in North America, each with its own distinctive call, finding true love in the midst of all this noise could be quite a feat. Luckily, different species of cicadas emerge as adults at different times of the summer, and even sing different tunes at different times of the day—sort of an insect version of a music festival.

Here in Wisconsin, we most often hear the "annual" cicada. These large green-and-black insects can be heard wherever there are tall shade trees, both in the city and the country.

A more famous cousin, called the "periodical" or seventeen-year cicada, usually gets most of the attention when the adults emerge from the ground every seventeen years. Luckily, all cicadas are harmless to plants, animals, and humans, since most do not even have mouth parts with which to eat (or bite) when they emerge.

All cicadas have unusual and interesting life stories. After mating, females lay their eggs in a slit they make in a tree. After they have hatched, the small grub–like larva fall to the ground, burrow in, and stay there from two to twenty years!

The periodical cicada spends exactly seventeen years burrowing through the soil, feeding on the root sap of trees. At an exactly prede-termined time, the insects tunnel up through the ground and crawl up the sides of trees and buildings. Mature winged adults emerge from a slit in the back of the larva and fly to the treetops. You might find the remains of a larva still clinging to the tree if you look closely where cicada are singing. They look something like brown, dried-up shrimp.

After spending seventeen years of its life as a grub in the dirt, the cicada has only one week or less to emerge as winged adult, mate, lay eggs, and then die. Occasionally, this is the time that people find this often heard but rarely seen insect, when they fall from the trees, ending a long and unusual life.

So, there you have it. Summer is officially proclaimed by the lowly cicada. Next time you hear the familiar *zeeerr, zeeerrr* ringing out high in the treetops, take time to glance skyward for a chance glimpse of an interesting member of "Wild Wisconsin." ▲

September

Autumn officially begins on September 23rd, the fall equinox, when the days and nights are equal in length. Although we may not notice the change, Wisconsin's wildlife is already preparing for the cold winter days ahead. Fall webworms hurry to complete their tent-like nests at the tips of tree branches, while below woolly bear caterpillars can be seen crossing busy highways in search of safe cover to hibernate.

Under September's full "harvest moon," also called the "fruit moon," cornfields are beginning to ripen and apple orchards are ready for picking. In the woodlands, black bears and woodchucks begin to gorge themselves with wild fruits, packing on extra layers of fat in preparation for their long sleep ahead. Gray squirrels are busy burying acorns for safe storage in the leaf litter of the oak forest floor.

As the days grow cooler, white-tail deer bucks feel the urge to rub off the fuzzy velvet covering the shiny white antlers beneath, and begin to spar with tree saplings in anticipation of the fall breeding season ahead. As the month ends, occasional frosts cause weaker flowers to wither, while more resilient plants like goldenrod and asters continue to flourish.

BARN OWLS
GHOSTS OF THE AUTUMN SKIES

Imagine a late-night stroll around the block on a dead-still, cold, frosty, autumn evening. As you pass the old neighborhood church, you pause to watch the bright orange harvest moon rising over and illuminating the parish cemetery, and take a moment to contemplate your own mortality. At that very moment, you suddenly hear an eerie, blood-curdling scream coming from church steeple. O *Shrreee* ... Too petrified to move, you glance skyward and are startled see a ghostly creature with piercing black eyes and a spook-white mask fly out of the steeple and silently glide through the moonlit sky.

Sounds like a page right out of a creepy horror novel, right? Actually, the scenario was a real-life drama that occurred right here in Wisconsin, at a church in Ozaukee County, a few years ago. But, just like the thousands of other "haunted house" tales told through the ages, the spook here was not from the world beyond, but was merely a harm-

185

less bird called the barn owl. Unlike most other owls that need large tracts of forest to survive, the barn owl actually prefers to live near people, making its home in man-made structures such as unused barn lofts, silos, vacant houses, sheds, and, of course, church steeples.

Barn owls are attractive birds with orange-gold plumage, nearly pure white underparts, and a heart-shaped facial disk. It's often called the golden owl or monkey-faced owl. Of course, barn owls didn't always live in barns and church steeples. Because of its nearly white plumage, biologists believe barn owls once lived on limestone bluffs. Barn owls are the most widespread of all owls, found throughout North and South America, Europe, Asia, and even Australia. Wisconsin is near the northern range of the barn owl, so unfortunately we don't see many of these interesting birds. Only a handful nest in the state each year.

Barn owls are often referred to as "living mousetraps" because they feed almost exclusively on mice, voles, shrews, and rats. In many countries, especially Germany, farmers erect special nesting boxes high in the dark corners of their barns to attract the owls.

Nesting pairs of barn owls raise large families of up to eleven babies at a time and need to catch twenty or more mice each night to feed their hungry offspring. Sometimes, female barn owls will begin to nest and incubate a second batch of eggs before the first youngsters are fully grown, doubling the demand for food from her exhausted mate, who tries to feed not only himself and the young hungry owlets, but the nesting female as well. No wonder wise farmers of long ago claimed that one barn owl was worth more than a dozen cats.

Although barn owls are thriving in some parts of the world, and even in a few areas of the United States, they are not doing well in many Midwestern states. Wisconsin placed the barn owl on its endangered species list in 1979 and soon after started an active ten-year reintroduction effort. The Milwaukee County Zoo raised several pairs of barn owls each year for the recovery effort. They were kept in old barns, fed mice, and when they had successfully nested and raised their young, were set free. The goal of the reintroduction was to encourage the barn owls to adapt to their new home and return year after year to nest. Unfortunately, many of the young birds did not survive, and those that did flew south of the state line and never returned. The program was discontinued a few years ago without the results hoped for.

The reasons for the barn owl's disappearance in Wisconsin are many. Modern municipal ordinances now discourage or prohibit the abandoned, ramshackle barns, silos, and "haunted" houses that were once common, eliminating many of the traditional nesting sites. Most new or remodeled barns are now sealed tightly with steel siding, and silos have closed fiberglass or aluminum roofs which block entry.

Biologists believe the main reason for the decline of the barn owl, however, is that there is simply not enough for them to eat in Wisconsin. Years ago, loose dry hay in barns, barnyard straw stacks, outside corncribs, open granaries, and large cow pastures created what amounted to year-round mouse and rat utopias throughout the state. The rodents were kept in check by a few mousetraps, a few lazy farm cats, and perhaps a couple of barn owls. Today, crops are harvested more efficiently and stored in almost vermin-proof areas.

In addition, both rural and city folks have grown almost completely in-tolerant of living with even a single mouse nearby. This phobia has spawned a multi-million dollar rodent extermination industry. A full array of chemical pesticides and mouse poisons are now used in every home and farm in America. Of course, the end result of this ongoing rodent warfare is an empty plate for the barn owl.

Barn owls remain an endangered species in Wisconsin, with little hope of the bird population recovering any time soon. The state's Bureau of Endangered Resources still offers a twenty-five dollar reward to any citizen who finds and reports an active barn owl nesting site, but this program isn't likely to drain the state's fiscal resources, since only one or two nesting pairs are found each year. Although barn owls were probably never very common this far north, due to our long, harsh winters, let's hope that we can find a way for these beautiful, ghostly birds to fly the moonlit skies of autumn once again, and, with their eerie, haunting shrieks, scare the keegeebers out of future generations of humans.

KESTRELS
TINY TERRORS OF THE SKY

Many people still call kestrels "sparrow hawks," even though these birds aren't particularly fond of eating sparrows and are not true hawks. Early English colonists named these tiny birds of prey sparrow hawks because they reminded them of a bird back home by the same name. Many years later, perhaps with the advent of eyeglasses, these early Americans took a second, closer look and noticed that the sparrow hawk actually resembles another European bird called a kestrel. Today, several hundred years later, we still seem unsure whether to call this beautiful bird of prey a sparrow hawk, as it is still listed in many bird identification guidebooks, or the American kestrel, which is now the more accepted name.

Whatever you call them, kestrels are certainly one of our most colorful and handsome birds. You've probably seen many kestrels, even if you haven't been aware of it, since they like to perch on utility lines along highways throughout Wisconsin. At first glance they look like to mourning doves, until you get closer and see their falcon-like shape, long, pointed wings and tail, and beautiful plumage. Although much smaller than their more famous cousin, the peregrine falcon, they share many of the same characteristics, including the distinctive black vertical stripe below the eye. Some biologists believe this stripe serves to identify it to other falcons, while others believe that this black marking may help the bird hunt for prey by reducing the glare of the sun, much as black eye grease does for football receivers and baseball fielders.

Kestrels are common throughout the state, but are especially abundant in areas with just the right mix of farms, fields, forests, and mild weather. Some kestrels spend the entire winter in Wisconsin, if they can find enough food, but most migrate in late fall to warmer climates with better hunting prospects.

Kestrels are loners, spending almost all their lives by themselves.

Even paired males and females have their own separate hunting territories, overlapping only during the mating and nesting season in late April to June each year. Unlike other falcons that lay their eggs on bare cliffs or on the tops of urban buildings, kestrels prefer to use tree cavities and sometimes even bird houses. Females pick the nesting site and incubate the eggs, while the male hunts to feed his nesting mate.

Being a ferocious bird of prey while only a little bigger than a robin, the kestrel is definitely a "small" game hunter. They are sometimes called grasshopper hawks, because they eat many of these and other insects during the summer season. Despite their small stature, however, kestrels are capable of catching larger prey such as mice, snakes, and small birds. Most of their hunting is done over open grassy areas, especially along roads and fields. Usually, if you don't see kestrels perched on power lines, they are in flight, hovering over a patch of grass, searching for mice or insects. When kestrels spot their prey, they dive straight down, pin it to the ground with their talons, and sever the head at the base of the neck in a quick and deadly *coup de grace*.

Kestrels have trouble finding enough undisturbed nesting and hunting areas because urban development has brought noise, people, pets, and disturbance to much of our rural landscape. In addition, our penchant for cutting down all the dead and hollow trees in our woodlots has further reduced the available nesting areas for kestrels and many other birds and mammals that need these natural cavities.

You can help restore some of these lost nesting areas by building a kestrel nesting box. Attach it with a strong wire to a tree at the edge of a wooded area, as far away from disturbance as possible. All they need is a simple, wooden, unpainted box, 9-12 inches square and 15 inches deep, an entrance three inches round or square, and some wood chips in the bottom. You might not get a kestrel to nest in it right away, but you're sure to be rewarded with some other critter using it, such as a screech owl, flicker, or squirrel.

With a little help from us, we can continue to enjoy watching these tiny terrors of the sky, hovering in the breezes along our roadsides, grassy fields and woodlots in their eternal search for grasshoppers and mice.

GULLS
SOARING TO NEW HEIGHTS

The year was 1848. A new religious farming community, the Mormons, were about to harvest their first crop in their new home in Utah, when disaster struck. A swarm of hundreds of millions of grasshoppers invaded their fields and began to destroy the harvest. It looked like starvation faced the new pioneers in the winter ahead. But then a miracle occurred, as described by historian Orson Whitney: "Great flocks of gulls suddenly appeared, filling the air with their white wings and plaintive cries ...All day long they gorged themselves until the pests were vanquished and the people were saved."

The Mormons believed the gulls were sent from heaven, and later they erected a large, towering monument to the gulls, "in grateful remembrance of the mercy of God to the Mormon pioneers." Whether or not the gulls were really heaven-sent or merely following their instincts by foraging for food from their home at nearby Salt Lake, is open for debate. Whatever the reason, the gulls did what gulls do best—eat.

Gulls are both predators and scavengers. Everyone has seen the huge flocks of gulls in farm fields, following the plow as it turns over the black earth, exposing grubs, worms, grasshoppers, and mice. Along our lakes and rivers, gulls are on constant patrol looking for dead or dying fish to eat. Like other scavengers, they seem to have no problem eating decayed flesh, but prefer fresh fish if they can get it. Gulls are also helpful in cleaning up edible garbage along our lakeshores as well as our urban parking lots, especially around fast-food restaurants.

Gulls are often referred to as "seagulls," but there are more than forty different species of gulls in the world, many of which never venture out to sea at all. Several different species of gulls can be found in Wisconsin throughout the year, but the two you're most likely to see are the herring gull and the ring-billed gull. Although both have the distinctive white-and-gray coloration and yellow beaks and eyes, the ring-billed gull is usually the most numerous and can be identified by its namesake, a ring around the tip of its beak. The herring gull is usually larger in size, and the adult has a red mark on its beak. Identifying immature gulls can be difficult, especially since it takes them up to four years to get their adult plumage. Until then, juveniles are mottled brown with dark beaks and eyes.

Gulls have been increasing in numbers at an incredible rate during the last century, keeping pace with our own population increase. They are incredibly adaptable birds, finding food everywhere man goes, including garbage dumps, city parks, and farm fields. With thousands of gulls found throughout Wisconsin, a common question is, "Where do they nest?" A few gulls nest on a isolated, rocky islands in the Great Lakes, but most of them head to more secluded spots in the far north and western great plains of Canada. The gulls we see in our area are either migrating to or from their nesting areas or are non-breeders that stay here throughout the year. Beginning as early as July, you can see breeding pairs and their brown, mottled, feathered young returning to our shores.

With the boom in gull populations, it's hard to believe that at the start of this century there were so few gulls that there was concern they would become extinct. Gulls had been shot in incredible numbers for food, and their eggs were taken for the frying pan by the hundreds of thousands each year. In addition, their feathers were prized for women's hats, which led to the mass destruction of many species of gulls. Help for the gulls came in 1916 with the Migratory Treaty Act between Canada and the United States, which gave protection status to gulls along with other shoreline birds.

Gulls still face many enemies, including natural predators such as egg-stealing crows and foxes. Gulls even prey on each other, by breaking open eggs or eating the hatchlings of their own kind. Some gulls fall victim to our modern-day technology as they become entangled in monofilament fishing lines and lures, or plastic six-pack can holders. Awhile back I rescued a gull struggling with a fishing lure hooked in its beak and foot. As I cut out the last of the hooks, the gull promptly thanked me by biting my finger hard, and then flew off to new adventures.

Gulls have lived side-by-side with us since our very beginnings, and have followed us wherever we have roamed. Despite some of their antics, and the trouble they get into within our urban sprawl, we would certainly miss these beautiful birds with their graceful flight and familiar call along the shorelines of our rivers and lakefronts.

RED FOX
CLEVER, CUNNING, CRAFTY

The red fox is known all over the world as being one of the most beautiful and intelligent animals in nature. Its attractive red fur, large bushy tail, bright yellow eyes, and uncanny ability to outwit and elude its enemies have made the red fox a favorite of lore and legend through the ages. The clever fox is often featured in popular literature, stories, movies, and even cartoons of nearly every culture on earth.

Despite their popularity, the red fox also has been relentlessly hunted, trapped, poisoned, and chased by man for centuries. Early settlers shot them on sight whenever they got too close to the hen house, while others trapped them for their luxurious pelts. In Wisconsin, red fox were once thought to harm game bird and small animal populations, and so, starting in the 1880s, the government began to pay bounties for each fox killed. The program was discontinued in 1963. Today, red fox populations are kept in check by established hunting and trapping seasons, providing outdoor opportunities for thousands of sportsmen each year.

Red fox are found throughout the state, but are more numerous in the agricultural areas of the southern and eastern counties. Although very common throughout their range, we rarely catch a glimpse of them, since they tend to avoid contact with people and especially our pet dogs. They're also difficult to observe because they hunt for prey almost exclusively at night. Red fox have special elliptical or slit-shaped eye pupils, similar to those of cats, to help them see better in low light. All other members of the dog family, including wolves and coyotes, have round pupils designed for daylight hunting.

Despite their normal fear of people and pets, a red fox family has claimed the backyard of my home as their territory for the past several years. They've even dug several large den holes within sight of our pet Siberian Husky's kennel, a mere forty paces away. Because they hunt under the cover of darkness, we usually don't see them at all, but in late spring and early summer they can often be seen sneaking through the yard during the early morning hours. This is the time of year that the exhausted parents must spend more and more time and energy hunting. They must find prey to feed their hungry litter of four to six pups back at the den. Although the young pups weigh only four ounces in mid-March or April, when they are born, they grow quickly and depend on both parents to bring them food. At nine months of age, they will be fully grown, ready to mate and have pups of their own by the following year.

Fox are known as excellent hunters, but are also efficient scavengers. They will eat just about anything, including carrion, road kill, and garbage. They're also topnotch mousers, catching hundreds of mice, voles, and rats throughout the year. Although they have excellent eyesight and sense of smell, it's their hearing that best helps them locate prey. A fox is able to hear a mouse squeak up to 150 yards away. In summer, red fox eat lots of insects and are particularly fond of wild strawberries, grapes, and other fruits. They also prey on rabbits, squirrels, woodchucks, and occasionally game birds, if given the opportunity. Studies, however, have shown that they don't affect game populations as much as we once suspected.

Except during the mating season in mid-December, red fox are loners, spending most of their time resting in woodlots and forests. They rarely use their underground dens for shelter except for raising their young and occasionally for shelter during heavy rainstorms. Fox prefer to stay out in the open, even during the winter when they curl up and use their long, bushy tails to protect their face and feet.

Although hunted, chased, shot at, poisoned, and persecuted for hundreds of years, the red fox has not only survived, but may even have increased its numbers. Its ability to adapt to the changing landscape, from wilderness to farms to suburbia, has allowed the red fox to find all the cover, rodents, roadkill, and garbage it needs to live side by side with us. They may not be as clever, cunning, or crafty as the old tall tales and stories lead us to believe, but in world where many other animals are struggling to survive, the red fox is smart enough.

WHITE-TAIL DEER
EVERY ANTLER TELLS A STORY

Buck fever. Any deer hunter knows the symptoms. Your heart beats harder and your breathing becomes heavy. You're nervous and your hands may even start to shake. All this is caused by the sudden sight of antlers, the bony outgrowth on top of a white-tail deer's head. With antlers, the bigger the rack, the greater severity of this temporary illness. For some reason, antlers can turn normal, able-bodied hunters into wet noodles.

Antlers are not "horns," even though many people refer to them as such. Horns grow permanently on animals such as cows and goats, and are made from keratin, the same stuff your fingernails are made from. Antlers, on the other hand, are grown and shed every year. They usually grow only on the male member of the deer family, including elk, moose, and white-tail deer, and are true bone made from calcium and phosphorous.

In early spring, as the days lengthen, special glands at the base of a buck's brain are stimulated by the increased day length, producing hormones that cause antlers to grow. Around April, the buck's head sprouts two knobs, which are covered with a special, soft, fuzzy skin called "velvet." The antlers grow rapidly throughout the summer, sometimes as much as a half-inch a day. Within a month, the first fork of the rack starts to form, followed by a second in about three weeks. While growing, the antlers are actually warm to the touch because of the large network of blood vessels that are gradually supplying bone salts to the expanding rack. You can see the marks left by these blood vessels in the lines and crevices at the base of antlers later, when they harden. Bucks are usually shy and reclusive during this time of year, since their antlers are soft, tender, and easily damaged. Even fawn bucks begin to grow antler-like knobs on their heads at only a few months of age. By fall, these little guys may have up to an inch of antler growth, giving rise to the common terms "nubbin" and "button" buck.

The number of points on the antlers has nothing to do with the age of the deer, except that a buck in its prime at four or five years of age will normally sport a larger rack. Antler size has a lot to do with the diet of the deer, however. Ample food usually equals good antler development, but not always. Just as with people, heredity has a large influence. Some people turn out to be the Arnold Schwarzeneggers or Robert Redfords of the world, and the rest of us, well ... don't. Deer with a good diet and the right genes will sport the biggest antlers.

By mid-September, as the daylight begins to shorten, the same glands that started the antler growth begin to shut it down, the antlers now beginning to harden and the velvet covering drying up. Bucks seem anxious to get the velvet off quickly, rubbing their antlers against small saplings and brush to clean and polish them.

Although they look like formidable weapons, antlers are used only for sparring with fellow bucks during the brief breeding period in fall. By early winter, a layer of cells at the base of the antlers begins to granulate and the antlers fall off. Most bucks in the state have dropped their antlers by December or January, although some of the younger ones might hold onto them longer. I've noticed that bucks along the warmer Lake Michigan shoreline seem to hold on to their antlers longer. I have photographed nice eight-point bucks well into the end of February, and even one time in March.

Antlers. From the ancient caveman drawings to modern wildlife paintings and trophies hung on hunters' walls, we've always been fascinated by these bony appendages. Why millions of us pursue getting them and decorating our homes with them is a question still unanswered. Perhaps it goes back to our ancient beginnings as roaming bands of hunters. Maybe we haven't fully evolved out of the need for things wild and free. Maybe we shouldn't.

LITTLE BROWN BATS
NATURE'S MOSQUITO TERMINATORS

Bats—they're evil, dirty, blind flying mice that get tangled in women's hair. Right? If you still believe these old tales, it's time to get the "bats out of your belfry," so to speak, and get the true story of the world's only true flying mammal.

First of all, bats are not flying mice. In fact, bats are probably more closely related to humans than they are to mice or other rodents. They are also not dirty, since they spend considerable time cleaning and grooming themselves, a trait not always shared by some of our own species.

The old adage "blind as a bat" is another misconception. Bats can see quite well during daylight and have exceptional night vision. Since they make their living catching and eating insects in mid-air at night, their eyesight alone would not be adequate, however. To help them locate their prey, bats have evolved into a sort of living, flying radar system called *echolocation*. While in flight, bats emit chirps at a rate of fifty per second, usually at a high pitch beyond our hearing range. These sound waves bounce off everything in the bat's path and return signals to the bat, pinpointing the location and size of everything from bugs to buildings. Thanks to this sophisticated system, bats are able to catch a moth or mosquito in mid-air in total darkness. The system also prevents them from flying into trees, wires, buildings, and other obstructions, especially women's hair.

Wisconsin is home to eight species of bats. One of the most common is the little brown bat, which is often found near cities and farmsteads because it likes to live in our attics, sheds, or any other available shelter. A few summers ago, a pair of little brown bats made their home under a small wooden sign attached to my kids' playhouse. Despite nearly daily disturbance by curious children in the neighborhood, the bats seemed content to roost in this unusual shelter.

October is a busy time for little brown bats in Wisconsin, as they spend more and more time feeding on insects to build up fat stores in their bodies. Unlike some bats that migrate to warmer climates, most brown bats remain in our state, hibernating through the long, cold winter. Where they hibernate seems to be a mystery, but most likely they find either a natural underground cavity or a suitably warm attic.

Little brown bats have incredible appetites and can eat six hundred mosquitoes in an hour, stuffing their stomachs with one-third of their own body weight. This would be comparable to an average person eating fifty pounds of food at one meal!

Fall is also mating time for the little brown bat. In a special adaptation to our cold climate, female bats can store the male's sperm for several months while hibernating. About March or April, the stored sperm is released and the female egg is fertilized. Unlike mice and other rodents that can give birth to dozens of babies each year, brown bats bear only one young at a time. The baby bats, called pups, are born in late May or June and spend the first few weeks of life suckling nourishing milk from mother bat. Once they are fully grown, the youngsters take wing and join the adults on nightly feeding flights.

For centuries, bats have been unfairly associated with witchcraft, sorcery, and death. It's hard to imagine Halloween, spooky movies, or haunted houses without them. Even today, people continue to fear these gentle, helpful animals. But things are changing. All over the country, Americans are finally catching on to the European practice of encouraging bats to their backyards by putting up special bat houses, much the same as we do for our feathered friends.

Maybe this interesting and beneficial animal will soon shake its dark and gloomy past and make its way into the hearts of mankind. Kind of like a "bat out of hell," so to speak.

THE GARTER SNAKE
A GARDENER'S BEST FRIEND

There are no two ways about it—you either love 'em or hate 'em. Maybe it's our Sunday school perception of the evil serpent in the Garden of Eden, or maybe we've just seen too many Hollywood movies filled with scenes of poisonous snakes threatening the hero. Whatever the reason, snakes just seem to bring out our emotions and fears as few other creatures can.

Despite their fearsome reputation, all snakes are generally very shy and would much rather slither quietly away to safety than confront a human. Wisconsin is home to many species of these gentle reptiles, nearly all of which are nonpoisonous. The only exception is the timber rattlesnake, which lives in the remote bluffs and cliffs in the southwestern part of the state, and the rare, endangered massasauge rattlesnake, which lives in only a few isolated marshes.

The most common snake you're likely to encounter in Wisconsin is the eastern garter snake, sometimes called a "garden" or "grass" snake. Like most other snakes, the garter is harmless and rarely bites, even when handled for the first time. Garters do have small teeth for holding on to their prey, but lack the fangs and poison associated with venomous snakes. Garter snakes do, however, have another defense to ward off their enemies, as our cat once discovered when it cornered one in our backyard. The snake emitted a foul-smelling musk that instantly repelled the cat and anything else downwind of it. The noxious odor remains potent for most of the day and cannot be washed off.

The garter snake is brightly colored with stripes of black, brown, green, and yellow or orange. This coloration led to its being named after the gaudy garters that were once fashionable to hold up gentlemen's socks.

Garter snakes emerge from hibernation in early spring, soon after the snow melts. They remain near their dens for several weeks and often mate in large numbers. My wife and I witnessed this natural spectacle a few years ago while hiking along a rocky gorge in Sauk County. We saw literally hundreds of garter snakes converging into one area from all directions, eventually massing into a large wriggling ball, sort of a reptilian orgy, I guess.

After mating, garter snakes spend the rest of the summer alone, foraging for food in the marshes, woodlots, and fields. The snakes tend to prefer damp places where they can find their favorite prey—frogs, toads, salamanders, and earthworms. Sometimes, especially in dry weather, garter snakes invite themselves into our backyards, probably seeking the moisture we apply to our lawns and gardens. Unfortunately, many snakes are killed by well-meaning but uninformed people during these times. Veteran gardeners, on the other hand, know to encourage garter snakes to live in their gardens and often build grass and mulch nests to offer them protection during the heat of the day. They know that garter snakes are superb predators of garden pests such as insects, grubs, slugs, and mice.

In August or early September, female garters give birth to their young. Unlike most other snakes, which lay clutches of eggs, the garter gives birth to her young live. They can give birth to more than seventy young at a time! Since garters can live to be ten years old, one female may produce five hundred or more babies in her lifetime.

Of course, not all these young survive. In addition to the threat of the gardener's hoe and lawnmower, many snakes are killed by farm machinery or are run over while crossing highways. Garters are also eaten by hawks, owls, raccoons, skunks, and even other snakes.

The next time you come across a garter snake, remember that this gentle reptile is not only harmless but is really very helpful to us. You may not come to love 'em but hopefully now you won't hate 'em, either.

AMERICAN TOADS
BACKYARD INSECT-EATING MACHINES

Few animals in nature have been so misunderstood and unfairly persecuted as the poor, lowly toad. Throughout much of our history, this unfortunate amphibian has been considered to be an ugly, evil creature in league with the devil himself. In the fifteenth and sixteenth centuries, when witches were being hunted, tried, and executed in both Europe and America, the toad's reputation probably hit rock bottom. People killed toads on sight in those days, believing that they were a witch's "familiar" or her evil spirit servant in animal form.

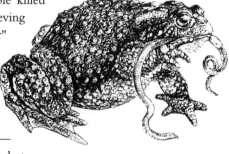

Nowadays, of course, we don't see too many witches flying around on broomsticks wearing black, pointy hats— except on Halloween night—but then again, the toad might be responsible for this, as well. It was well known to people during the Dark Ages that witches could make themselves invisible by outlining a crooked cross on their bodies with a magic lotion concoction made out of toad spittle. Toads were also believed to have a magical jewel hidden inside their heads called a "toadstone." These precious jewels were set in rings and were thought to change color in the presence of poisoned food or drink; they also had healing powers. Even Shakespeare wrote about these mythical toadstones in some of his plays and poems. Today, we are far too sophisticated and educated to believe in any of this mythical nonsense, yet many still believe that you can somehow get warts from handling toads, despite all the scientific and medical evidence to contrary. Old folklore and myths die hard, even in modern times.

Aside from all the lore and legends, toads are really just harmless members of the amphibian family, with more than two hundred different species worldwide. Unlike their frog cousins that have soft, colorful, moist skin, toads have rough, warty, dry skin that is usually brownish in color to blend in with the earth. Despite their plain exterior, most toads have beautiful, jewel-like golden eyes, especially the American toad, which is the only one native to Wisconsin.

Toads prefer to live on dry land. They don't need wetlands as frogs do, except in spring when they must return to their ponds and marshes to mate and lay eggs. Because of this, toads can be found nearly anywhere there's a little vegetation, cool damp soil for hiding, and plenty of insects to eat—such as in our backyards. Here, they dig shallow depressions in the earth and simply wait for prey to come within range of their sticky, super-quick tongues. Smart gardeners welcome toads in their gardens, since they know that these amphibians are finely tuned insect-eating machines. A single toad can eat more than ten thousand insects in a single summer, and will eat just about anything else it can catch, including spiders, slugs, earthworms, and even smaller toads and frogs, if they can swallow them.

During the hot, dry days of summer, toads retreat into the leaf litter and soil to escape the heat, but until recently nobody had a clue as to how these cold-blooded creatures could survive the deep freeze of our Wisconsin winters. Toads spend nearly every waking moment of spring and summer gorging themselves on food, and then in October dig a foot or so into the earth to spend the winter. Biologists have discovered that toads can tolerate extreme cold temperatures because their cells contain a chemical called glycerol—the same stuff we use in our automobile radiators in winter. With this natural antifreeze, as much as 35 percent of their body mass can turn to ice, and they can still come out of hibernation alive and well in spring.

Of course, not all toads survive extremely cold winters, and those that do survive meet new challenges and threats after hibernation. Many predators, including hawks, owls, crows, and snakes, eat adult toads, their eggs, and tadpoles. Mammal predators such as fox, raccoons, coyotes, and domestic dogs and cats also try to eat toads—but usually only once. Toads have a fairly potent defense mechanism built into their bodies. When they feel threatened, such as when a dog picks one up in its mouth, the toad releases a bad-tasting alkaloid poison from its skin. This usually causes the dog to spit it out unharmed and gag, sneeze, and cough for a while, with no permanent damage to either animal. This tactic doesn't work too well against humans, of course, since we rarely pick up toads with our mouths. But the toad has a backup plan in store for us by releasing the contents of its urinary bladder into our hands when we catch it—a gross and surprisingly effective defense.

Are toads really the evil, occult creatures of witchcraft, or are they merely harmless insect-eating amphibian friends of gardeners? Are they ugly, revolting animals with warty, wrinkled skin, or have they merely mastered the best camouflage nature could provide for their peaceful existence in our own backyards?

Neither evil nor ugly, the familiar American toad deserves a better reputation as an integral part of Wisconsin's great outdoors.

HORNETS
Hᴀɴᴅsᴏᴍᴇ, ʜᴜɴɢʀʏ ᴘᴇsᴛs

They're everywhere. You can't escape these unwelcome guests at your backyard barbecue. They appear at your favorite picnic spot, sneaking a sip of your soda or helping themselves to your hamburger. No doubt about it—the bees are back!

Although they look similar to bees, with their attractive yellow and black markings, these pesky insects are actually members of a large family of insects called vespids, which include hornets, wasps, and yellow jackets. Most of us have a hard time telling one species from another, but basically hornets are the ones that build their papery nests in trees. Yellow jackets also build paper nests, but usually construct them in underground cavities.

Our summer encounters with hornets are usually friendly, since they tend to build their nests high in trees and away from people. On the other hand, the hornet's close cousin, the paper wasp, seems to seek us out, often building its single-layer nest under the eaves of our homes and garages. The wasps are usually mild-mannered, unless you venture too close—especially, it seems, with an aerosol can of wasp-killer in hand!

Yellow jackets are by far the most aggressive of the bunch. They will not hesitate to chase after you if they feel threatened, such as when a hiker or hunter unknowingly stumbles onto their underground nest. Unlike honeybees that sting only once and then die, yellow jackets can sting repeatedly. Although painful for awhile, a single sting or two has no long-lasting effects to most of us, although a large number of stings can make some people quite ill. Multiple stings may even be fatal to those with severe allergic reactions.

Only the females of the species have the ability to sting. In fact, the life cycle of hornets and yellow jackets reads like a bad script from an old Amazon Women movie. The entire organization and operation of the community is run by the females of the species. It all begins in early spring, when a lone queen builds a small nest with hexagonal cells and lays an egg in each. In a week they hatch into larvae and the queen feeds them bits of caterpillars and flies until they emerge as adult but sterile females. From then on, the queen concentrates on producing more young while each new batch of sterile females takes over the chore of enlarging and building the nest, hunting and feeding, and tending to the young.

The large papery nests hornets build in the treetops are amazing feats of insect engineering. The paper-like material is made as the insects strip away pieces of fiber from exposed wood, boards, weed stems, and discarded paper. The fiber is chewed up by the female workers along with water and their own saliva and formed into the gray-colored nests. The nests are even coated with a substance that helps them shed water. The insects were probably the world's first and original recyclers, since they chew apart the insides of their own nest to reuse the material over and over again in enlarging the nest. In late summer, the queen lays eggs that develop into fertile females and, for the first time, males. It appears that the males' only purpose in life is to eat and mate with the fertile queens. After mating, the queen stops laying eggs and the workers not only stop caring for the young but may eat them as well. The daily routine of nest-building also stops and the entire population of insects starts spending more and more time away from the nest in search of food. For some unknown reason, their former preference for caterpillars and flies now changes to a desire for sweet and greasy foods.

This is the time of year when our paths often cross with hornets and yellow jackets. What were once a few hundred queens in spring have turned into hundreds of thousands of hungry adults on the wing, all searching for food. At the same time, we humans are out in force at barbecues, picnics, county fairs, and sporting events. Children are returning to school with lunch boxes filled with candy bars, snacks, and sweet juice packs. The result is the inevitable conflict between man and insect, as they attempt to help themselves to our great outdoor feasts.

Then one day it happens—the first big, hard frost. With the exception of the few fertilized queens, the entire colony of yellow jackets and hornets dies. Even the large paper nests are abandoned, never to be used again. Complaints about the insects stop, and everyone forgets about them once more as we enter the winter season. But somewhere in a crack, crevice, or building is the hibernating queen, ready to bring on another generation next spring. Like it or not, they'll be back. You can count on it.

WOOLLY BEAR CATERPILLER
NATURE'S WEATHER FORECASTER

Want to know what kind of weather is in store for us, this coming winter? You could just tune in your favorite television mete- orologists and listen to one of their long-range forecasts. Or you could ven-

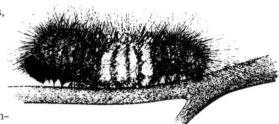

ture out into your own backyard and look for nature's orig- inal weather forecaster-the woolly bear caterpillar.

"Woolly bear" is a generic name we give to pretty much any fuzzy caterpillar with long, bristly fur. Actually there are hundreds of species of woolly bears, almost all of which belong to the same insect family called tiger moths. They come in a variety of colors, some almost pure white or yellow, others reddish-brown or even black.

According to the folklore, however, the only true "weather worm" is the woolly bear caterpillar of the Isabella moth. This is the one that has a reddish-brown band in the center of its body and jet-black fur at both ends. Legend has it that the local weather can be predicted by looking at the width of the fuzzy, reddish-brown band on this particu- lar caterpillar. A narrow band means we're in for a long, cold winter, while a wide band indicates a mild winter ahead. This folk belief was studied years ago by researchers at the American Museum of Natural History, who compared the woolly bear forecasts with those of the best meteorologists over a period of several years. To their surprise, the woolly bear turned out to be more accurate in predicting winter weather than the professional meteorologists—much to the delight, no doubt, of non-scientists everywhere. Some also believe that rainfall amounts can be predicted by observing the width of the caterpillar's black bands. A small band at the head means little rain early in summer, while a wide black band at the tail end would indicate lots of rain coming late in fall.

Woolly bear weather forecasters are actually the larvae, or worm stage, of the Isabella moth, one of the most common moths in North America. The adults are small, yellowish insects with wingspans of only two inches. They have rows of black spots on their bodies and wings.

Because they fly mostly at night and hide during the day, we rarely get to see one. After mating and laying eggs, the adult moths die and the familiar black-and-brown woolly bear caterpillars hatch and spend the summer munching on their favorite plants. Lucky for us, woolly bears eat mostly backyard weeds, and to their credit are especially fond of dandelions and plantain.

Although you can find woolly bear caterpillars anytime from spring through summer, we usually see more of them in late summer and early fall as they frantically cross busy roads, sidewalks, and gardens, seemingly in a hurry to get somewhere. This is the time of year that kids and adults alike enjoy picking up these harmless, fuzzy bears, to watch as they crawl up an arm or coil up into a fuzzy ball. These late-season woolly bear caterpillars are the last brood to hatch for the year, and they are busy searching for a good, sheltered spot to spend the winter. Woolly bears are one of the very few insects in the world actually to hibernate as a caterpillar, which explains why they need the warm, fuzzy hair coat in order to survive.

One fall, I collected several woolly bears caterpillars and put them in a jar with plant food for a temporary display at a local nature center. Within a few weeks, the caterpillars curled up in a ball on the bottom of the jar and appeared to be dead. Despite spending the entire winter in the unheated building in sub-zero freezing temperatures, the woolly bears eventually thawed and by late spring came out of hibernation, good as new. After eating some fresh, green dandelions, they began to spin cocoons, using a special silk they secrete and mix with the long hairs from their own bodies. Within a few weeks they emerged as adult Isabella moths, and I was able to release them into the wild again.

Woolly bear caterpillars had always been the traditional and trusted weather forecasters, going back to the time of our great-grandparents and beyond. Of course, today we are all too sophisticated to believe such nonsense and rely instead on our weather satellites, computer model programs, and an army of professional, highly educated and trained meteorologists to give us accurate weather forecasts. On the other hand, now that I think about it, today was supposed to be clear, calm, sunny, and warm, according to last night's forecast. I'd be outside right now looking for a real woolly bear "weather worm." but it's just too darn cold, windy, and rainy!

CRICKETS
EASY-LISTENING SERENADES

"To have a cricket on the Hearth is the luckiest thing in the world."

—Charles Dickens, 1841

In England, the sound of a chirping cricket in the house was welcome, since it was thought to bring good luck to the occupants. Whether or not good fortune shines on a house that harbors a cricket is open to debate. More than likely, however, at least one resident of the house is sure to get lucky—the cricket, itself.

Crickets find a smorgasbord of good things to eat in our homes, including food scraps, crumbs, and pet food, and also are known for eating unusual things such as cotton garments, rubber products, and leather goods. One cricket in the hearth might be okay, but hundreds in the house could spell trouble.

Despite the occasional damage they cause, crickets are probably one of mankind's favorite insects. For some 1,500 years, people in the Orient have kept crickets for house pets, much the same as we keep gerbils or parakeets in our homes. Here in America, Walt Disney's animation of Jiminy Cricket has made this cartoon character a favorite of many generations of children.

With some nine hundred species worldwide, the cricket's chirp is a universal experience heard everywhere on earth, except in polar regions. Their soothing nightly serenades are so familiar that many of us aren't even conscious of hearing them, sort of like the sound of street traffic or maybe the television playing in your home.

In many ways, it's too bad that we've tuned out the cricket's song, since it is the longest and most complicated sound made by any insect. Different species have individual calls, and even individual crickets can make several different calls. In Wisconsin, you're most likely hearing the mating call of the common black field cricket. The sound is produced only by the male

Jim McEvoy

crickets, in a sort of monotonous "Here I am, baby" call to attract females. Of course, like their human counterparts, trying to attract females can also attract contenders, and fights among males are common as they struggle to win the attention of the cutest female crickets.

Male crickets produce their chirping sound by rubbing their wings together. Although useless for flying, the wings are specially designed with rough, textured areas that the cricket uses in a sort of file-and-scraper manner to fiddle its music. Crickets usually speed up their chirping rate during hot weather, and slow down or stop altogether when it cools down. They are sometimes called "temperature crickets," because of their ability to gauge the temperature accurately. If you count the number of chirps a cricket makes in 15 seconds and add this number to 37, it will about equal the outside temperature.

Because crickets are so weather—and temperature—sensitive, we often don't hear them until late summer. In cool summers, we hardly hear them at all in the evening, but then they are usually chirping loudly earlier in the day, when it's warmer. As fall approaches, the nightly and daily serenade gradually decreases. And then, one day, the chirping stops altogether, usually right after the first hard frost. The cricket's soft body cannot withstand the freezing temperatures and the entire cricket population dies long before the first snows appear, with the exception of those lucky crickets in your house.

Before they perish, female crickets will have safely laid their eggs in the soil, to insure that another generation of crickets will hatch the following season. In one of the many quirks of nature, the parents of one generation never get to see the new generation they produce. Young crickets hatch as orphans in late May or June, and have to fend for themselves by eating plants and dead insects. By late summer, the males grow wings and begin the familiar and eternal serenade once more.

FALL WEBWORMS
NATURE'S TINY TENTSHOW

The circus is back in town! No, not the kind with dancing horses, clowns, and wild animal acts, although this circus does have tents, colorful acrobats, high-wire acts, and even tigers. Well, it has tiger moths, anyway. You can spot the tents of these miniature insect circuses by late summer in trees and shrubs all over Wisconsin. The builders and performers of these tiny tent shows are one of our common tiger moth larvae called the fall webworm.

As adults, fall webworms are pretty nondescript moths, usually plain white with orange abdomens and wingspans of only two inches or so. Unlike most other moths or butterflies, it's the caterpillar or larvae stage of the fall webworm that catches our eye. Fall webworms have the unusual ability to spin silk and build webbed tents around the leaves of trees they feed on. Inside the tents you'll find dozens of colorful, yellow, fuzzy caterpillars with shiny black heads, munching away at the foliage during the daytime and spinning more webs during the evening hours to enlarge their nest. When they've finished gorging themselves with food, they abandon the nest to pupate. They leave behind a dirty, empty web tent filled with leaf skeletons, bits of leaf clippings, fecal droppings, and the molted skins they shed as they grew larger.

Fall webworms are one of the few insects to construct these unique silken tents. Biologists suspect they do so to protect themselves from predators while they're feeding, although many birds such as yellow warblers and other predator insects such as hornets seem to have no problem plucking them from their tents. Another common insect that builds a similar nest is the tent caterpillar, which also transforms into a moth. You can tell the difference between the two by the location of the tent. Fall webworms are sun-lovers, always building their nest over the outside of leaves near the tips of the branches, and feeding inside the safety of their tents. I guess you'd have to say they would rather eat at home in bed. Tent caterpillars, on the other hand, like to go out to eat, leaving the safety of their tents to feed on leaves all over the tree. Unlike webworms, they always build their nests in the forks of branches, not over the leaves. In addition, tent caterpillars are fussy eaters, usually feeding only on choke cherry, black cherry, or some other fruit tree. Fall webworms have such robust appetites that there aren't many trees or shrubs they won't eat, except evergreens. Some of them even build their tents and feed on weeds and wildflowers.

Backyard gardeners are often upset about the appearance of fall webworms in their trees, worrying that these insects are harmful to their landscape plants. Actually, unless the insects completely defoliate the trees, they are not usually harmed in the long run, although their appearance may not be the best for a while.

If webworms are bothersome to you, there are dozens of chemical products you can purchase at garden centers to destroy them. Or, if you want to save some money and protect the environment, you can merely hand-pick them or snip off the leaves on which they appear. Although not a serious threat to our native trees, fall webworms are one of the very few native American insects that have crossed the ocean and actually invaded a foreign land. The aggressive webworms have become serious pests in the Orient, causing problems in the Asian silk industry by defoliating mulberry trees and competing with valuable Japanese silkworms.

Fall webworms perform daily in trees or bushes throughout the state, beginning in late summer, but by fall they disappear and spin their cocoons in preparation for the oncoming winter. But not to worry, they'll be back. By late spring, thousands of webworm moths will emerge and lay up to nine hundred eggs a day in clusters on tree leaves. Within a week, the tiny webworms hatch out and begin to build web tents. The circus will be back in town once again. ▲

OCTOBER

October

Fall colors usually peak in northern Wisconsin by early October. Gradually, day by day, the woodlands are set ablaze in brilliant hues of reds and yellows, like a slow-moving forest fire spreading southward to the state line.

October also brings the first killing frosts of the season, clearing the air of pesky mosquitoes and signaling red bats to migrate south. Although the nights are chilly, the days are often warm and sunny, providing some of the most pleasant weather of the year.

White-tail bucks become restless as the mating rut peaks near the end of the month under October's "hunter" full moon. Sportsmen and their faithful retrievers march through cornfields in hopes of flushing up a colorful ring-necked pheasant rooster or search the aspen groves for a quick wing-shot at a ruffed grouse.

By the time Halloween's full "blood moon" rises in the autumn sky, high-flying Canada geese can be heard late into the frosty evenings as they stay one step ahead of old man winter, right at their tails.

SCREECH OWLS
DON'T GIVE A HOOT

"Now at sundown I hear the hooting of an owl. This is my music each evening. It is a sound admirably suited to the twilight woods, suggesting a vast undeveloped nature which men have not recognized nor satisfied."

—Henry David Thoreau, Walden Pond, 1851

The haunting call of an owl on a crisp and cold autumn night can be at once startling and comforting. Through the ages, these creatures have been associated with the dark, mysterious night we tend to avoid. Many ancient legends associate owls and their eerie calls and shrieks with witches and ghosts, which were believed to sail through the darkness of night in the form of an owl. On the other hand, the hoot of an owl can be comforting, as well, reassuring us that there is at least a bit of wilderness we have yet to conquer or turn to our own purposes.

Usually, when we hear an owl at night, it's

one of our common "hoot" owls, such as the "who cooks for you, who cooks for you all" call of the barred owl, or the deep base "who's awake, me too" hoot of the great-horned owl. But there's one owl that really doesn't give a hoot at all about hooting. The eastern screech owl prefers instead to belt out an eerie shriek or whistle that sounds more like a horse's whinny than a traditional owl call.

The screech owl is a small, pigeon-size bird that looks like a miniature great-horned owl with its large ear tufts and piercing yellow eyes. Its plumage has two color phases, some owls entirely gray, others more reddish-brown in color. Screech owls are found throughout the state, but avoid heavily wooded areas such as the northern evergreen forests. They prefer the small woodlots and open farm fields of southern Wisconsin, although they may also be found in the suburbs and city parks of major metropolitan areas. Screech owls never seem to be abundant anywhere, probably because of the limited number of nest hole cavities available to them. They prefer to nest in natural hollows in tree trunks, although they will also use abandoned sheds and barns. Since screech owls don't migrate, they need shelter year-round for roosting during the day, for nesting, and as protection from predators and severe weather.

Despite their size, screech owls don't seem to fear humans greatly, and will often dive-bomb an intruder who ventures too close to their nesting hole. I discovered this, first-hand, as a young boy on my family's farm in Manitowoc County. One day, while exploring and climbing an old apple tree in our orchard, I discovered a large hollowed-out cavity in one of the dead branches. Naturally, as most boys that age would do, I stuck my head inside the cavity, and to my surprise (and terror) I saw a pair of bright yellow eyes staring back at me. I'm not sure who flew out of that tree faster—me or the startled screech owl.

In late winter, when screech owls begin to search for mates, their nesting holes become even more important than usual. Males try to attract females by catching prey and leaving it in or near the nesting cavity, in a sort of wine-and-dine courtship. Eventually the female will lay four to six white eggs and incubate them while the male continues to feed her on the nest.

Once hatched, the young owlets have ferocious appetites. The parents must hunt throughout the night, catching June beetles, large moths, crickets, and grasshoppers, as well as mice, shrews, rats, snakes, and frogs, to satisfy the owlets' constant hunger. Screech owls also hunt small birds, especially abundant species such as English sparrows, which are plentiful in both farmyards and urban areas. They're able to take sparrows right off their roosts at night, even under the eaves of buildings.

If all goes well, the young screech owls will be ready to take wing by the end of June, but they, too, will need nesting cavities of their own. Without some protection they are harassed endlessly by blue jays and crows, or attacked and killed by hawks during the day and by larger owls at night. Many are also hit by automobiles as they chase insects into the headlamps of oncoming vehicles.

Screech owls are one of the few birds of prey that we can actually help to survive in our own neighborhoods. We can leave a few dead trees standing in our woodlots or along fence lines, for the owls to use as nesting cavities. Unfortunately, most of the old apple orchards that used to provide nest sites are long gone, and modern orchardists don't allow dead wood in their trees. In addition, most old wooden sheds and barns are either being torn down or fitted with weather-tight steel siding with no cracks or crevices for nest sites. Recently, people who give a hoot have come to the aid of screech owls by building wooden nesting boxes and installing them on the sides of living trees. Plans for nesting boxes are available at most nature centers and county extension offices, or at the public library.

Perhaps, with a little help from us, these mysterious little featherballs with their hauntingly beautiful call will continue, for generations to come, to send a shiver down someone's spine on a dark autumn night. Perhaps they will always provide Thoreau's "music each evening" to the ears of people who enjoy nature.

RING-NECKED PHEASANTS
WISCONSIN'S FAVORITE GAME BIRD

Autumn just wouldn't seem like autumn without frosty mornings, golden fields of ripe corn, and the start of the pheasant-hunting season. Few other sports can match the heart-stopping excitement of a ring-necked pheasant exploding from cover with its startling *cuck-cuck-cuck* cackle as it sails over the cornstalks and cattails. Whether you hunt with a shotgun, camera, or pair of binoculars, the gaudy ring-necked pheasant is certainly a feast for the eyes. While the females are drab brown, the male roosters have beautiful iridescent, greenish-black heads, long striped tail feathers, shiny copper-colored breast plumage, bright red face wattles, and, of course, the distinguishing white ring around their necks. It's easy to see why pheasants are members of the same colorful family of birds that includes its near cousin—the peacock.

Although it seems as if the familiar ring-necked pheasants have always been a part of our Wisconsin autumn scene, it wasn't that long ago that they were not even found in the state, or anywhere else in America, for that matter. Unlike our native game birds such as the ruffed grouse and the turkey, the ring-neck was introduced to our continent from the Orient more than a century ago. Back in 1881, our then-American counsel general in Shanghai, China, Judge O. N. Denny, decided to ship thirty ring-necked pheasants to his home state of Oregon. The birds adapted so well and proved so hardy that soon hundreds more were literally "shanghaied" from their mainland China homes and shipped across the ocean to be released in the wilds of America.

Pheasants were first released in Wisconsin in 1916 at a site in Waukesha County, and soon spread throughout the southeastern part of the state. The birds seemed to adjust well to our climate, thriving in the countryside mix of farm fields and wetlands. Several years later, the State Conservation Department began raising and stocking pheasants, a program that continues to this day. More than 100,000 birds are now raised annually and released throughout Wisconsin by state and local conservation clubs.

Despite these massive stocking efforts, however, wild pheasant populations started to decline in the 1940s and have never fully recovered since. Why the pheasant population could not sustain itself after so many years of success remains somewhat of mystery. Some said it was due to the intensive draining of wetlands after World War II. Others blamed changing agricultural practices such as early summer mowing of hayfields that destroy pheasants' nests before the chicks can hatch, and the increased use of pesticides and herbicides. Still others put the blame on increasing populations of predators such as fox, skunks, raccoons, hawks, owls, and domestic dogs and cats. Some are even convinced that after so many years of rearing pheasants on game farms, we've simply bred the wildness out of the birds and they are now simply unable to survive, breed, and nest in wild. Whatever the reason or combination of reasons, it's generally agreed that the traditional put-and-take system of game farm pheasant rearing is not helping the wild population of birds.

But the end to the ring-necked pheasant story has yet to be written, and may in fact just be starting—again. In recent years, wildlife biologists have introduced wild strains of ring-necked pheasants from the state of Iowa into several southeast Wisconsin counties in an attempt to reestablish a truly wild population. Another project involved the stocking of imported Manchurian ring-necked pheasants from the Jilin Province of China. So far, these latest immigrants to America are doing fine, especially in areas that have undergone habitat improvements.

Some of us "seasoned" sportsmen can remember the good old days, back in the early 1970s and earlier, when pheasant populations were high and hunters harvested more than a half-million birds a year. Memories of frosty mornings spent in cornfields and cattail marshes with relatives, good friends, good and not-so-good bird dogs, and the wild and wary ring-necked pheasants run deep in some parts of the state. We hope that new efforts will once again restore the pheasants to our countryside and allow a whole new generation of sportsmen and women the opportunity to form their own cherished memories of Wisconsin's favorite game bird.

RUFFED GROUSE
NO ORDINARY BIRD

"There are two kinds of hunting: ordinary hunting—and ruffed grouse hunting"
—Aldo Leopold

If you spend enough time in Wisconsin's great outdoors, you're sure to experience many unforgettable moments. But if you chase after grouse you can almost count on something out of the ordinary to happen. I had one such experience years ago while grouse hunting in the Baraboo Hills of Sauk County. I had just climbed to the summit of a high, wooded ridge when I saw it coming. Far below in the distance, I could see the brown autumn landscape magically turn white, even though it wasn't snowing. While watching in awe at this unique natural phenomenon, the white wave of hoar frost came up and over the ridge, gently passing through me and covering my clothes, my gun, even my beard with large, intricate ice crystals. As I turned to watch the woods behind me turn into a sparkling, frosty, winter wonderland, a ruffed grouse suddenly exploded from a nearby blackberry patch. Instinctively, I raised my gun to fire, but instead merely watched the beauty of the bird rocketing through the white underbrush, leaving a trail of falling ice crystals like the exhaust of jetliner in the upper atmosphere. It was one of those experiences in nature I'll never forget, and likely never experience again.

Ruffed grouse, sometimes called partridge, are the most abundant game bird in Wisconsin, found in nearly every county in the state. The birds are named after the dark collar feathers, called ruff, around their necks. Both male and female grouse are similar in size and plumage, with gray coloration that on some birds tends toward a reddish-brown. The male has an unbroken black outer band on its fan-like tail, while the female has this same band broken by two brown center tail feathers. While both make a chicken-like "puck, puck" call while browsing on the forest floor, males make a peculiar sound of their own, called drumming. In spring, they climb onto stumps or large fallen logs where they fan their tails, strut back and forth, and flap their wings against the air, creating a loud booming sound that can be heard a mile away on quiet mornings.

The elaborate and alluring courtship display of the drumming male ruffed grouse eventually attracts several hens. After mating, the hens will lay and incubate up to a dozen eggs at a time in a small depression on the forest floor, usually next to a tree or stump. As soon as the little ping-pong ball-size chicks hatch, the hen herds them away from the nest and out to the grassy forest edges to feed. Although young grouse eat lots of insects as hatchlings, they will eventually learn to eat more than six hundred different kinds of plants, including berries, leaves, nuts, and a grouse's all-time favorite food—aspen tree buds. Biologists have estimated that a single grouse can eat more than 1,300 aspen buds in one day. Like deer, grouse feed on the move, never browsing long enough in any one aspen tree to do any significant damage.

Ruffed grouse were hunted by Native American Indians and early explorers for food, but were never very plentiful until European settlers began to cut down the mature woodlands of America, creating brushy clearings for pioneer trees such as aspen to sprout. Today, grouse still thrive in actively managed public and private lands where pulpwood is harvested by clear-cutting blocks out of the forest. But in many other areas, grouse populations continue to drop due to the loss of forest habitat. Even in the best of conditions, grouse numbers tend to bottom out every ten years or so, and then gradually build up again in a never-ending natural cycle still not fully understood.

Many ruffed grouse fall to human hunters, and are also prey for hawks, owls, fox, coyote, and just about any forest animal with canine teeth. In addition, grouse can often be their own worst enemy by falling victim to their own peculiar habits. In autumn, grouse often make newspaper headlines by flying into automobiles on the highway, slamming into the sides of buildings, or crashing through living-room picture windows. Explanations of this unusual behavior range from the belief that the birds become intoxicated on the fermented berries, to their simply not recognizing the reflection of the surrounding landscape mirrored on house windows. But nobody knows for sure.

A few years ago, I decided to rekindle my hunting experiences with these goofy game birds by trying another wild grouse chase at a nearby marsh. After an hour or so of pushing through some tough swamp brush, I finally flushed two grouse in front of me. Unfortunately, this occurred at the exact moment that a dogwood branch snapped back, bounced off my right eyeball and knocked my hat off. After stumbling along half-blind for another half hour or so, I stopped under cedar tree, cradled my gun, and reached into my pocket for a handkerchief, only to be caught off-guard again by a grouse exploding in flight from his perch a few feet above me. As I turned around to try and take a shot with my one good eye, I broke through the thin marsh ice and went up to my knees in swamp muck and water. Sensing defeat, I decided to forfeit the game and go home. As I limped back to my truck on my wet, frozen foot, nearly blinded by one eye swollen shut and the other filled with a constant stream of tears, all I could think about was Leopold's old adage—there's ordinary hunting ... but then again, there's ruffed grouse hunting.

GRAY (HUNGARIAN) PARTRIDGE
BEER BARON BIRDS

A violent storm was surging on Lake Michigan that December day in 1863, when the floundering steamship Huron finally ran aground at Whitefish Bay. On board, the ship's captain, Fredrick Pabst, pondered whether to continue his hazardous career of sailing the Great Lakes or accept his father-in-law's offer to join his brewery business in Milwaukee. As most everyone knows, the rest is history. The Pabst Brewery and its "blue ribbon beer" became one of the largest and best known companies in the nation. But what most people don't know about is the Pabst family's contribution to sport hunting in Wisconsin, especially the introduction of a new game bird to the state called the European gray partridge.

Gray partridge are small, plump birds, not much larger than a pigeon. As their name suggests, much of their plumage is gray in color, although their wings and sides are a mottled cinnamon-brown. Between 1910 and 1929 more than five thousand of these birds were imported from Europe and released in Waukesha County, all because of the persistent efforts of one man—Col. Gustav Pabst, son of Fredrick Pabst and then president of Pabst Brewery. Gray partridge were also released in other parts of America during this period, and today their numbers are highest in the Dakotas, Montana, and into the Canadian provinces. Many of the birds were imported from Germany, Sweden and Russia, but the majority came from Hungary, giving rise to their common name, Hungarian Partridge, or "huns" among hunters.

In Wisconsin, Col. Pabst's original partridges flourished, eventually increasing their home range over the entire southern part of the state. They are now most numerous in the eastern counties bordering Lake Michigan. Here, gray partridge find all they need for food and shelter on the many small family farms scattered throughout the region. Gray partridge are seed eaters, feeding on ragweed, brome grass, dandelion, alfalfa, and clover, as well as waste corn, wheat, and oats. Although they will eat some standing grain crops, studies have shown that their preference for noxious weed seeds more than offsets any damage to agricultural crops.

In spring, gray partridge pair up and look for nesting sites. Because they dislike the heavy cover of marshes or woodlands, they look for dry sites in large, open, grassy areas to scratch out their dirt nests and lay eggs. Unfortunately, these nesting sites are often in the middle of hay fields, and many nests are destroyed long before they're able to hatch out a brood of chicks. But when they do succeed, gray partridge can increase their population quickly, since females often lay eighteen to twenty eggs in a single nest. Once hatched, the young stay with the adults in family groups called coveys. To protect themselves from predators, gray partridge always spend the night in covered-wagon formation, their tails in the center of a circle, their heads pointed out, always alert to danger from any direction.

The gray partridge is probably the state's single most difficult game bird to hunt. I've taken a few birds in the past, usually stumbling upon them by accident while pheasant hunting in open hay fields, but I've found that to hunt these birds successfully often requires more luck than skill. Their short, cupped wings give them exploding flying power exceeding 45 miles per hour as they speed away, rocking and turning, more like tiny sidewinder missiles than game birds. Usually, a hunter has a chance to get off only one or two shots before the covey flies out of range and glides a half-mile or more, disappearing into the next hay or stubble field. Even if you take the time and effort to stalk them, the now "educated" birds will usually fly up ahead of you, far out of range.

Gray partridge populations have always had their ups and downs, and they seem to have had a few bad years recently. Weather can play a role, especially if severe cold, heavy snow cover, or ice storms prevent them from getting at weed seeds in winter. Although a few "huns" might make it into the game bag, biologists have found that hunting does not have much of an impact on their populations. They do have other predators, especially during the nesting season, when fox, skunks, crows, owls, hawks, and cats can take their toll. But their real enemy seems to be themselves and their insistence to nest in hay fields rather than safer areas. Modern hay harvesting techniques have allowed much earlier and more frequent cuttings of hay fields, reducing the opportunities for game birds such as gray partridge to nest successfully. Recent studies have shown that the nesting success rate for gray partridge is often less than ten per cent, if they use hayfields, and even worse if they nest along line fences where predators can find them.

Hungarian partridge are one of those imported game birds, such as the ring-necked pheasant, that few expected to succeed but have beat all the odds, anyway. Today, the autumn landscape just wouldn't seem complete without these interesting little game birds winging their way over the corn stubble and hayfields of southern and eastern Wisconsin. Col. Pabst might be surprised that his efforts, almost seventy years ago, continue to provide some exceptional and challenging hunting opportunities for thousands of outdoor enthusiasts. No doubt, he would also be pleased to see a successful "hun" hunter sit down to a delicious wild game dinner complete with—what else?—one of his famous "blue ribbon" beverages.

MALLARDS
WORLD'S MOST SUCCESSFUL DUCKS

Most hunters remember vividly their very first mallard duck hunt as if it were yesterday. Although I had jump-shot wood ducks and teal from farmland ponds and creeks as a boy, my first real mallard duck hunt didn't occur until many years later, while I was attending college at Stevens Point. There, my roommate Terry and I spent countless hours roaming the vast Mead Marsh state wildlife area, practicing what we called "primitive" duck hunting—no boat, no dog, no decoys, just hip boots, shotgun, and the ability to walk for miles through knee-deep swamp. We decided that our ultimate goal that school year would be to enjoy "exceptional" hunting while at the same time earning "acceptable" grades in our college courses, even though we suspected our priorities might be viewed as a bit backwards by our university professors.

It was early in the afternoon on a bright and sunny October day when I sat down in a flooded stump field after a long, tiring trek into the marsh. While emptying one of my leaking boots and scanning the blue skies, I spied a flock of ducks far in the distance make a sudden turn and head towards me. With no cattail cover nearby to hide in, I backed up against a dead snag and watched as the flock barreled its way into the stump field at what seemed like their top flying speed of sixty miles per hour. Luckily, the lead drake mallard decided to drop elevation and set his wings for a landing just past my location. Not being an expert, or even an acceptable pass shooter at the time, I'm not sure who was more surprised when the drake tumbled out of the sky at the sound of my old 16-gauge Mossberg shotgun.

Common among most hunters, retrieving downed game can often bring out emotions of not only joy and excitement, but also just a bit of remorse and reverence for taking such a beautiful animal from the wild. Mallards are certainly one of our most attractive ducks. The drake has a bright green, iridescent head with an olive-colored bill, and a white ring around its neck. Its breast feathers are a beautiful chestnut color with gray-to-white plumage over the rest of its body, except for the blue patches on its wings and black, curled underfeathers near its tail. All this is supported by bright orange legs and webbed feet. Later that night, I got a chance to see the mallard's attractive plumage more closely, as I attempted to dry-pluck all ten thousand of its feathers (yes, someone once counted), a chore certainly designed by nature as revenge on the hunter.

Although we think of the common mallard as being an all-American duck, it's really the most numerous and widespread of all waterfowl in the entire Northern Hemisphere. Mallards are true cosmopolitan ducks, living in such distant and diverse places as Europe, Russia, India, Siberia, China, and Japan, to name just a few. They were even introduced into the wilds of Australia and New Zealand.

Mallards have always had a close tie to mankind, and remain one of the most hunted species on earth. They are wary birds and can be difficult hunt in the wild because of their exceptional color vision and natural fear of man, yet they can also be tamed. The Romans are credited for being the first to raise mallards as a source of meat and eggs. In fact, nearly all forms of domestic ducks are believed to be descendants of the wild mallard.

Today, as more people take an interest in wildlife and begin to feed mallards in urban water settings, more and more mallards are becoming civilized. Unfortunately, this has led to the problem of too many semi-domestic ducks creating messes on lawns, beaches, and golf courses, a problem all too familiar in cities throughout the country. Many flocks now even refuse to migrate south for the winter as long as they can find food and some open water.

In autumn, mallards are busy gathering in small flocks, feeding and preparing for migration. Most drakes have already grown their colorful breeding plumage in contrast to their summer "eclipse" or mottled brown plumage. In July, both males and females go through a complete molt and lose their primary wing feathers, making them flightless for a few weeks. Most of the year's young ducklings have been flying for some time, by then, and gradually take on breeding plumage as well.

Mallards usually nest during the last three weeks of April, enabling their young to learn to fly before the hot, dry weather of August dries up their ponds and marshes. Besides the threat of drought, mallards have many other dangers to overcome. Skunks, raccoons, and fox regularly destroy their nests before the eggs get a chance to hatch, while in the water snapping turtles and larger game fish lay waiting for the newly hatched ducklings. Nesting failure can run as high as seventy percent some years. Because of the wide variety of foods they eat, the many types of habitats they can survive in, and their ability to live along side of man, mallards are the most successful ducks in the world.

The sun was almost below the horizon at the end of that first mallard duck hunt by the time Terry and I crawled out of the marsh. We cased our guns, fell exhausted on top of one of the dikes in the wildlife area, and just quietly watched the sky turn from pink to purple as darkness approached. Suddenly, wave after wave of ducks of every kind flew over our heads, quacking, peeping, and whistling as they settled into the marsh for the night. We sat on the dike and watched in awe this seemingly endless natural spectacle until way after dark. I guess we learned an important lesson that day, one we couldn't have been taught in the classroom. There's a whole lot more to life and duck hunting than just filling the game bag. Something spiritual that wise, old-time hunters have known for years, and the rest of us just have to discover in ourselves.

NIGHTSHADE
WITCHES' SECRET INGREDIENT

Halloween just wouldn't be the same without the image of witches flying through the spooky night sky on their broomsticks. Even though we now consider them merely part of the fun of a happy children's holiday, there once was a time when witches were not only believed to be very real but much feared as well. According to folklore, witches had to rub a magic ointment all over their bodies in order for them to fly off to do their evil deeds. The traditional ingredients of this flying ointment usually included items such as hemlock, aconite, cinquefoil, a pinch of baby fat, some soot, and of course the all-time favorite secret ingredient used by witches and sorcerers alike—deadly nightshade.

Modern researchers once attempted to duplicate some of these ancient nightshade recipes and try them on themselves. What they discovered was that, although they certainly couldn't fly through the air, the concoction did have a powerful narcotic and hallucinogenic effect, creating the illusion of flight in some. In other words, even though witches could never actually fly on their broomsticks, they no doubt got high enough on the fumes of these powerful drugs that they surely believed they had flown, when they awoke the morning after.

Nightshades are common wild plants that often grow in backyard gardens, along buildings, farmyards, fence lines, moist woodlands, and waste areas throughout Wisconsin. Except for our native black nightshade, also called American bittersweet, all the nightshades were introduced to this country from Europe and the Middle East and have now escaped into the wild. The term "nightshade" refers to the early use of the plant centuries ago by the noblewomen of Renaissance Italy, who dropped the juice from the nightshade's ripe berries into their eyes, causing the pupils to dilate and making their eyes appear large, dark, and alluring.

With common names like poisonberry, bittersweet, and black or deadly nightshade, you might suppose that these are plants you might want to learn to recognize, perhaps avoid. All nightshades contain powerful poisonous alkaloids, especially in their berries. If eaten in large enough quantities, these poisons can interfere with the body's nervous system, virtually shutting down both blood circulation and breathing, resulting in a quick death.

The most common nightshade in Wisconsin is the European bittersweet, which grows as a vine and has heart-shaped leaves. In summer, the plant sprouts purple flowers with bright yellow stamen centers that later transform into stalks bearing green berries. As autumn approaches, these berries ripen by turning yellow, then orange, and eventually a bright, shiny red. Unfortunately, these poisonous berries look very much like small, juicy cherries, especially to children. I can remember tasting them myself as a kid and discovering why they're called bittersweet. At first bite, the berries have a sweet, sugary taste, but that is quickly followed by a sour, bitter taste that makes you pucker up and spit them out.

Despite their dark, sinister reputation as a poison and their association with witchcraft and death, nightshades aren't all bad. The nightshade family includes some of our favorite garden vegetables, including potatoes and eggplant, although it took until the mid-19th century for us to finally trust the idea of eating one of the most famous nightshade vegetables of all—tomatoes. Nightshades have also been used for centuries as a source of some our most useful modern drug compounds. No doubt you have some product in your medicine cabinet right now that contains a nightshade-derived drug, such as atropine, commonly used in cold medicines and sleeping pills. Research continues today for more uses of nightshade, such as a variety of the plant in Wisconsin being studied for its tumor-inhibiting properties in the fight against cancer.

Like so many plants we simply call weeds today, nightshade once played an important role in our ancestors' lives, from its use as a reliable cure-all home remedy to that of a beauty enhancer for young women. Perhaps nightshades will someday be better known as the plants that launched a new miracle drug rather than as the narcotic, poisonous weed that helped propel evil witches into the air on their broomsticks.

But, just in case, I'd keep an eye skyward on Halloween night. You never know.

WITCH HAZEL
THE HALLOWEEN TREE

I remember the first time I saw it. I thought I had discovered some sort of freak of nature. Here was a small crooked tree ablaze with bright yellow flowers blooming in late October! After all, everyone knows that autumn is the time of year when trees shed their leaves and go into their dull, dormant state—not flower as if it were springtime.

To satisfy my curiosity, I snapped off a twig and looked it up in a tree identification book that evening. My discovery turned out to be a pretty ordinary small tree called "witch hazel." Although the tree is fairly common, it is hardly ordinary, having the distinction of being our only woody plant that blooms in late autumn and sometimes even after the first snowfall.

Over the years, I've learned more about this oddity of nature. The tree grows throughout the state in rich hardwood forests such as those in the Kettle Moraine State Forest, in southeastern Wisconsin, but I've also encountered it growing in almost pure sand soils along Lake Michigan. It has smooth bark and oval, waxy, toothed leaves that are usually shed by the time the tree starts to bloom in fall with dull yellow, stringy blossoms. Witch hazel's branches usually have twin seedpods, which are still maturing from the previous year. When ripe, the pods burst open, throwing the shiny black seeds several feet from the parent tree—another mystery of this unusual tree.

The tree's colorful name conjures up images of witchcraft, sorcery, and an evil past, although some researchers believe its common name was actually derived from an old English word meaning "pliable" or "weak," having nothing to do with witches. Others believe that the tree was named by superstitious colonists. One can only guess at what these early settlers thought when they found a tree in full bloom at the start of winter, when all the other forest vegetation was dead or dormant. How could the tree's delicate yellow flowers survive the bone-chilling and killing frosts each night? Only witchcraft could have explained or caused such an eerie event, especially so close to Halloween.

Besides being an interesting oddity of nature, witch hazel has a long history of medicinal uses. Indians taught colonists how to make medicine out of an extract of the tree's bark, twigs, and leaves. The substance was used for a variety of ailments, but most often for healing bruises and swellings. Although many of the wild plant concoctions from long ago have been abandoned in favor of modern drugs, witch hazel continues to be used to this day. It is still listed as an official drug, and is sold by the millions of gallons each year for use in a variety of products today. If you look closely at the labels you'll find witch hazel listed as an active ingredient in everything from shaving lotions and vaginal douches to lotions for insect bites and sprains.

Perhaps witch hazel does indeed have nothing to do with witches or witchcraft, but the Halloween tree will always hold a special kind of magic in the autumn woodland of Wisconsin.

WHITE-TAILS
GUESS WHO'S COMING TO DINNER

Remember when you put up that bird feeder in the backyard a while back? You've probably had some success attracting a few of the common winter birds, such as cardinals, chickadees, and blue jays, but no doubt you also got your share of uninvited critters—English sparrows, starlings, or those pesky house finches. Possibly the first to find your feeding station wasn't a bird at all, but one of the neighborhood raccoons, opossums, or more likely the plague of all bird feeders—squirrels.

Having dealt with all of these animals in my bird feeder at one time or another, I thought I had seen everything, until recently. Deer had always visited our bird feeder to lap up any of the cracked corn or sunflower seeds that may have been spilled onto the ground. But one winter day, a young doe, with her first fawn at her side, suddenly got a burst of inspiration and taught herself a trick that to this day has not been duplicated by any of the other neighborhood deer. She discovered that by balancing on her back legs and hopping around she could twist her neck, turn her head sideways, and reach inside our platform bird feeder to lap out the seeds with her long tongue. Although I tried raising the feeder by a foot and a half, she was still able to reach into it, since an adult doe can stand a full six feet or more on her hind legs.

White-tail deer aren't known for their keen intellect or reasoning skills, but as any farmer or gardener can tell you, they sure seem to have a high I.Q. when it comes to finding something to eat. Deer are browsers, feeding mostly on leaves, buds, twigs, fruit, and foliage of just about anything that grows. They also eat seeds, mosses, lichens, fungi, grasses, farm crops, and sometimes even animal matter such as snails and small fish. I was pretty skeptical about deer eating fish until I saw two young bucks eagerly munching small dried fish called alewives along the Lake Michigan shoreline a few years ago. Deer are also fond of aquatic vegetation. I've seen them belly-deep in rivers and marshes eating water plants and pond scum during the summer.

There are certain foods that deer will do almost anything to get. If you're trying to raise crops in deer territory, it seems that their favorite food is corn, alfalfa, winter wheat, soybeans, or whatever else you plant.

If you have a garden near a wooded area, you know that deer eagerly eat your peas, beans, cabbage, sweet corn, or pretty much anything they can get at. A few years ago, after trying to deer-proof my own garden with a succession of failed deer repellents, contraptions, and fencing schemes, I finally installed an expensive electric fence as the ultimate solution. When the deer eventually learned to leap over this fence, too, I planted a large white flag right in the middle of the carrot patch, admitted defeat, and let them finish off the rest of the garden.

Although sometimes causing extensive damage to garden and agricultural crops, most deer prefer woodland foods if they're available. In the forest, deer are dainty feeders, nipping a twig here and plucking a leaf there, always on the move from one feeding area to another. Favorite wild foods on their menu are white cedar, aspen, maple, blackberry, dogwood, white pine, sumac, wild grape, and hundreds of other native plants. But the all-time favorite food of deer in Wisconsin has to be acorns, especially the sweeter white oak acorns. In fall, acorns can make up over eighty percent of the white-tail's diet, and if left undisturbed the deer may not even leave the oak woods to feed or bed down anywhere else. As long as the food is falling right out of the sky around them, why should they leave?

Deer must eat ten to twelve pounds of food a day in order to survive. As a survival technique, deer must fill their stomach with eight or nine quarts of forage in only one or two hours of feeding, which they accomplish mostly in the early evening hours and again just before daybreak. They also feed at night, especially when the moon is bright or when they have been hunted hard during the daytime. Deer have evolved on this "fast food" feeding frenzy schedule to avoid being caught out in the open and exposed to predators. They are also keenly aware that they are vulnerable while feeding because they can't hear well while chewing food. If you've ever sat quietly on a deer stand or in a blind, you can relate to this, remembering how hard it is to hear the woodland sounds around you when you are munching on a sandwich.

Like other ruminants, such as cows, deer have a four-chambered stomach. After nipping off vegetation, they quickly chew it once or twice and swallow it for storage in their paunch or stomach. Later, when in safer cover, they regurgitate it in the form of moistened balls of cud about the size of an orange. After chewing the cud for another forty times or so, they swallow it again, and it is then churned and digested by the billions of microorganisms that live in the deers' stomachs.

In late summer, as the days begin to get shorter, deer eat high-protein, high-fiber food to store as fat for the winter. They carry some of this extra fat just under their skin on their belly, back, and hams, just as people do. But they also have the ability to store it in large quantities around abdominal cavity organs and even in net-like structures around their intestines.

Unlike people, who spend much of the winter trying to get the extra weight off their bodies by exercise and diet programs, deer have no problem using up their fat stores during the long, cold days. They go through the winter with little to eat except the low-protein and less digestible forage of twigs, dry grasses, and evergreens. If the winter is unusually long or severe, their fat reserves might become exhausted, leading to the sad but inevitable fact of starvation. No wonder that deer take advantage of the quick and easy nutritious snacks they find in our farm fields, gardens, and backyards. Maybe that's why I don't get too upset when my seed-stealing doe returns to my bird feeder each year. A few pounds of seed lost here and there seems insignificant compared to the real life-and-death struggle the white-tail deer must endure to keep its fragile flame of life lit against the icy, howling winds of an unforgiving Wisconsin winter.

GRAY SQUIRRELS
LOVE 'EM OR LEAVE 'EM

When it comes to gray squirrels, the world is pretty much divided up into two camps—squirrel lovers and squirrel haters.

Squirrel haters often refer to gray squirrels as "tree rats" and spend enormous amounts of time, money, and frustration trying to keep them out of their bird feeders and gardens. They usually don't step on the brakes when a gray squirrel makes a dash across a busy city street, and may even be tempted to swerve a bit in the squirrel's direction.

Squirrel lovers, on the other hand, affectionately call gray squirrels their little "bushy tails" and don't mind their daily raids on the backyard feeder. They even buy corncob feeders and special squirrel snacks for their beloved rodents.

All squirrel lovers don't like them for the same reason, however. While some pamper and protect their bushy tails from danger, others see them in a more culinary sort of way—such as the main ingredient in squirrel stew, for example. Hunting gray squirrels for food and sport has always been a favorite pastime for many outdoorsmen. A recent survey showed that Wisconsin hunters spent some 800,000 days afield hunting squirrels, harvesting more than one million each year.

If you like sleeping late in the morning, squirrel hunting or squirrel watching may be right up your alley. Gray squirrels aren't very active until well after sunrise, and then have another surge of energy in mid-afternoon. But don't be fooled. Wild squirrels are not like their fat and lazy city-park cousins, and can be difficult to hunt. They are smart and quick to escape if they sense a predator approaching. Some call them "timber monkeys" for their unbelievable aerial acrobatics as they leap fearlessly from tree to tree, high in the forest canopy.

The Chippewa Indians called the gray squirrel *ah-ji-dah-mo*, which means "tail in the air." The squirrel's large, bushy tail has more uses than a Swiss army knife. Sometimes it's used as a rudder to balance in the treetops, sometimes as an umbrella to shield itself from the sun or rain, and other times as insulation from the cold winds.

By the time European settlers arrived, squirrels were said to be able to travel from the Atlantic Ocean to the Mississippi River without once touching ground, thanks to the vast, unbroken virgin forests. Squirrels were so numerous that every few years huge migrations occurred throughout their range, including several dozen right here in Wisconsin. One spectacular migration was recorded by naturalist Ernest Thompson Seton in 1842, in southwestern Wisconsin. He determined that the migration route was 130 miles wide and 150 miles long, involving some half a billion squirrels. Nobody knows for sure why these mass migrations occurred, but they probably were related to overpopulation and food supply.

Squirrel numbers plummeted as the forests were cut down and the land was turned into farm fields. In addition, many communities, including some in Wisconsin, offered bounties for killing squirrels to protect corn crops. By 1901, there was concern that the gray squirrel might even become exterminated. Luckily, due to hunting regulations, squirrel populations rebounded quickly, and they are now probably the most numerous game animal in the state.

Gray squirrels are fun to watch in autumn, as they scurry around gathering and burying acorns. Because they don't hibernate, squirrels must store plenty of food to survive the long winter months. How they relocate buried nuts after several months was once a mystery, but if you watch them closely you'll learn their secret. After squirrels dig their hole and drop in the acorn, they push the nut down with their nose before burying it. This leaves a scent on the acorn that they can detect later, even through the leaves, ground, ice, and snow. Of course, they don't always find all of their acorns, which accounts for the millions of oak seedlings that sprout each spring in the forest.

In December and January, the gray squirrel's attention turns from acorns to other squirrels, as the breeding season starts. After mating, females hole up in tree dens and give birth typically to three babies during the cold month of February. The newborn squirrels arrive in this deep-freeze world of snow and ice without hair and with their eyes and ears closed. Luckily, mother squirrel has her warm winter fur coat and fluffy tail to keep them warm until spring. Gray squirrels also have a second late-spring breeding season, the young born in early summer.

Whether you love them or hate them, you've got to admire the intelligence and ingenuity of gray squirrels. They have figured out pretty much every seed feeder known to mankind, and they have survived all our extermination efforts of the past. Someone once said, "When, in the end, man finally extinguishes himself; the squirrels will take over." I believe it.

RED BATS
FROM EEK! TO CHIC

Bats don't have a very positive image here in the U.S., but throughout the Orient these shy and gentle creatures are considered the symbol of happiness and joy. Next time you visit a Chinese restaurant, look for the stylized bats that often adorn decorations and rice bowls. The bats represent the four blessings of ancient Eastern culture: old age, wealth, love of virtue, and a natural death.

Bats may be beautiful to biologists that research them, but I'll be the first to admit that they are not exactly nature's cutest creatures. Maybe it's their wrinkled humanoid face, hairless skin-covered wings, or the way they bare their sharp teeth when cornered. If there is such a thing as a "beautiful" bat, the common red bat found right here in Wisconsin would have to come close. One author described the red bat as "among the world's most beautiful mammals" because of its long, attractive, angora-like reddish orange fur.

Red bats are common throughout the state, perhaps even more numerous than the better known little brown bat, yet few of us have ever seen one. Unlike brown bats, which have the unpleasant habit of congregating in large colonies in our buildings, red bats stay clear of human structures. They even avoid roosting in caves, preferring to hide in trees in forests or right in our own backyards. There they hang upside down by one foot with their wings wrapped around them, making them appear like dead leaves in the tree. Red bats are loners, rarely even roosting with another bat, except during the mating season in October.

In May or June, red bats give birth to two or three babies, called "pups." These tiny bats cling to their mother's fur for the first few weeks of their lives, and even ride along as she flies out to hunt for food at night. You've probably seen many red bats, since they're usually the first ones to take flight, even before the sun has set, and are larger than brown bats. I once measured the wingspan of a red bat and found it to be over eleven inches.

All bats have ferocious appetites, eating hundreds of thousands of insects during their lifetime. They eat mostly night-flying insects such as moths, beetles, flies, and especially mosquitoes. Bats can eat more than six hundred mosquitoes an hour, and stuff themselves with up to a third of their own body weight each night. An average person would have to eat fifty or sixty pounds of food every day to match the appetite of a bat.

As Halloween approaches each year, people tend to think more about bats, along with spooks, goblins, haunted houses, and all the other superstitions and folklore that tend to reinforce our fear of these gentle, harmless creatures. Although some bats stay in our area and hibernate, the red bat must migrate to warmer climates, and most have probably left the state by the end of October. Like migrating birds, bats use natural migration routes such as the shores of the Great Lakes to guide them south. Some observers along Lake Michigan have found that red bats make use of autumn storm fronts to propel them along the route, sometimes speeding along at up to eighty miles per hour.

Bat watching has long been a favorite pastime in Europe, and is becoming more and more popular in America, as well. Many people now encourage bats to live in their backyards by putting up special bat houses. Besides being fun to observe, bats help control those pesky insects, and are far less costly that those annoying electric bug zappers.

Bats may never become the symbol of happiness and joy in America, but our attitude towards them is changing. As someone recently said, in recent times bats seem to have gone from "eek! to chic" nearly overnight.

RACCOONS
NATURE'S MASKED BANDITS

Christopher Columbus was the first to document the "clown-like mute dogs" he found during his first voyage to the New World in 1492. Like other Europeans, he had never seen a raccoon, so it's easy to imagine his confusion over this odd, dog-like animal that never barked. Columbus was so impressed by these masked, ring-tailed animals, he even took several live raccoons with him on his return voyage to Spain. Native American Indians traditionally hunted raccoons for food and clothing. Recently, archeologists uncovered bones of both raccoons and humans, lying side by side, dating back some ten thousand years. The name raccoon was eventually adopted as the English pronunciation of the Indian word for the animal, *arocoun*. Raccoons were important to early settlements in America. Famous coonskin-capped pioneers such as Davy Crockett and Daniel Boone helped forge a new nation.

Raccoons are one of those uniquely American animals that live just about anywhere there is enough food and water, from southern Canada to Central America. Although raccoons are now found throughout Wisconsin, there was a time not too long ago when they were nearly trapped and shot out of existence. They were in the most trouble during the 1920s, when coonskin coats were a fad for college kids, since it took at least fifteen hides to make one coat, and both prices and demand were high. From 1936 to 1950, raccoon populations were so low that the Wisconsin Conservation Department sponsored a raccoon propagation program to help restore the population. Today, with proper management and set harvest seasons, hunters and trappers have an abundant and healthy raccoon population once more.

Raccoons are creatures of the night, doing most all of their foraging and prowling from dusk to dawn. During the daylight hours, they spend their time curled up in their dens or other resting spots, including tree cavities, high in the branches of trees, and in buildings and barns where they won't be disturbed. When foraging, there really isn't much that is not on the raccoon's menu, since they eat pretty much anything, plant or animal, dead or alive. Their favorite snacks include crayfish, clams, insects, grubs, carrion, frogs, earthworms, small birds, mice, berries, nuts, and fruits of all sorts. Despite what you've heard all these years, raccoons do not have to wash their food before they eat it. In fact, they rarely do this at all, except when in captivity.

Raccoons have taken advantage of our urban sprawl and farmlands with their nightly raids on our crops and garden vegetables, especially sweet corn. They seem to delight in using their cunning and intelligence in figuring out how to pop off nearly every type of garbage can lid ever invented. With forepaws almost as flexible as human hands, raccoons have little difficulty opening cooler latches or picking up food items and carrying them off into the woods. They are also fascinated by shiny objects. They pick up and manipulate most everything they can get their hands (paws) on.

The raccoon's uncanny ability to break into our food storage areas and carry off the bounty is almost legendary in our state park and forest campgrounds. Every camper seems to have a story to tell involving the antics of these little masked bandits and their midnight raids on campsites and coolers. One of the more unusual raccoon raids I've encountered during my years working as a ranger in state parks occurred at Devil's Lake State Park several years ago. The original complaint we received from the camper was that someone broke into his tent and stole his silver money clip and eighty dollars in cash. Upon investigation, I found a large hole chewed through the back of his tent and a long trail of potato chips, hot-dogs, buns, and eggs leading into the nearby forest—a typical raccoon burglary trademark. After a friendly lecture to the camper about keeping his food in his car rather than his tent, I helped him pick up the long line of food and litter. About two hundred feet from the campsite, I noticed a shiny object among the broken eggshells. Yup, there it was, the silver money clip intact with the missing eighty dollars. Apparently, the little masked bandits had finally moved up to petty theft of cash.

Fully-grown raccoons may reach three feet in length and weigh up to forty pounds. They have few enemies except for man and his dogs during the hunting season. Quite a few are killed while crossing highways, especially in spring when they are on the move looking for mates, and again in fall when they're busy searching for food. As winter approaches, raccoons seem to eat nearly anything and everything to build up their body fat before the cold weather starts. Because they don't hibernate, raccoons must have plenty of stored fat to get them through those howling winter storms and deep freezes ahead. During the winter they keep a low profile, getting a lot of sleep, but by early spring they're up and around, hungrier than ever. It's unlikely that these masked bandits will ever figure out how to spend their stolen cash, but when it comes to raccoons, I wouldn't bet any money on it.

GARDEN SPIDERS
BACKYARD GOOD-LUCK CHARMS

If you wish to live and thrive,
  let a spider run ALIVE.

—Old English rhyme

Spiders are one of nature's creatures that are almost universally disliked and feared. Like snakes and bats, we've delegated them into the category of all the creepy, crawly critters we try to avoid when possible. Despite the negative image we have of spiders, nearly every country in the world holds a nearly identical superstition: It's bad luck to harm a spider.

Why so many of us dislike spiders is a mystery. After all, they are very beneficial to mankind because of their enormous appetite for flies, mosquitoes, and grasshoppers. In fact, a single spider can kill some two thousand insects in its short lifetime. Luckily, humans are not on the menu of any spider, and they rarely bite or bother us in any way, other than to build their webs in areas where we don't want them. Because of this, spiders are routinely killed (or carried outside by the superstitious), a chore that seems to be universally assigned to the eldest male of the household.

Of the dozens of species of spiders that live in the Wisconsin, one of the easiest to recognize is the black and yellow argiope (ar-JY-o-pee), better known as the common garden spider. Although these spiders look dangerous with brilliant yellow and black warning markings on their large bodies, they actually are a threat only to insects and they should never be killed.

Like other spiders, only the female garden spider spins a web. They're the large, ornate, circular webs with zig-zag support strands in the center that you find in your vegetable or flower gardens. The large yellow-and-black female can usually be found sitting head-down right in the center of the web, waiting for an insect or fly to jump into her trap. As soon as she feels the vibration of a struggling insect in the web, she pounces on it, injects a poison to paralyze it, and then wraps the victim in silk until it looks like a miniature mummy. Garden spiders have no teeth, not even a mouth, and must slowly suck the juices out of their prey to feed.

Male garden spiders are small, brown dwarfs, only a quarter the size of the female. The courtship and mating ritual of this odd couple is bizarre, and can even be fatal for the male. Since the large female has such poor eyesight, the little Romeo must approach carefully and gently pluck out his code on the strands of her web. If he's not careful, the female may mistake him for just one more struggling insect ensnared in her web, and he might end up as her meal instead of her mate. Even if he is recognized, the poor little fellow might be killed, anyway, if she is not in the mood for amour. Eventually, one of the males is lucky enough to be accepted and mate with the female, after which he struggles to make a quick exit off the web. Honeymoons are short in the world of spiders. In fact, the female often attempts to kill and eat the male after mating has taken place.

After this brief romance, the female garden spider leaves her web and lays up to eight hundred eggs to assure another generation of spiders for next year. Before dying in a few weeks, the female wraps the eggs into pear-shaped egg sacs with yellow, coarse silk to protect them. In spring, hundreds of little yellow spiderlings hatch and spend the next two years growing and maturing until they, too, can produce their own kind, although only a few of them are lucky enough to survive that long.

Spiders are interesting creatures with which we share our homes and yards. Despite our fumigating, poisoning, and swatting, they still survive in tremendous numbers, and most likely always will. Whether you decide to squash or spare the spiders around your house is up to you. Just remember the old English rhyme—and good luck ▲

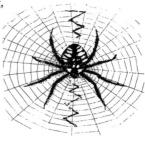

November

NOVEMBER

French trappers and Indians called November's full moon the "beaver moon." Fur-bearing animals such as fox, otter, and beaver grow thick, luxurious coats this month, in anticipation of the quickly approaching winter.

As autumn draws to a close in Wisconsin, every living thing seems to sense the urgency of the season. There is so much to do and so little time left before the snows arrive. Farmers rush to harvest their golden fields of ripe corn, while flock after flock of geese glide down into the stubble to glean the waste grain left behind.

In the forest, red squirrels are busy hiding the last of their winter supply of pine cones, while cedar waxwings gulp down a few more wild berries before heading farther south. Turkeys stuff their gullets with newly fallen acorns and gather into larger flocks to find more sheltered areas in which to spend the winter.

By the time Thanksgiving week arrives, the first permanent snow cover often blankets much of the state, just in time for the annual deer hunt. Hunters, dressed in blaze orange, light up nearly every woodland in their quest to match wits with the elusive white-tail deer. Late at night, the newly fallen snow shines like a million sparkling diamonds under the bright light of November's full "frost moon."

WILD TURKEY
RETURN OF A NATIVE

Had Ben Franklin gotten his way in 1782, the wild turkey—not the bald eagle—would have become the national emblem of the United States. Franklin argued that eagles were common in almost every foreign country, while the wild turkey was peculiar "only" to our shores. Although the congress voted down his proposal in favor of the eagle, Franklin was accurate in describing the turkey as a true all-American bird that's been part of our country's landscape for a long time. Just how long was recently discovered when some turkey bone fossils, ten million years old, were uncovered by archaeologists.

Wild turkeys are impressive birds, the adults standing three to four feet tall and tipping the scales at up to 25 pounds. Despite the popular belief that turkeys are flightless, these large birds can propel themselves into the air like mini-helicopters and fly straight away at speeds of up to 55 miles per hour, even though they would rather run. Turkeys are attractive birds with iridescent bronze feathers that shimmer all the colors of the rainbow in the sunlight. You can tell the male or "tom" turkey from the female by their leg spurs and also by the fleshy wattles on his head, colored a patriotic red, white, and blue. The tom also grows a bristly mass of modified feathers out of his breast, called a "beard," but this can't always be used to identify males, since a few hens also grow them.

Turkeys were probably misnamed centuries ago in Europe because they were mistakenly believed to be imported from Africa through the country of Turkey, as guinea fowl were. In reality, the breeding stock of all domestic European turkeys originally came from wild flocks of American birds, which were captured and sent overseas by the Spanish when they conquered Mexico. Others believe that turkeys got their name after the soft turk-turk-turk sound they make as they flock and feed.

Whatever the reason, everybody "talks turkey" in November, as we celebrate Thanksgiving day. The holiday was first celebrated in 1863 when Abraham Lincoln took time from his grim duties of overseeing a bloody civil war to proclaim the last Thursday of November as the official Thanksgiving Day, in commemoration of the Pilgrims' feast of 1621. The date was later moved up a week earlier by President Franklin D. Roosevelt because he felt it was too close to Christmas. But for whatever reason, Thanksgiving just wouldn't be the same without the turkey as the guest of honor.

Early settlers to Wisconsin found turkeys plentiful, especially in the open woodlands of the southern part of the state. Flocks of thousands were common and market hunters could shoot several hundred in a day for sale to city markets. But the unregulated shooting and the clearing of the oak woodlands to make way for croplands eventually led to the disappearance of these native game birds. The last wild Wisconsin turkey was seen near Darlington, Lafayette County, in 1881. Since then, several private and government efforts to reintroduce wild turkeys into our state were attempted, but all failed. Then, in 1974, DNR wildlife officials worked out an agreement with Missouri in which we agreed to trade some our native ruffed grouse in exchange for a few shipments of their wild turkeys, which were released in the southwestern part of the state. Not only did these transplanted birds survive, but were so successful that their offspring are now found in two-thirds of the state, and their populations are large enough to support both spring and fall hunts.

Part of the success of the turkey's comeback was the restoration of many of the oak forests that were leveled in the 1800s, and also the ability of turkeys to eat just about anything available. Although they prefer insects, berries, seeds, acorns and other wild foods, turkeys are also fond of helping themselves to agricultural crops. But, in the dead of winter, when the fields are plowed under and the acorns are buried under ice and snow, turkeys must often resort to some drastic measures to survive. Some of the largest flocks I have ever seen were in farmers' fields, digging through recently spread cow manure in the winter, searching for undigested kernels of corn.

Another reason they've been so successful is that turkey hens are excellent mothers. Although they lay a dozen or so eggs in ground nests, and can abandon them if disturbed, once they hatch out a brood they aggressively defend them from predators. I saw this myself a few years ago, when we lived in southwestern Wisconsin. One morning I looked out the window and saw our tough, old tomcat cornered in the garage by two mean-looking hen turkeys that kept him at bay while their nineteen chicks took turns dusting themselves in our garden and eating grasshoppers off the lawn. As far as we could tell, that cat never tangled with turkey hens after that.

Perhaps it was just as well that Franklin's dream of having the wild turkey become the national emblem of the federal government never came to be. After all, being called a turkey has now become a pretty unflattering slang term for a fool, a flop, or a failure. On the other hand, considering the endless bipartisan bickering and shameless political shenanigans that have gone on in Washington, D.C., over the years, maybe old Ben had the right choice, after all.

CEDAR WAXWINGS
NOMADS OF THE BIRD WORLD

They're called the "happy wanderers" of the bird world, always on the move, restless and anxious to get on to greener pastures. Cedar waxwings seem to appear magically overnight in our woodlands, fields, and backyards, searching for berries, cherries, grapes, or any other fruit they can find. Because they are flock feeders, cedar waxwings usually move as a group through the bushes and trees, gorging on berries. If you watch them long enough, you might see their peculiar habit of passing fruit from one bird to another, seemingly to make sure that all get their fill. Waxwings call to each other while feeding, and if you listen closely you can hear their *seee*-call, which sounds like a combination of a hiss and a whistle.

I first encountered these colorful avian gypsies years ago as a young boy, as I explored the dark, mysterious cedar-tamarack swamp near my grandparents' farm. I remember thinking then, as I still do today, that cedar waxwings are proba-bly the most handsome birds in nature. They have sleek bodies, soft-colored plumage in various shades of grays, browns, and olives, a yellow-tipped tail, and a crested head and black facemask. A few years ago, when an injured waxwing was brought to me, I had a chance to see up close why the bird is called a wax-wing. The tips of the wing-lining feathers are covered with a drop of brilliant red, plastic-like material. Bird watchers of yesteryear thought these shiny red drops looked like sealing wax, and hence the waxwing's common name.

Because cedar waxwings are often seen nesting and feeding in our lowland forest areas, I always assumed they were named after the white cedar trees that grow there. Actually, the first part of their name comes from their relationship with an upland tree called the red cedar, which, as it turns out, is not a cedar at all but a juniper tree. Instead of pro-ducing the familiar pinecones, like other evergreens, the red cedar bears juicy, bluish berries that cedar waxwings relish.

For most of the year, waxwings roam the countryside in flocks, but in spring they pair up and settle down a bit. But even then, they tend to be unpredictable and sometimes don't bother to start nest-building until late June. Unlike other birds, cedar waxwings don't bother to defend a nesting territory, often leaving the nest to flock with other waxwings to feed. Usually they have a second nesting right after the first brood is fledged. In keeping with their erratic nature, however, they might not get around to it until late September or even October, when most other birds are beginning to fly south for the winter. Nevertheless, once November and December roll around, many waxwings migrate as well, some going as far south as Central America. On the other hand, some waxwings seem content to sit out the winter right here in Wisconsin, usually in southern and southeastern part of the state, and usually in urban areas or wherever they can find a steady supply of berries still left on the trees and bushes.

Cedar waxwing were once used for food and slaughtered in great numbers for city markets. Even as late as 1842, America's foremost naturalist and bird enthusiast, John James Audubon, wrote about eating waxwings in a very matter-of-fact way. "They fatten and become so tender and juicy as to be sought by every epicure for the table," he said.

Lucky for cedar waxwings, most of us now prefer domestic poultry rather than songbirds for our dinner table, and cedar waxwings are now protected by state and federal laws. Today, these happy wanderers are welcome in our backyards, and are fun to watch in the wild as they continue their never-ending search for that perfect berry patch.

SCAUP *or* BLUEBILLS
THE REAL THANKSGIVING BIRDS

So you're planning to host Thanksgiving dinner for family and friends, and you're feeling a bit stressed out. Well, imagine having to put on a feast for fifty of your neighbors and ninety local Indians, such as the Pilgrims did at their first Thanksgiving in 1621. With no grocery store, you'd have to grow, hunt, or harvest whatever you needed for your meal. There would have been no milk, butter, cheese, or beef, since cows were not brought along on the Mayflower. And there would be no bread, since the wheat flour supply had long since run out. Luckily, the local Indians had taught you how to grow and prepare boiled pumpkins and corn, but pretty much everything else had to come from the surrounding wilderness. For the main course, you probably would have served venison seasoned with boiled wild cranberries.

But what about roast turkey? Despite our long holiday tradition, there's no record of wild turkey being served at all, at the first Thanksgiving feast. One of the Plymouth colony's members, Edward Winslow, wrote, "Our harvest being gotten in, our Governour sent foure men 'fowling,' so that we might after a more special manner rejoyce together, after we had gathered the fruit of our labour."

Since the Plymouth colony was located along the shores of Cape Cod Bay, the hunters were more likely to shoot waterfowl such as geese and ducks, than turkeys. One of the wild ducks that no doubt found its way to that first Thanksgiving feast was the scaup, better known to today's hunters and birdwatchers as the "bluebill," so named because of the color of its bill. Scaup are still one of the most abundant ducks in America. Despite their large numbers, however, not many of us get to see them up close, since they prefer to rest and feed in deeper marshes and lakes far from the shoreline.

Scaup can be seen in Wisconsin in large numbers during the spring and fall migrations, often congregating offshore in large rafts of hundreds of birds. They're the black-and-white ducks with the bright yellow eyes you may have seen bobbing up and down in the waves of Lake Michigan or other large bodies of water. Females have mottled brown plumage with a white patch behind their bill. Both the greater and lesser scaup can be seen in our state, but they're difficult to tell apart.

Like all diving ducks, scaup have their legs placed toward the rear of their bodies, which makes walking awkward but allows them to be excellent swimmers. They feed mostly on aquatic plants such as wild celery, pondweed, and wild rice, and they can dive to depths of 25 feet or more, far more deeply than most other ducks.

Scaup make up an important part of the duck hunters' harvest each year, since they visit smaller lakes and marshes to feed. They may seem awkward fliers, at first, since they need to run along the surface of the water to get up enough momentum to launch themselves into the air. Once in flight, however, their wings beat rapidly, making a whistling sound as they propel the birds at fifty miles an hour, twisting and turning low over the water, making for a difficult target.

Although a few scaup may nest in Wisconsin, most prefer to head northwest into the Dakotas, Canada, and Alaska to breed. Once there, the male scaup puts on an elaborate courtship display to attract females. He bows his head, opens his bill wide, and makes a loud, *scaup-scaup* call, giving rise to his namesake. After mating, the female incubates her eggs alone, while the male abandons her and returns to join the "boys" at a nearby lake or marsh to molt. In the past, the size of some of these molting concentrations could be incredible, one lake in Saskatchewan holding an estimated 25,000 scaup per mile of shoreline. Unfortunately, scaup numbers have not been that dramatic in recent years, and biologists are carefully monitoring their populations to find out why.

Scaup might be called the ultimate procrastinators of the duck world. During the spring migration they slowly make their way northward, following larger rivers and Great Lakes shorelines from March way into June. They're usually one of the last ducks to get around to nesting, and then they don't bother to migrate south again until the ice starts to close in on their ponds. Even then, they may linger until December to finally migrate south. A few don't bother to migrate at all, staying right here in Wisconsin in Lake Michigan's waters through the winter.

Late fall is a good time to look for scaup off our state's coastlines, but eventually most of the birds do manage to make it to the southeastern states. There they winter from Florida up the Atlantic coast as far north as the Chesapeake Bay, Long Island, and of course the Cape Cod Bay of the Pilgrim's Plymouth Colony, just as they have for countless generations. A few short months later, we get to see these colorful black-and-white-ducks bobbing up and down along the lakes and rivers of Wisconsin once again, as they make their leisurely trip back north— all in their own sweet time, of course.

CANADA GEESE
HONK IF YOU'RE A GOOSE HUNTER

It was a goose hunt like no other before or after. Even now, years later, it still seems like a surrealistic, slow-motion dream. My hunting buddy and I were stalking a large flock of geese feeding in a hilltop cornfield. We were crawling on our bellies as we inched our way up a grassy ravine towards the noisy flock of birds. We'd move a few feet and then freeze, as flock after flock set their wings to glide over us and land in the field ahead. When we finally stood to shoot, we were startled to find ourselves in the middle of several hundred, if not a thousand, Canada geese. Almost at once, the entire field around us exploded into a black and white whirlwind of flapping wings, bobbing heads, and the ear-piercing noise of hundreds of honking geese taking flight. After we regained our composure, we attempted to pick out a single target in the mass of birds that seemed to be whizzing in all directions like an exploding fireworks display. In the end, one of us shot three holes in the clear blue sky and the other shot once and got doubles.

Hunts like this would have been commonplace in Wisconsin in the early 1800s, when market hunters killed hundreds of thousands of geese to ship to stores and restaurants. But by the turn of the century, the year-round hunting with no bag limits, coupled with the draining of marshes to create farmland, had all but exterminated our state's wild goose population. Despite new laws to establish hunting seasons, Canada goose populations did not rebound quickly. As late as 1942, the Horicon National Wildlife refuge station counted a mere 450 geese at the marsh.

But things have changed since then, with sportsmen and women leading the way to preserve important wetland areas such as Horicon Marsh, and to push for nationwide controls on hunting waterfowl. Today, thanks to these efforts, both hunters and birdwatchers can enjoy the thrill of seeing some of the 500,000 geese that pass through Horicon Marsh each year.

Canada geese have an advantage over other waterfowl because most of them prefer to nest in the remote, far north tundra areas of Canada, far from the disturbance of man. Geese breed when they are two years old, and usually mate for life. They are aggressive defenders of their territory and are very protective parents. After their goslings are grown, they tend to flock together in family groups. All Canada geese pretty much look alike, but their size depends on which of the eight races they belong to. Some, at three or four pounds, are only slightly larger than a duck, while others, such as the giant Canada goose, can tip the scales at eighteen pounds or more.

Most geese migrate in spring and fall, but recently in some areas of the state, especially the southeastern counties, more and more geese can be seen almost any time of the year. These are giant Canada geese that have decided to nest here in Wisconsin, making them a familiar sight in urban areas from Green Bay to Milwaukee. Some don't even migrate in winter at all, if they can find open water and food. With their flocks now numbering several thousand and growing, it's hard to believe that back in the 1930s, giant Canadian geese were thought to be all but extinct, except for a few birds kept in captive flocks. Today, wildlife managers are searching for solutions to reduce the flocks, because of the mess geese make when they take over golf course greens, parks,and swimming beaches, leaving their droppings on our clean, manicured lawns.

Although some geese may remain in Wisconsin all year, most migrate south in autumn to wintering grounds in southern Illinois, Kentucky, and other Mississippi River refuges. Exactly how millions of geese can find their way from the arctic tundras to the southern water-fowl areas and return again in spring remains one of the great myster-ies of nature. Biologists know that geese rely on landscapes, waterways, and even the position of the sun and stars to find their bearings during migration. But how they can navigate on dark, foggy days with heavy overcast clouds, is still a riddle. Some have even speculated that geese have some sort of natural, built-in compass system.

Geese tend to fly in V-shaped formations, which act to break up wind resistance and cause an uplift from one goose to another, making flying easier. Since the lead goose gains no advantage from this forma-tion, the flock breaks up occasionally and a new leader shifts to the front of the V.

There are few sights and sounds in nature that can cause us to pause and contemplate life and the change of seasons like a flock of honking geese heading south for the winter. Author and naturalist Sigurd Olson described it best:

"Suddenly out of the north came the sound I had been waiting for, a soft, melodious gabbling that swelled and died and increased in vol-ume until all other sounds were engulfed by its clamor. Far in the blue I saw them, a long skein of dots undulating like a floating ribbon pulled toward the south by an invisible cord tied to the point of its V."

LICHENS
TAKING A LIKIN' TO LICHENS

And when the dew had gone up, there was on the face of the wilderness a fine, flake-like thing. When the people of Israel saw it, they said to one another, "What is it?" for they did not know what it was. And Moses said to them, "It is the bread which the Lord has given you to eat."

—Exodus 16, The Bible

After only two and a half months into their exodus from Egyptian slavery, the Israelites were exhausted and near starvation. Their leader, Moses, had promised that God would send them bread, but instead they found a flaky, wafer-like plant that grew on the desert sands. The Israelites called it "manna" and found they could indeed make a nutritious bread from it, which they did for the entire forty years they roamed the wilderness in search of a homeland.

Today the Biblical manna from heaven is believed to have been a common desert lichen that not only still grows in North Africa, but is still used by roaming nomadic tribes of the region to make bread. The plant is one of the 20,000 different species of lichens that grow everywhere from the hottest deserts to the coldest regions of the Arctic. Lichens are probably the most common, yet least noticed, plants on earth. They're the colorful blotches you see growing on trees, rocks, cliffs, buildings, gravestones, and even right on the ground. Some are soft and leafy, while others are hard and coral-like.

Lichens are one of the longest-living organisms in the world, some estimated to be over 4,500 years old. They are also probably the slowest-growing plants in the world, many growing as little as a half-millimeter a year, although most grow much more quickly. Most lichens reproduce themselves by cloning or producing microscopic clumps of cells that get blown into the atmosphere by the wind. Some are washed back down to earth to start new colonies, similar to those that may have appeared in the biblical account of the raining of "manna from heaven."

Wisconsin is home to hundreds of different lichens. One of the easiest to spot is called rock-tripe. These are the colorful green, orange, or yellow blotches you might see growing on the boulders along old rock fence lines, or on older tombstones at the cemetery. Another common lichen in Wisconsin is called lungwort, which grows on everything from trees to house shingles. Lungwort is usually green, brown, or even bluish in color, and is very leafy-looking. One of my favorite lichens is called British soldiers, which are tiny tree-like lichens with bright red caps, often seen growing on the ground or on the top of old tree stumps.

Although lichens look like plants, they have no roots, no leaves, and no vascular system. What they really are is a combination of two separate organisms—algae and fungus. The fungus is the outside part of the lichen that you can see. It acts as a sponge and can absorb water right out of the air. It also provides minerals to the algae living within it. In turn, the algae produce sugars and starches that the fungus needs to live. Lichens can be eaten by both animals and people, but since most are dry, juiceless, and bitter unless they are first parboiled, they are definitely an emergency wilderness survival food.

In addition to their value as food, lichens have been used for centuries for dyes and medicines, and are still used in some cosmetic powders. Probably their most important role, however, is that of a natural environmental monitor. Like canaries in the coal mines, lichens can warn us of toxins in the air we breathe. They are especially sensitive to the sulfur dioxide commonly spewed from coal-burning power plants. Clean, breathable air and healthy-looking lichens go hand in hand, but when the lichens disappear, as they have in some large, polluted cities— watch out.

Few other living organisms in nature are as overlooked as the lowly lichens that grow all around us. Next time you're on one of your outdoor adventures, keep an eye out for these colorful, interesting plants. Who knows, with some practice, you may even take a likin' to them.

WHITE CEDAR
THE TREE OF LIFE

Imagine you're a member of a 16th-century expedition led by the French explorer Jacque Cartier. The year is 1557 and you find yourself deep in the Canadian wilderness. Winter is setting in and the members of your expedition party are sick from scurvy, too weak to go on. With no medicine, no food, and a thousand miles from the nearest settlement, what would you do?

Luckily for the Cartier expedition, help came from a tribe of friendly Indians who revived them with a drink of a vitamin C-rich tea, brewed from the leaves of the white cedar tree. The Frenchmen were so impressed with this seemingly magical tree that they named it *l'arbe de vie*, the "tree of life." Later, they carried white cedar saplings back to France, and the tree eventually became a favorite ornamental throughout Europe.

White cedar trees are pyramid-shaped evergreens with the ragged, twisting, reddish bark. You see them in city parks, golf courses, or maybe on your front lawn. Unlike most other evergreens that have stiff, prickly needles, white cedar has soft, scale-like leaves covering its branches. American Indians most aptly called it *Oo-soo-ha-tah*, meaning "feather leaf."

White cedar is native to most of Wisconsin, except the southwestern part of the state. The tree is found in the wild only in southern Canada and the Great Lakes area. It grows best in the mucky soils of shallow swamps and marshes, but can also do well in upland hillside sites. White cedar is sold by tree nurseries for ornamental plantings under the name *arborvitae*, with more than fifty varieties on the market.

Near the turn of the century, white cedar was considered an important timber tree. In 1899 alone, some 95 million board feet of cedar was cut for fence posts, shingles, boxes, poles, boat and canoe planking, water tanks, fish net floats, and many other uses. Before the days of treated lumber, cedar was one of the few woods that were naturally rot-resistant. The tree was also used by American Indians for medicine and for construction where a lightweight, strong, and durable wood was needed, such as in making framing for birch-bark canoes.

Although some cedar is still harvested today for use in split-rail fencing and rustic log home construction, the tree is no longer considered an important timber tree. Farmers now use steel or treated wooden posts for fencing, boxes are made out of cardboard, boats and canoes are built out of aluminum or fiberglass, and cedar shingles are rarely used on roofs these days. In addition, the tree grows very slowly and usually only in very wet soils and in other areas that are difficult to harvest. Cedar can live up to three hundred years, growing to impressive heights. A Wisconsin record cedar tree in Manitowoc County was found to be 92 feet high with a trunk circumference of 12½ feet.

Today, white cedar is probably most important as a food source for deer during the winter months. In many areas, the dense stands of cedar are the primary wintering areas for deer, providing not only food and cover from enemies, but shelter from the howling winds and subzero temperatures. Unfortunately, the white-tail deer's appetite for white cedar is also contributing to the tree's demise. With deer populations at all-time highs during the last two decades, white cedar has not been able to reproduce itself in many areas of the state. As soon as a cedar seedling sprouts, it is eaten by browsing deer. In addition, many existing white cedar trees have been stripped of their leaves as far as the deer can reach on their hind legs. This browse line is usually about five feet from the ground and can easily be seen in areas of high deer concentrations. Time will tell if the great cedar swamps of lore and legend will become just another chapter in history, and whether cedars will survive only as an ornamental tree in our backyards and manicured golf courses.

In a true paradox of our times, the tree of life must now struggle for its own life. But maybe we can find a way to keep this historic and interesting native tree in our forests for future generations of both people and deer.

PORCUPINE
NATURE'S OWN PINCUSHION

Porcupines are one of the few creatures on earth that never seem to have to worry about where their next meal will come from. In fact, it's been said that a porcupine never starves, since it can eat pretty much anything in the forest. Porcupines eat a variety of woodland plants and fruits during most of the year, but because they don't hibernate like many other rodents, they must change their diet dramatically in winter. Luckily, nature has provided porcupines with large and sharp front teeth, similar to those of beavers, allowing them to gnaw and eat the bark and twigs of forest trees such as aspen, maple, pine, or nearly any other tree. This natural pruning doesn't usually cause any permanent damage to the forest trees, although porcupines sometimes do their gnawing in orchards and tree farms.

Porcupines are often considered pests because of their fondness for anything salty to chew on. This includes pretty much anything we humans touch, since we leave our salty perspiration residue on tool handles, leather boots, and much more. Many a camper has learned the hard way about the porcupine's passion for salt when they discover their canoe paddle handle chewed to a stub overnight. For some reason, porcupines also seem to be fond of eating the glue or resin used to bond plywood. Years ago, when I was a ranger in the northern forests, I routinely had to repair many trail signs, bulletin boards, and restroom plywood siding that had gnawed on by these animals.

Porcupines are often perceived as being clumsy and dim-witted, probably because of their slow waddle, but once off the ground they are agile tree climbers. Almost any predator, including man, can outrun a porcupine, but catching them is a whole other matter, since their bodies are covered with 30,000 needle-sharp quills, most of which are hidden by soft guard hairs. Despite popular belief, porcupines can't actually throw their quills, but if a predator comes too close for comfort, they will turn their back and swat their tails at them. Once impaled in the skin, the sharp quills are difficult to remove, since the tips are covered with barbed scales. If not pulled out, the quills will work themselves more and more deeply into the body and can eventually be fatal if they reach the heart, liver, or other vital organ of an animal. If stuck in the mouth, the quills can prevent the victim from eating. Animals as large as mountain lions, bears, wolves, and even eagles are known to have died from porcupine quills. Only a few predators such as the fisher—a member of the weasel family—are able to kill an adult porcupine, and then only if they're able to attack the porcupine's soft, quill-free underbelly.

Porcupines were once common in most of Wisconsin and throughout the Great Lake states, but as the forests were cut near the turn of the last century they were pushed farther and farther north. Once exterminated from an area, porcupines are slow to recover, since they don't reproduce as quickly as other rodents. Adults spend most the year living alone, except in mid-October, when they pair up, rub noses, and (carefully) mate.

Usually, only one cub is born in spring. Baby porcupines are born with a full set of quills but, lucky for the mother, the quills are soft at birth and don't begin to harden until later. Today, porcupines are still common in our northern forests, but are rarely seen due to their nocturnal habits. They spend the daylight hours sleeping high in the treetops, and usually wait until after dark to travel and eat. Although they have an excellent sense of smell to help them find their favorite foods, porcupines have poor eyesight, explaining why we most often see them as casualties along busy forest highways.

Porcupines have always fascinated mankind. They were used by Native Americans as an important food source, and their quills were used to decorate clothing, moccasins,

247

sewing baskets, and even war bonnets. Porcupines have also been the subject of countless stories and legends told over campfires of long ago.

It's hard to imagine another animal that nature has endowed so well with tools for survival . The porcupine's nearly impenetrable pincushion of sharp quills that protects it from nearly every predator in the wild, and its ability to eat almost anything, virtually assures that this animal will continue to thrive in Wisconsin's forests for centuries to come.

RED SQUIRRELS
SOUNDING THE WOODS ALARM

It happens every time. You tiptoe silently through the dark, early-morning forest to your favorite deer stand. You've masked your odor with the latest cover scent, and you're wearing your best camouflage outfit. With gun, bow, or camera in the ready position, you're sure to see some action, since your presence in the woods was undetected.

Right?. . . WRONG!

Suddenly, a red squirrel appears on a nearby branch, chattering in that high-pitched, high-volume warning call that only they can do so well. Not content to scold you at a distance, the squirrel moves closer and closer in short jumps, continuing his loud chattering, foot stamping, and tail flicking. No doubt about it—the jig is up, you've been spotted.

Red squirrels, also called pine squirrels, are aggressive, bold, high-energy animals that scold nearly all intruders into their territory, including humans. Like blue jays and crows, red squirrels are part of the alarm system wired into most all woodlands. Because of their defensive nature, red squirrels often find themselves fighting with much bigger squirrels, such as gray and fox squirrels.

Because red squirrels are so small, they are often mistaken for babies of the larger species of squirrels. Even fully-grown adults rarely tip the scales at more than half a pound. The squirrel's common name refers to the reddish fur on its back and tail. The underside of the squirrel is white, as are the distinctive rings around its eyes. Because of its high-strung disposition, the red squirrel always reminds me of fuzzy, wind-up kid's toy with its spring wound just a little too tightly.

The red squirrel's high metabolism rate requires that it eat high-energy food and lots of it. When not fighting with other squirrels or scolding hunters, the squirrel spends most of its time collecting and storing seeds, nuts, mushrooms, and pinecones. Unlike other squirrels that bury individual nuts throughout the forest, the red squirrel prefers to store his winter supply in huge piles. You can often find their pine-cone caches stacked three feet deep and several yards across. Pine squirrels also seem to have favorite eating spots that are easily identified by the mounds of spent pinecone seeds piled up around trees or stumps. Some of these piles are several feet high, representing probably many generations of squirrels over a period of years.

Red squirrels make their nests in tree hollows, if available, but also build leaf nests in treetops. Unfortunately, they are not shy about using storage sheds, garages, or even attics, which often puts them in conflict with humans. Females give birth to four or five babies, usually in May. Occasionally they will have a second litter in fall. Baby squirrels are born naked and blind and are weaned and cared for by the mother until late summer, when they are chased off to find their own territory. Young squirrels are often at greatest risk at this time, many falling prey to hawks, owls, fox, and domestic pets. Once fully grown, however, few predators seem to be able to catch them. The pine martin was once the only true predator of the red squirrel. The martin was almost exterminated from Wisconsin, but is now being successfully reintroduced in the northern part of the state, thanks to an abundant population of red squirrels.

Red squirrels are most plentiful in northern evergreen forests, although they seem to be almost as common in hardwood lands and along stone fences next to cornfields in the southern part of the state. They also help themselves to backyard bird feeders and will often go to great lengths to get at their favorite birdseed. A couple years ago I had an ambitious red squirrel that not only chewed through our garage doorframe, but also gnawed into a thick plastic barrel to get at my birdseed. I now have to keep my birdseed in a metal container with a weight on top.

Luckily, red squirrels, like hyperactive children, have short attention spans and quickly tire of chattering and scold-

249

ing hunters and hikers that dare to invade their home turf. Eventually, they move on to more daring challenges—but not before "sounding the woodland alarm."

CHIPMUNKS
NATURE'S REAL CHIP AND DALE

It seemed like one of those funny old "Chip and Dale" cartoons, except that I was the ever-gullible Donald Duck. For some reason, every time I bought a box of dog biscuits and set it on a shelf in the garage, the biscuits seemed to disappear mysteriously, almost overnight. At first, I accused each of my three children (Huey, Dewey, and Louie) of feeding the dog too many treats, and later blamed the dog herself for sneaking the snacks, but I could never catch any of them in the act.

Then, one day while I was splitting firewood in the backyard, I noticed a chipmunk scampering away from me in a zigzag route from tree to tree, heading towards the garage. At the same time I saw a second chipmunk sneaking out of the garage in the opposite direction, heading right for the woodpile where I was sitting. As he got closer, I could see a colorful bone-shaped dog biscuit clenched in his teeth, the ends of the biscuit sticking out from both cheeks. Apparently, this chipmunk tag-team relay had been going on for some time. No doubt their tunnels under my wood stack were piled high with these stolen goods. Although Donald Duck would have spewed out a flurry of expletive adjectives at this point in the cartoon, I couldn't help but just laugh aloud at this comical solution to the mystery.

Wisconsin is home to two kinds of chipmunks. The eastern chipmunk is the larger of the two, and is more common in the southern part of the state, while its smaller cousin, the least chipmunk, is found in northern forests. Both are similar in appearance, with long, alternating, brown, black, and white stripes, reminiscent of the old-time prison uniforms, and a black mask over their eyes. A perfect outfit for the little thieves they can be at times.

Chipmunks communicate with each other with a loud, high-pitched chipping sound that can go on for several minutes. Most people assume the chipmunk's common name derives from this sound, but it was actually named after the Chippewa Indian word, *chitmunk*, which means "head first," referring to the way they descend trees. Although they are good tree climbers, chipmunks prefer to be on or under the ground most of the time. They dig long networks of tunnels that may stretch thirty feet or more, with several escape routes and cozy nesting chambers.

Besides their appetite for dog biscuits, chipmunks like to eat nuts, acorns, berries, and even insects, earthworms, and mushrooms. Chippers that live near urban areas or farms may steal some corn, wheat, or seeds from backyard bird feeders, but they rarely do much damage. Actually, their appetite for harmful pests such as June bugs, slugs, snails, and cutworms more than compensates for their occasional raids of our crops and gardens.

Chipmunks don't store much body fat to prepare for winter, and don't go into a true hibernation. Because of this, they work tirelessly all autumn, collecting nuts and seeds to store in their underground bunkers to get them through the cold season. To help them accomplish this incredible chore, chipmunks have large, stretchable cheek pouches which they use to carry large loads of food back to their burrows. A chipmunk can easily stuff more than thirty kernels of corn or seventy sunflower seeds into its mouth all at one time. Once stored in the chipmunk's underground chamber, this food supply is like money under the mattress. They even build their grass-lined sleeping nests right on top of their piles of seeds and nuts, and can literally snack in bed all winter long.

Chipmunks emerge from their cozy underground burrows in early spring, and immediately search for mates to begin raising families. Even though they have two litters of five or more young each year, most of the young will not survive to the end of the summer. Chipmunks are eaten by fox, coyotes, hawks, owls, cats, dogs, and just about anything else bigger than themselves. Although adult chipmunks can outrun most of their enemies, they can't hide from predators such as snakes and weasels, which can squirm right down into the chipmunks' underground tunnels.

Except for our pets, automobiles, and an occasional kid with a BB gun, chipmunks don't seem to be greatly threatened by people. Someone once said that chipmunks consider us as nothing more than a necessary nuisance—a willing provider of peanuts and a source of the bonanza of food that they gladly steal from our houses, backyards, picnics, campsites, and, as I discovered, the box of dog biscuits in my garage.

FOX SQUIRRELS
COUNTRY BUMPKIN COUSINS

So you say you'd really like to spend some time hunting this weekend, but you can't stand the thought of setting your alarm clock for four o'clock in the morning. You say crawling out of your warm, cozy bed and stumbling through the cold, dark forest to your deer stand, or sloshing through the damp, pitch-black marsh to the duck blind, has lost some of its appeal? If so, there's a perfect Wisconsin game animal for you—squirrels.

The familiar gray squirrel is probably the most abundant and most hunted of all the squirrels, with an estimated harvest of more than a million taken each year in Wisconsin alone. Just like most of us, gray squirrels hate to get up early in the morning and are usually not up and about until at least sunrise. But if you're a really lazy—er, sleepy— hunter, the gray squirrel's bigger cousin, the fox squirrel, might be even more your style. Fox squirrels don't bother to crawl out of the sack until even later in the morning—sometimes not until eight o'clock or later. Because they are sun-lovers, fox squirrels remain busy throughout the day, even over the warmer noon hour when most other squirrels have slipped back into their dens or crawled high into the treetops for a long midday snooze. Then, unlike gray squirrels that become active again just before nightfall, fox squirrels retire early for the evening. Most of these sleepyheads crawl back into their nests or dens by 6 P.M., even during the long daylight hours of summer.

Fox squirrels are named after the color of their fur, which resembles the rusty brown color of the red fox. Sometimes they're called "yellow-bellied" squirrels because of the orange-yellow hue of their lower bodies. Fox squirrels can be found nearly anywhere east of the Rocky Mountains where they can find a food source. They are the largest squirrels in North America, adults tipping the scales at up to three pounds. Like other squirrels, they eat acorns of all kinds and are especially fond of hickory nuts. They also eat berries, wild fruits, and, as any

Fox squirrels might be called the country bumpkins of the squirrel world. While most squirrels need large tracts of dense, mature woodlands to survive, fox squirrels actually prefer to live in open agricultural areas, as long as there's a small woodlot or nut- bearing trees available for food. Because of this, fox squirrels have actually expanded their range westward and northward over the years, almost replicating the pattern of early pioneer settlers as they cleared forests and developed new croplands. Some fox squirrels might spend their entire lives in and around a single oak or hickory tree, along a fence line. Because they are not as agile tree climbers as their gray cousins, fox squirrels spend much of their time on the ground, but have extremely good hearing and eyesight and are rarely caught off guard. True to their rural roots, fox squirrels prefer country living and are rarely seen in urban areas, unlike the gray squirrel, which seems to have adapted all too well to the city's backyard birdfeeders and gardens.

Years ago, many kids, including myself, first learned to hunt by matching wits with fox squirrels along the fence rows and woodlots of a relative's farm. There, by waiting patiently under a big hickory tree, and with a little luck, a fox squirrel or two might eventually make it home to our dinner table. But fox squirrels have more threatening predators than a few kids with beat-up .22 rifles or shotguns. Because they don't venture out after dark, fox squirrels can avoid owls and most other nighttime predators. But during the day, hawks often pluck squirrels right off their trees, while on the ground, fox, coyotes, dogs, and cats can take their toll.

Despite these threats, the most devastating enemy of all to fox squirrels is a poor or failed nut crop from the trees it depends on for survival. Without being able to store a good harvest in fall, the squirrels have to remain active all winter, searching farther and farther from its den to find food, making them greater targets for predators.

Today, most kids live in urban areas and unfortunately no longer have ties to the family farms many of us had only a generation ago. A young person's first hunt, if they hunt at all, might be to sit for hours on a boring deer stand on a cold, November day at a crowded public hunting area. Although there's nothing wrong with this, I can't help think that these kids and adults are missing something, if that's the only hunting experience they ever get. Maybe what's missing are those long, warm, sunny September days of long ago. Spending time all alone observing nature, exploring the cornfields, fence lines, and woodlots of a Wisconsin farm, trying to out-fox the local fox squirrels. There's still time to get out and enjoy an old-time squirrel hunt. But remember, don't forget *not* to set the alarm clock.

LADYBUG
NATURE'S LADY LUCK

It was a dark day for the peasants of Europe during the Middle Ages, and all seemed lost. A plague of plant-sucking aphids were swarming the countryside destroying their crops. With winter fast approaching, the threat of famine for both man and beast seemed certain. Without modern pesticides to fight the insect pests, the farmers could do little more than pray for a miracle. As the legend goes, the peasants prayed to the Virgin Mary for help. Soon after, millions of tiny beetles arrived, ate all the aphids, and saved the day. Ever since then, these colorful little bugs have been called "lady" bugs or ladybird beetles, after the Virgin Mary.

Today, ladybugs are still welcome in our gardens and farm fields because of their ferocious appetite for aphids, potato bugs, plant lice, and other crop pests. Many gardeners still order boxes packed full of ladybugs from mail-order catalogs to release in their gardens. Although mature ladybugs eat plenty of garden pests, their offspring are even more beneficial. When hatched, ladybug larvae live up to their nickname of "aphid-wolves" by devouring every insect pest they can catch. Biologists have estimated that a single ladybug may eat more than five thousand aphids during its two-year lifespan.

Ladybugs are probably the most universally recognized insect on earth, with more than two thousand species known worldwide. Most of the 150 species here in the United States are the familiar round-shelled variety that look like tiny, orange M&M's, but some are brown, red, yellow, green, and even black in color. Almost all ladybugs have between two and fifteen spots on their colorful wing shells, but the two- and seven-spot kinds are the most commonly seen. The number of spots on a ladybug has always been a source of superstition. German farmers used to count the spots on ladybugs to forecast the success of their crops. Fewer than seven spots meant a big harvest was ahead. Still others believed that the familiar seven-spot ladybug represented the seven joys and seven sorrows of Mary.

Unlike most other insects, ladybugs are one of the few bugs that most people actually like. In almost every country in the world, people believe having a ladybug in the house is a good omen, and that to harm or kill one will bring bad luck. This ancient superstition has transcended the ages even into modern America. Many people, including me, can remember being asked to carry these lucky beetles out of their mom's house unharmed, while the run-of-the-mill bugs were squashed on sight. Ladybugs have also made their way into our literature, as in this familiar verse:

"Ladybird, Ladybird fly away home,
Your house is on fire and your children are all gone;
All but one, and her name is Ann,
And she crept under the frying pan."

Nobody knows the origin of this dark and mysterious children's rhyme. Some believe it began centuries ago in England when farmers used to burn hop vines, usually full of ladybugs, after the harvest.

In fall, you often see several dozen or even hundreds of ladybugs all in one location. As autumn approaches, ladybugs stop eating and flock together to migrate to their wintering areas. Sometimes after a windstorm off Lake Michigan, I've found thousands of ladybugs of all sizes and colors littering the shoreline, hanging onto to driftwood or other debris. Most likely, these were migrating ladybugs that got blown out of the sky and washed ashore while en route.

In recent years we've seen a huge increase in the number of ladybugs in Wisconsin. Unfortunately, most of these are not our native ladybugs but an alien look-alike invader called the Asian lady beetle. These aggressive beetles were imported from the Orient in the 1970s in an attempt to control the pecan aphid in Georgia, but have since spread like wildfire throughout the country. They were first seen in Wisconsin in 1992, and have now become a common pest in nearly every house and office, especially in fall, when they move indoors to find a warm and dry place to spend the winter.

Although they look helpless and would seem to be easy pickings for predators, ladybugs have a few tricks up their sleeves. If threatened, they can release or squirt drops of yellow, stinky juice from the joints of their legs to repel the attack. Their brightly colored shell is a clear warning to most predators to stay clear of them. Ladybugs hibernate together, sometimes by the hundreds, under leaf litter and grass for safety. They seem to find strength not so much in numbers, but in the awful stench they can produce together to ward off enemies during their long winter sleep.

Most of us seem to have a soft spot in our hearts for ladybugs. For centuries we've made jewelry, clothing, and toys, and decorated our homes with their likeness. We encourage them to live in our gardens and farm fields to help us control harmful insects. Even the sight of a ladybug can cheer you up, especially when one is found inside your house in the middle of winter.

Some would say that all these ladybug superstitions and folklore belong back in the Dark Ages, and that carrying bugs out of our homes unharmed is just so much foolishness. On the other hand, we seem to need all the luck we can get these days, so I don't think I'll take a chance.

DADDY LONG-LEGS
LONG-DISTANCE RUNNERS

Like most farmboys years ago, I spent many fun-filled hours in pursuit of all sorts of creepy, crawly critters in the great outdoors. One of my favorite captures was the daddy long-legs, or harvester spider, as it sometimes called. With long, thread-like legs some thirty times as long as its body, the daddy long-legs could be a real challenge to catch. The spider is able to move rapidly up and down walls and trees, and can even run on top of grass blades. Once caught, however, daddy long-legs never bite, and they become nice pets—at least until a more interesting critter crawls by.

Many people have fond memories of the daddy long-legs. Even those who find all other spiders repulsive seem to have a special fondness for these creatures. With some three thousand species of daddy long-legs worldwide, you are almost certain to have one (or one hundred) in your backyard, no matter where you live. Chances are that you saw them in fall as you washed the windows on your house or raked leaves in the backyard. Some people make the mistake of killing daddy long-legs, thinking this will reduce the number of spider webs around the house. In reality, daddy long-legs don't even spin webs, and, in fact, do you a favor by killing and eating the other spiders that do make webs.

Daddy long-legs are technically not even spiders at all, but members of a large family of spider-like creatures, including mites and ticks, in the class Arachnida. This formerly little-known family reached celebrity status a few years ago, when a popular Hollywood movie "Arachniphobia," became a box-office hit.

Besides not being able to spin webs, daddy long-legs differs from its spider cousins in other ways. While spiders have two body sections and up to eight eyes to search for prey, the daddy long-legs has only one oval body section and only two eyes. Its eyes are mounted back-to-back on top of its body—similar to a gun turret on a warship.

Since daddy long-legs don't have the ability to trap their prey in webs, they must run down and capture them—a feat made possible by their long legs and great speed. Favorite meals include insects, caterpillars, mites, and smaller spiders, which they catch and pierce with their large beak-like jaws, sucking the juice from their victims' bodies. As is often the case in nature, however, the hunter sometimes becomes the hunted. Daddy long-legs are occasionally eaten by larger spiders and centipedes, but are rarely eaten by birds, toads, or other, larger predators because of their ability to release a smelly liquid from behind their front legs, making them just too distasteful to eat.

Another survival trick, familiar to farmboys and other such predators, is the ability of daddy long-legs to drop a leg off their bodies to escape capture. The lost leg often twitches and quivers for a few seconds to further confuse the predator and allow enough time for a quick getaway. Unfortunately, daddy long-legs are not able to regenerate a new leg as many spiders can do, but they seem to get along fine minus a leg or two.

In autumn, daddy long-legs congregate in large numbers near sheltered areas, where they mate and lay their eggs. In the northern areas of their range, including Wisconsin, all the adults die by late fall. By this time, however, their eggs have been laid. Next spring will bring a new generation of daddy long-legs, and also another crop of boys and girls to chase after them, just as children always have and probably always will. ▲

December

December ushers in the official start of winter on December 21st, the winter solstice and shortest day of the year. As each day grows colder than the one before, the rare beauty of the winter landscape is reshaped and sculptured over and over by the howling winds and shifting snowdrifts.

At night, the light of December's "cold" full moon casts a blue hue over the frozen woodlands and glimmers through the crystal-clear icicles. Far in the distance, the barred owl's familiar "who cooks for you" call can be heard, while nearby, curious deer mice scurry under the moonlight in search of a midnight snack of wild seeds. By dawn, the rap-tap-tap of downy woodpeckers drilling in old tree snags breaks the frosty silence of the forest, and the woodlands come alive with the animated antics of colorful cardinals, black-and-white cottonball chickadees, and loudmouth blue jays.

As the holidays approach, the crunch of footsteps can be heard in forests and evergreen farms throughout the state, as tree hunters search for that perfect balsam fir or scotch pine to harvest. By the time December's full moon illuminates the long, cold winter nights, the trees will be trimmed in brilliant decorations and twinkling lights, bringing nature's beauty indoors and providing hope for warmer days ahead.

DOWNY WOODPECKERS
LITTLE JACKHAMMERS OF THE FOREST

Take a hike on a brisk, early winter morning in almost any Wisconsin woodlot and you'll notice something different in the air. The frantic rush and color of autumn has disappeared under a blanket of snow, and everything seems frozen in a world of silence. But just when it seems that every living creature has either flown south for the winter, or has holed up snug in some underground burrow, you hear a faint *tap-tap-tap … tap-tap-tap*. High in the treetops you spy a small black-and-white bird with a red patch on its head, busily pecking away at a dead snag. More than likely, this tiny, feathered jackhammer will be our state's smallest and most common woodpecker—the downy.

Like other birds that choose to remain behind in our winter wonderland, downy woodpeckers are well equipped to survive the bone-chilling cold, snow, and ice. During the day, their fluffy feathers and insulating down keep them warm as they hop and fly from tree to tree in search of food. Often, they join flocks of chickadees and nuthatches as they check every branch in the woods for insect eggs, cocoons, mites, and spiders. At night, downies return to the shelter of their nesting holes inside dead or hollow trees.

The downy, like other woodpeckers, has a unique, built-in set of tools to help it survive in the wild. Its chisel-shaped bill allows it to chip away behind bark and into solid wood to get at burrowing insects such as ants, larvae, and beetles that make up more than 75 percent of its diet. It also has a heavy, thick skull that gives it the extra weight it needs to chisel wood, sort of like the swing of hammer. To support this drilling, the downy's foot has two long toes on top and two on the bottom, to help anchor the bird onto the sides of trees, and a short, stiff tail to brace itself. Once a hole is drilled, downies use their long, sticky tongues tipped with barbs to spear and extract insects.

Occasionally, the downy's slow, methodical tapping turns into a loud, rapid *prrrrr . . . prrr,* called drumming. You might have heard these excited bursts of tapping while you were hiking through the woods. The drumming is used by downies to warn other woodpeckers to stay out of their territory, or sometimes merely to keep in touch with their mates. Downy woodpeckers are able to increase the volume of their drumming by using drumming posts such as hollow trees, dead limbs, power line poles, and sometimes even the rainspout on your house.

Downy woodpeckers live solitary lives for much of the year, males and females living apart in separate nesting holes. But by late winter they unite and start looking for a suitable nesting tree in which to raise their young. In the world of downy woodpeckers, a house is truly a home, and not just any old dead tree will do. In fact, if the pair cannot agree on that perfect tree they may separate again. Irreconcilable differences, I guess.

Once the downy pair does find that "tree of their dreams," they both begin the long chore of excavating a nesting hole, chip by chip. After nearly two weeks of work, the nesting cavity will be about eight inches deep and ready for occupancy.

After the female lays four or five white eggs, both parents share in incubating them, taking one-hour shifts. When hatched, downy babies are blind, naked, red-colored, and pretty homely looking—but within a few days their feathers grow in and they are transformed into cute black-and-white miniatures of their parents. Only the male downy grows a red patch on the back of his head.

Besides being the most common woodpecker, downies are also among the most friendly birds in our region. They don't seem to mind sharing their territories with people, and are found in parks, gardens, farmlands, and even urban areas. Downies eagerly come to backyard bird feeding stations, especially in late winter when their wild food sources are running low. Although they sometimes snatch up sunflower seeds, if you really want to attract downies you should have a suet feeder. Beef suet is cheap and usually available at the meat counter at most grocery stores. Just stuff it in an old plastic mesh orange bag and hang it on a tree. Or you can purchase metal holders and pre-shaped blocks of suet at wild bird centers and most hardware, garden, and department stores. Many other birds, such as blue jays, chickadees, nuthatches, and starlings, will enjoy your suet feeder as well.

The downy woodpecker's busy antics at the birdfeeder are fun to watch, if you're able to attract them to your backyard. If not, take that brisk winter hike into the woods and listen for the *tap-tap-tap* of Wisconsin's favorite woodpecker.

HOUSE WREN
NATURE'S GOOD-LUCK CHARM

The wren, the wren, King of all birds,
On St. Stephen's Day, Is caught in the furze.

This curious rhyme about catching a wren in the furze or "bushes" was sung long ago in the British Isles and in France by roving bands of young boys on the first day of Christmas, December 26th, also known as St. Stephen's Day. According to this odd custom, on this day the "wren boys" of Christmas would go out at night and beat the bushes with poles to chase out the small birds roosting there. Whoever managed to kill the first wren became the group's king for the day and carried the dead wren tied with colorful ribbons on top of a pole. At daybreak, the wren boys brought their tiny trophy back to town, stopping at each house along the way to present a single wren feather to the woman of the house in exchange for ale, food, or some sort of present. Killing or harming a wren was normally considered a sacrilege at any other time of the year. On St. Stephen's day, however, it was not only acceptable, but any household that was visited by the wren boys was said to be assured of good luck for the year to come. At the end of the day, the tiny wren corpse was given a proper burial somewhere in the local church cemetery. Fortunately for wrens everywhere, this odd and somewhat barbaric custom is now a part of the past.

Wrens are the small, perky, brown birds with the familiar upturned tails you've probably seen in your backyard or local park. If you haven't seen a wren, no doubt you've heard one, especially in spring when the males sing in what can only be described as a loud, nonstop outburst of bubbly melody. The Chippewa had a long and descriptive name for the wren, *O-du-na-mis-sug-ud-da-we-ski*, which meant "a big noise for its size." With at least fifty different species of wrens worldwide, and nine of them in the United States alone, you don't have to go far to see a wren. In fact, you really don't need to look for them at all since they usually find us, instead—especially the house wren, which is probably the easiest of all birds to attract to your backyard.

Over the years, the house wren or "Jenny wren," as the English colonists called them, have endeared themselves to many of us because of their eagerness to nest in the birdhouses we put up for them, no matter how crudely built they may be. In some areas, competition for birdhouses from the larger English sparrows and tree swallows can be fierce, but you can eliminate this problem by keeping the entrance hole to your birdhouse to one inch in diameter, or about the size of a quarter, which will allow only wrens to enter. Even if you don't provide a birdhouse for them, wrens may show up in your backyard, anyway, and are known for building their nests in the oddest places—over light fixtures, inside old tires, even inside the pockets of clothes hung on the wash line. Most wrens, except for the marsh wren, nest in tree cavities in open brushy woodlands, but when given the choice they seem to prefer our artificial nest boxes. They have adapted so  well to suburban living that they are now our most common backyard bird, and their numbers are still increasing each year.

House wrens start to nest as soon as the males arrive in spring, usually in early May. The male selects a territory and builds several nests at the same time by filling every available nesting box or tree cavity to the top with short straight twigs. Female wrens arrive later and select males to pair with by choosing one of his nests in which to lay her eggs—but not before some major redecorating. Female wrens, like their human counterparts, are never satisfied with the male's crude attempt to set up house. She immediately begins to undo all his work by tossing out every twig and rebuilding it herself, which usually leads to a lot of chatter and scolding between them. Eventually, the nest is completed, peace is restored, and the female adds a soft lining of feathers, hair, and soft grasses to the nest, where she lays six to eight tiny eggs with reddish-brown speckles.

One of the best times to watch house wrens is right after their eggs have hatched. Both parents make hundreds of trips a day to and from the nest with food to satisfy the ferocious appetites of the hatchlings, and they don't seem to mind if we watch them. Wrens are probably the gardener's best friend, since 98 percent of their diet is made up of insects. It's fun to watch them bring wriggling caterpillars to the nest, or the hundreds of other kinds of insects they eat, including cabbage worms, weevils, crickets, and a variety of bugs and beetles.

You probably won't find any house wrens on the first day of Christmas in Wisconsin, since most have already left our state for warmer climates by the middle of October. There have been reports of the "winter" wren, the same species hunted on St. Stephen's Day in Great Britain, overwintering in Wisconsin, but they're not too common. In a few short months, however, these loud, hyperactive little busybody brown birds will be back, belting out their endless bubbling melodies in nearly every backyard across the state, bringing a smile and, we hope, good luck to you in the year ahead.

BARRED OWLS
TEDDY BEARS OF THE FOREST

"Who cooks for you? . . . Who cooks for you-all?"

Repeat this sentence aloud in a throaty, high-pitched voice, and you'll make a pretty good imitation of one of Wisconsin's most common owls—the barred owl. Not to be confused with the barn owl, which is a rare and threatened species in Wisconsin, the barred owl lives just about everywhere in the state, although few people ever get a chance to see one in the wild.

Barred owls spend most of the daylight hours perched silently in the treetops. They are almost invisible to us because of their exceptional camouflage of black-streaked gray-and-brown feathers that blend right into the bark of tree branches. The owl's common name—barred—refers to the black lines or bars that mark its plumage, especially under the chin and breast feathers. Unlike most other owls that have large, piercing, yellow eyes, barred owls have dark brown eyes, giving them a softer and friendlier appearance. They also lack the pointed tufts of feathers on the head, called ears or horns, that many other owls have. Because it is so attractive, the barred owl is often affectionately called the "teddy bear" of the owl family.

Barred owls are true homebodies, rarely leaving their territories, each approximately one square mile, except in winter when food may be scarce. Like most other owls, barred owls are night-hunters. Although they don't have the radar-like echo location that bats have, they can still pinpoint the location of a mouse or other prey with incredible accuracy, using their exceptional hearing and eyesight. Owls cannot see in complete darkness, but they do have excellent low-light night vision which allows them to see quite well even on overcast, moonless nights.

Like most other birds of prey, barred owls swallow their food whole or in chunks. Their digestive track does the rest, separating the nourishing soft parts from the hard bones, teeth, and hair, which are regurgitated as the familiar owl pellets you might find under one of their roost trees.

Despite being such a common owl species, very little is actually known about the barred owl. We do know that they prefer to live in woodlands, but they will readily move into urban areas in search of prey. Not much is known about the owl's love life, either, except that it's quite a noisy affair. Sometime in February or March, the birds start a variety of mating calls and screeches in addition to their regular who-cooks-for-you routine. They also spend a lot of time displaying to their mates by bowing and spreading their wings. I've even seen them fighting on occasion.

Barred owls prefer to nest in holes of trees, but, if holes are unavailable, they will use the open nests of hawks, crows, or even squirrels. Usually, two or three eggs are laid and both parents incubate them. The first chick to hatch usually has the best chance to survive, since the parents begin feeding it before the other eggs have hatched. In years when prey is in short supply, this young owlet may be the only one to live, its smaller, weaker siblings literally starving to death right in the nest. Although shocking to us, this is nature's way of assuring that at least one healthy owlet survives to adulthood rather than producing a whole nest of weak, underfed birds that would likely not survive the winter.

We have always associated owls with an image of wisdom, probably because their eyes are on the front of their face, making them appear humanlike. The adage of the "wise old owl" comes to us from old folklore and superstition. In reality, owls are neither wise, nor do they live to be very old. Although barred owls are top-notch night-hunters, they can be fairly accident-prone, as well. They are often seen swooping past a car's headlights chasing a mouse across the road, seemingly unaware of the danger of the oncoming vehicle. I once found a freshly killed barred owl severed in half on a railroad track. Apparently, even something as large and noisy as a freight train did not deter this owl from focussing on its prey. In addition to accidents, many younger owls do not make it through their first winter, starving because of a shortage of prey and the extreme cold.

Barred owls are protected by federal and state laws, which make it illegal to shoot, disturb, or even possess one of their feathers. This protection has helped bring back their numbers, but owls must still contend with the loss of more and more of their habitat to development and logging. In addition, they are often poisoned when they eat insects and rodents contaminated by pesticides.

Despite all the odds against it, barred owls continue to thrive in Wisconsin. Hopefully, in the future we will always be able find places to hear the barred owls ageless question:

"Who cooks for you? Who cooks for you-all?"

MOURNING DOVES
WISCONSIN'S BIRD OF PEACE

"Four calling birds, three French hens, two turtledoves."

This familiar old English Christmas song lists all the treasured gifts given by someone's true love, including a pair of turtledoves, better known to us as mourning doves.

Mourning doves are found throughout Wisconsin but are more common in the southern part of the state. The doves are smaller and more slender than regular pigeons, and have a distinctive long V-shaped tail. Male doves are handsome birds with their beautiful rose-tinted breast and grayish head, while the females are mostly brown in color.

You might find a mourning dove nesting in your backyard in spring or summer, especially if you have tall evergreen shrubbery in which they build their flimsy stick nests. Mourning doves lay only two eggs and both the male and female take turns incubating them. Young doves in the nest are fed "pigeon milk," which is a nutritious, whitish liquid regurgitated by the parents. Doves mate for life, and are very affectionate towards each other both during and after the nesting season. This has led to the almost universal designation of doves as the symbols of love and peace throughout the world.

By early winter, most mourning doves in Wisconsin have already migrated to warmer climates such as Florida or Texas, but not all. For some reason, many doves do not migrate at all, spending the winter right here in the snowbelt. You can see them in small flocks throughout rural areas, feeding on waste grain and weed seeds, or perched on utility lines. In the city, mourning doves spend their winter days visiting bird feeders, scratching the ground in search of spilled cracked corn and millet seeds.

The birds' common name refers to the familiar, mournful sound of their cooing. They can also make very loud whistling sounds with their wings, which has startled more than one hunter or birdwatcher while stalking the fencerows and cornfields in search of other game.

Doves have always been regarded with reverence, even by ancient people who drew pictures of them as far back as 3100 B.C. Doves are mentioned many times in both the Old Testament and New Testament of the Bible, and were a common offering in the temples of Jerusalem and other holy places. Nearly everyone knows the story of Noah's ark and the dove that returned with an olive branch, signifying that dry land was nearby. Since those early days, both the olive tree and the dove have been symbols of peace.

Many years ago, the Wisconsin State legislature adopted the mourning dove as the official state symbol of peace, and the birds were listed as a protected species. Recently, however, a controversial change in state law has allowed a mourning dove hunt in Wisconsin. The birds will now be hunted, just as they are in most other states.

Mourning dove populations will most likely be able to survive the newly created hunting season. After all, they are already hunted during the day by a nearly every hawk and falcon that can catch them. At night, they are at risk of being picked off their nests and perches by owls. Raccoons, opossums, crows, squirrels, and blue jays regularly destroy the doves' eggs or eat their young. Despite all their enemies, mourning doves seem to be doing quite well and are even increasing in numbers, especially in urban areas where more and more people enjoy watching them at their backyard feeders.

Whether you think of the mourning dove as a welcome visitor to your backyard feeder, or a game bird to provide food for your family, no doubt these gentle birds of peace will be around for many years to come.

SCOTCH PINE
AMERICA'S FAVORITE CHRISTMAS TREE

The arrival of the winter solstice on December 21st, the shortest day of the year, coupled with the start of the long, harsh winter ahead, must have been a time of great fear and anxiety for our distant ancestors. We can only imagine their thoughts as the season's cold, snow, and darkness trapped them in its icy grip. Would the gods ever return the warm summer sunshine and allow the forests and fields to turn green again? Would there be enough food in reserve to last until spring?

To appease these spirits of nature and reassure themselves that winter wouldn't last forever, families gathered together in each other's homes on the eve of the solstice to sing songs, eat and drink heartily, burn a symbolic yuletide log, and decorate their homes with evergreen boughs. Part of this ritual often included cutting a fresh evergreen tree to bring inside the house as a symbol of nature's rebirth. Of course, all this was many centuries ago, during the dark, unenlightened days of our poor, ignorant ancestors. Today, most modern, educated, and sophisticated people, such as we, celebrate the season by ... er, well, pretty much the same way. The only difference is that somewhere along the way, probably in Germany, this ancient pagan custom was combined with a new religion, and a new holiday featuring the Christmas tree was born.

Wisconsin has long been recognized as one of the top three states in growing Christmas trees. Although native trees such as white pine, spruce, and balsam fir are still popular, the number one best-seller year after year is usually a European import—the Scotch pine. Named after the ancient highland forests of Scotland, the Scotch or "Scots" pine is found throughout Europe and east into Asia where they grow into tall forest trees, sometimes in dense stands. One famous Scotch pine forest in Siberia ranks as the largest single-species forest in the world.

Scotch pine was introduced into America in an effort to reforest cutover areas, soon after we had leveled most of our own native timber after the turn of the century. They were chosen because of the tree's amazing ability to thrive and grow in almost any type of soil, even nearly pure sterile sand. They grow so well, in fact, that Scotch pine can often become a nuisance in some areas by crowding out native trees and plants. Unfortunately, the Scotch pine turned out to be a failure as a timber or pulpwood tree in America, because it tended to grow crooked and have serious disease and insect problems. Although you can still find some larger trees growing in forests throughout the state, most Scotch pine is used in wind-shelter belts around farm fields, or planted in backyards and city parks as ornamental trees.

With everything going against it and a reputation as an inferior timber tree, you'd think the Scotch pine would have disappeared many years ago. But leave it to American ingenuity to make a buck off a failed forestry experiment. A few clever tree growers started to shear a few trees and test the Christmas-tree market, instead. The only problem was that most Scotch pines tended to turn yellowish in autumn, right before they were to be harvested. Growers even tried to market them as "golden pines" for a while, but nobody wanted a yellow, sickly-looking Christmas tree. Eventually, greener looking strains of Scotch pines were developed, although some are still sprayed with green colorant before being sold. Scotch pines also had the advantage of being able to grow in the warmer climates of the southern states, where our native cold-loving spruces and firs couldn't survive. In time, the new, fast-growing, and moderately priced Scotch pines became the all-time favorite

Christmas tree in America.

In Europe, Scotch pines are valued for their natural beauty. The tree's huge, low-slung branches and attractive, reddish, onion skin-looking bark have long been revered. Even the famous 18th-century poet, William Wordsworth, extolled the virtues of Scotch pine by referring to it as an "enchanting tree with its often gnarled and twisted silhouette set against a winter landscape or moonlight shadows."

Each December, many of us continue to enjoy the beauty of a simple tree by bringing a little of nature indoors with us in celebration of one of the oldest traditions known to mankind. No doubt, our pagan ancestors would probably feel right at home with us.

BALSAM FIR
THE AROMA OF CHRISTMAS

Grandpa's Christmas trees were never much to look at. Some might even have called them ugly, since they were short, unshaped, scraggly-looking, balsam firs he cut fresh, right out of the cedar-tamarack swamp near my grandparent's home. But, to me, those simple, homely wild balsams were enchanting, especially when decorated with strings of cranberry and popcorn, antique ornaments, and homemade paper stars. The balsam fir always held its needles long after being cut, and it filled the house with that unmistakable Christmas evergreen aroma. Even today, I can't resist crushing and smelling balsam needles as I hike by one of the trees, since it brings back Christmas memories of long ago.

Sure, we've gone through the fads of the shiny aluminum trees of the 1960s and the synthetic plastic and vinyl Christmas trees of the 1980s. You know, the one you paid a small fortune for, rationalizing that you would never again have to pay high prices at the tree lot or pick needles out of your carpet. But, after a few years of putting up the exact same tree, and buying the evergreen-scented aerosol sprays to make it smell like Christmas, many people are going back to buying a real tree again. And more often than not, the tree we choose is the traditional balsam fir.

Balsam fir is the only native fir tree to grow wild in our state, thriving especially in the vast swamps of the great northwoods. They also grow well in southern Wisconsin, and are planted as ornamentals and, of course, in huge plantations for the Christmas tree industry. You can identify a balsam fir is by its shiny needles, which are dark green on top and lighter beneath. Balsam fir needles are flat and blunt, compared to the triangular and sharp needles of similar-looking spruce trees. Balsam fir always grows cones on the very top of the tree and starts to release its seeds by autumn.

Back in the logging days of the 1800s, balsam fir was spared from the axe because its wood was too weak to use for building material. Later on, it was harvested for use in making a turpentine used in varnish production, and now it is used in the paper-pulp industry. Another use of balsam comes from the sticky sap that oozes from blisters on its bark. This resin is commercially sold as Canada balsam, and is used to mount specimens on microscope slides and to fasten optical lenses together in a crystal-clear natural glue. Many old-time loggers used the balsam's soft, sweet-smelling needles to stuff their mattresses and pillows. Even today, the fragrant needles are used to make aromatic souvenir pillows for tourists, a way for them to bring a little of the northwoods home with them. Some people believe that the aroma of balsam fir needles in their pillow can keep them from catching a cold. Even the Potawatomi made balsam pillows for the same reason, centuries ago, as did the Hurons, who called the balsam "cough root," considering it one of their most valuable remedies for colds.

Today, most of us don't own our own woods where we can cut down a balsam fir for Christmas, as Grandpa did years ago, but there are plenty of alternatives. You can buy them right off the Christmas tree lot in town, or you can cut your own fresh tree at the many tree farms throughout the state. They shouldn't be hard to find, since Wisconsin ranks third in the nation in Christmas tree production, producing some three million trees a year.

Of course, these are the highly trimmed, perfectly shaped trees. If you want a truly wild, authentic balsam fir, there are still places you can harvest one right out of the woods. Several of the northern Wisconsin state and national forests sell tree-cutting permits. One is the Northern Highland and American Legion State Forest in Oneida and Vilas counties, where a permit for a few dollars allows you to cut either a balsam fir or spruce. The Nicolet National Forest, in Oconto County just north of Green Bay, also sells permits to harvest trees. Permits may be purchased at the ranger stations in the forest during the week, or by mail. Although it may be a long drive and will probably cost you more than a tree you can buy at the corner lot, if you include gasoline costs, your Christmas tree hunt is sure to be an outdoor adventure to remember.

Who knows, maybe your old-fashioned, fresh-cut balsam will indeed prevent you from getting a cold this year—unless you catch one going out into the cold, snowy northwoods to cut your tree, that is.

WEASELS
NATURE'S FOUR-OUNCE KILLERS

I remember, as a young boy on my family's farm, my first encounter with a weasel. It was a cold winter morning as I began my predawn chore of feeding and watering the chickens. It was still dark out, when the hens are normally still roosting and the chicken coop is silent—but not on this morning. As I opened the door to the coop and turned on the light I discovered a wild scene of cackling, terrified hens, and the grisly sight of several dead chickens lying on the floor. The dead hens' necks had been torn open and blood was splattered everywhere—the trademark of a weasel attack.

I later learned that such raids on chicken coops by weasels are not that uncommon, with some reports of fifty or more hens killed in a single night. Because of stories like these, weasels are often thought of as bloodthirsty killers that kill for pleasure. But nothing could be further from the truth. Weasels prefer to hunt and live in woodlands, far from man, where they feed on small rodents and rabbits. Since they don't hibernate or even slow down during the winter season, they must actively search for prey every day. And when prey becomes hard to find, they occasionally find their way to farmsteads, where they find an abundant supply of mice and rats to eat, especially under outbuildings such as chicken coops.

Because a weasel's next meal is always uncertain, and may be weeks away, this animal has evolved into an expert killing machine that takes advantage of prey while it is available. That's why they kill far more than they can eat at one time and drag off the rest to save for later. In the wild, they might kill an entire nest of mice or young rabbits at one time, eat what they can, and store the rest for later. Unfortunately, this same instinct kicks in when they find their way into a chicken coop, even though they can't drag their prey out of the building. Weasels are often described as "furry snakes" with legs. Their long, slender bodies help them crawl into the burrows and tunnels of mice, rats, and rabbits. Although they weigh a mere four ounces and are only a little bigger than a chipmunk, they can kill prey much larger than themselves. They're able to do this by their lightning speed in pouncing on their victim's back, digging in with their hind feet and biting the base of the neck.

There are three species of weasels that live in Wisconsin, including the long-tailed weasel found in the southern part of the state, the short-tailed or ermine found mostly in the north, and the tiny, fairly rare least weasel.

The weasel's fur is predominately brown in color for most of the year, but in winter, in northern states such as Wisconsin, its coat turns pure white to match the snow, with the exception of the black tip of the tail. When its fur is white, we call the weasel an "ermine." Although the weasel is still trapped today, its fur is not as important as it was centuries ago, when "ermine" fur trim was an essential feature of coronation robes and crowns for kings and queens. The use of ermine fur for royalty came out the old legend that the ermine would rather go through fire than filth, making it a symbol of purity and dignity. Even in the New World, the ermine's fur was prized by Native American chiefs, who used it to decorate their war bonnets.

The weasel has many enemies besides man. It is often caught and killed by house cats, dogs, fox, owls, hawks, and even its bigger cousin, the mink. Most of its predators do not eat the weasel, however, since it has offensive scent glands similar to those of its cousin, the skunk. Weasels are solitary animals, living and hunting alone except during the short breeding period.

Through the ages, weasels have been portrayed as villains, probably due their mysterious, sneaky habits and exceptional killing ability. Even today, they are often portrayed as the bad guys in cartoons, Hollywood westerns, and children's literature. They're even part of our every day slang language, since nobody wants to be called a "weasel," which is defined by Webster as a cunning, sneaky person.

Despite my negative experiences with weasels years ago on the farm, I've decided to view this predator not as a villain, but just another interesting member of our rich Wisconsin outdoor heritage, a commitment I don't intend to "weasel out of."

SNOWSHOE HARES
GHOSTS OF THE CEDAR SWAMP

I saw him far in the distance. Like a white ghost gliding in and out of the dark, frozen landscape of the cedar swamp. It was the first snowshoe hare I had ever seen, and he seemed larger than life, with his bright, white fur contrasting against the bare ground we had that winter. Only the tips of his ears, nose, and glistening eyes were black.

In a normal winter, the snowshoe would have been almost impossible to see against the snow-covered landscape. During most of the year, snowshoes are brown in color, but as the days shorten in autumn, the animal's glands begin to alter the color of its fur. By early winter, the snowshoe has grown pure white tips over its brown undercoat fur.

The snowshoe hare is much larger than its smaller cousin, the cottontail rabbit or hare, and prefers to live in large, wooded swamps and marshes in remote areas. Snowshoes have lots of odd behaviors, but none as bizarre as their mating rituals. At the onset of the breeding season, male and female snowshoes take turns leaping over each other again and again, while urinating on their mates in mid-air. I guess this is sort of the flowers, candy, and candlelight dinner part of the snowshoe's courting behavior. Unlike cottontail rabbits, which build nests and give birth to naked, helpless, blind babies, the snowshoe hare's youngsters are born fully furred, with their eyes open. They don't build any particular nest, so the tiny hares must be ready to venture into their new world and even eat on their own within a few days of birth.

When I lived in northern Wisconsin, seeing a snowshoe hare was a common sight. They're usually so abundant in the northern forests that there's often a year-round snowshoe season with no bag limit.

Snowshoe hares once inhabited nearly every swampy, wooded area, all the way south into Milwaukee County. But seeing one in the southern part of the state is now a rare sight. Nobody knows for sure why snowshoe hares have disappeared from their southern range, but some biologists believe their disappearance may have been related to competition for food with the white-tail deer. Both snowshoe hares and deer like to eat grasses and tender tips of woody plants such as cedar, willow, alder, and even pine and spruce in winter. Most animals have a hard time finding food in the deep snows of winter, but the snowshoe, as its name implies, can hop on top of the snow with its oversized feet. The more it snows, the higher the snowshoe can reach to nibble on brush and cedar. Some believe the combination of the large increase in the deer herd, combined with the lack of deep snow during our recent mild, dry winters, may have hurt the snowshoe's chances for survival.

Unlike cottontail rabbits that dive under brush piles or into underground burrows when chased, the snowshoe's main defense is to just sit still and try to remain unnoticed. They have no special home or nest and don't use underground tunnels. They rest in hollowed-out areas called "forms," which can be under stumps or low-hanging evergreen branches. When a predator comes too close, snowshoes dart out of these forms and run along their own network of trails and runways that they've packed into frozen highways, leaving behind the heavier predator stumbling through the deep snow. Snowshoes are powerful runners, getting up to speeds of thirty miles per hour and able to leap fifteen feet. Perhaps the lack of deep snow for so many years has made it easier for predators such as fox, coyote, and especially unleashed pet dogs to catch snowshoes. In addition, the snowshoe's fur unfortunately turns white whether there's snow on the ground or not, making them easy targets for predators to spot in years of little snow cover.

Happily, snowshoe hares are still abundant in Wisconsin's northern forests, but their disappearance in other areas is a reminder that the ecosystem we live in can be fragile and ever-changing. Perhaps some day, with a little help from us and a lot of help from nature, the ghost of the cedar swamp will return once more.

DEER MICE
NOT A CREATURE WAS STIRRING

"T'was the night before Christmas, when all through
the house, not a creature was stirring, not even a mouse."
—Clement C. Moore, 1822

Whether you live in a tumble-down shack or a mansion, eventually you will be adopted by one of mankind's most loyal, ancient, and constant companions. No, not a dog—a house mouse.

Regular, run-of-the-mill house mice are the little gray rodents with the naked tail that hitched a ride to America along with the first colonists from Europe. If you happen to live in a more rural or wooded area, however, you might be "lucky" enough to be adopted by another mouse, this one a native to Wisconsin—the deer mouse.

The deer mouse and its lookalike cousin, the white-footed mouse, are actually pretty handsome animals—for vermin, anyway. They both have attractive chestnut-brown fur and pure white undersides. Their large, black, beady eyes, big ears, and furry tails make them look like miniature versions of gerbils.

Despite being cute-looking, deer mice are usually not welcome guests in our homes because of their passion to eat or chew on just about everything. In the wild, deer mice prefer seeds, nuts, fruits, berries, mushrooms, and insects. But by late fall, when their easy-to-get food is running low, they roam more widely in search of new feeding grounds. If your house happens to be within their territory, you can expect some hungry guests at this time of year. How attractive our homes must be to them, offering warmth, a roof over their heads, crumbs and food scraps in the kitchen. And, if they're really lucky, maybe there will be a dog or cat-food dish to raid.

Because deer mice don't hibernate, they must have plenty of food to keep their high-energy bodies warm during cold weather. To help them through the lean, long days of winter, they store food in small piles or caches throughout their territory.

I had some first-hand experience with a deer mouse food cache several years ago, when I was stationed at Devil's Lake State Park. Our park secretary liked to keep an open dish of M & M candies and peanuts on the office counter for visitors. Occasionally, all the goodies in the dish would disappear overnight, with the blame usually directed at the night patrol rangers. This went on for weeks until, one day, the office copy machine shut down and wouldn't restart. Imagine our surprise when the service technician dismantled the machine and called us to see the problem—a huge cache of M & M's and peanuts piled high inside the copy machine.

Although deer mice eat just about everything, they themselves are on just about every other critter's menu, as well, including owls, hawks, fox, coyotes, snakes, and shrews. In captivity, deer mice can live up to eight years, but in the wild, most survive less than a year. To compensate for being preyed upon so heavily, deer mice reproduce quickly, usually having four litters a year. Except for the months of December and January, every time of the year is the breeding season for deer mice.

A couple of years ago, at Kohler-Andrae State Park, I found a mouse nest in one of the park's bluebird houses. Inside was the mother mouse along with five of her newly born, naked babies that looked like tiny pink jellybeans. Deer mice build large, round nests of shredded plant material, and despite being very clean and well groomed, themselves, they don't bother to keep their nests clean, even using them as a toilet. Because of this, the female has to move the whole family to a new nest when the old one becomes too fouled.

I let the mice live in the birdhouse for a few more weeks, but since the bluebirds were returning, I had to evict them and put the whole family a cage in the nature center, where park visitors were able to watch them for a short while before we released them. Deer mice babies grow up quickly. By the end of their fifth week they are already mature, and by the seventh week they are ready to seek out a mate and raise a family of their own.

It must have been an exceptionally magical night in Clement Moore's poem, if not even a house mouse was stirring. After all, mice spend most of the daylight hours curled up in their nests asleep, but when darkness falls or the lights go out in the house, it's "party time." Because of their nocturnal nature, deer mice don't make good pets. Also, if they're caged, they can't abandon their foul, mousy-smelling nest, and someone (like you) will have to clean it out for them. Better to leave the wild in the wild, where they belong.

Now, if I could just convince my local deer mice to live in the wild instead of sneaking into my house.

MUSKRATS
MATRIARCHS OF THE MARSHES

You no doubt have heard of the "Attack of the Killer Bees" or the "Attack of the Swamp Creature," maybe even the "Attack of the 50-Foot Woman," but I bet you've never heard of the "Attack of the Mighty Muskrats." Yes, that's right, muskrats, those cute, fuzzy little animals that look like miniature beavers, found in nearly every river, stream, pond, and marsh in Wisconsin.

I was once a disbeliever myself, even though my co-workers at the state park where I worked had told me the tale of how a lone muskrat once chased a ranger off a bridge in the park. Apparently, the muskrat charged him, snarling and clicking its chisel-like teeth, much to the delight of another ranger safely sitting in a truck, laughing at the spectacle. Naturally, I chalked it up as one of those exaggerated tall tales of yesteryear. But then, a few summers ago, an urgent radio message came in from the park office: "There's a vicious muskrat in Campsite 76 that won't leave."

When I arrived at the campsite, sure enough, there it was—a musk-rat with an attitude. After several attempts of trying to coax the animal back towards the marsh, it decided to turn around and return to the same campsite and crawl up and onto the engine block of the camper's car. Eventually, we managed to get it back on the ground and I tried to capture it in a steel garbage can. Apparently, that was the last straw for the muskrat and it charged right towards me at high speed, hissing, snarling, and clicking its teeth. Luckily, I had the garbage can cover to use as a shield and ward off its attack. Eventually, I did manage to capture the critter and bring him back to the marsh, but not without a few chuckles from other campers enjoying the show.

Despite their occasional aggressive behavior, muskrats normally spend quiet and peaceful lives, cutting and eating cattails, bulrushes, and other aquatic plants in Wisconsin's marshes and streams. Because they are mostly nocturnal in their habits, we rarely get to see muskrats in the wild. Often, the only evidence that they're even around are the lodges they build in the marshes. These structures are similar to beaver lodges, except they are much smaller and are made out of marsh plants such as cattails, instead of sticks and mud. Inside, the lodge has a hollowed-out chamber that is used for resting, complete with underwater escape tunnels. Muskrats that live in rivers usually dig their burrows into the sides of the stream banks instead of building a lodge.

In winter, muskrats hole up in their cozy lodges under a blanket of ice and snow. Since they don't hibernate, muskrats must continue to search for food throughout the winter. Unlike the beaver that caches piles of branches underwater to eat, muskrats don't store food for the winter. Despite this, most of them seem to find enough to survive by eating plant roots, clams, and crayfish under the ice. If necessary, they can even begin to eat their own home as a last resort. Occasionally, muskrats sneak on top of the ice through the breather holes they maintain, and make an overland food raid to a nearby corn or alfalfa field.

Although life under the frozen marshland seems pretty safe and secure, there are many hazards muskrats must face every day. Predators such as hawks and owls can catch them if they venture out onto the ice, fox and coyote occasionally dig them out of their lodges, and mink can attack them even under the water. Probably more of a threat to the muskrat is a major change in the weather. If it's unusually dry and the water table drops, the ice in the marsh may freeze all the way to the bottom and their lodges will be exposed to the cold wind and predators. A few winters ago, several muskrats found themselves homeless when an early thaw and unusual winter rainstorm flooded out a river marsh near my home. One of the flood victims made its way to my backyard and decided that the snowdrift next to my house would make an ideal substitute for his flooded lodge. "Muskie," as my kids called him, became an instant celebrity of sorts and lived off fallen birdseed and cracked corn from under the birdfeeder until his icehouse melted away about a month later and he could return to the marsh.

Muskrats, like other rodents, can reproduce quickly and in large numbers. They start looking for mates in late winter and breed from then all the way through summer. One female muskrat may have three or four litters and produce up to twenty or more offspring in a year. At that rate, it wouldn't take long for muskrat families to eat themselves out of house and home, if populations weren't kept in check by predators and other natural controls. In addition, many muskrats are taken during the annual trapping season from mid-October to the end of December. Muskrat pelts have rich, brown fur that was once sold as "Hudson Bay Seal." It is still in high demand in the manufacture of women's coats, especially in European and Asian markets. Wisconsin trappers harvest and sell millions of dollars worth of muskrat pelts each year, making the muskrat our state's number one fur-bearing animal.

Despite all the pressure on muskrat populations, biologists believe that most of them are under-harvested, especially in years when pelt prices are low. In those years, if muskrat populations are not kept in check by predators or the weather, nature turns to less attractive methods of population control, such as disease, parasites, and starvation.

Muskrats react to overcrowding by leaving their homes and wandering many miles overland in search of new marshes or rivers in which to live. This is usually the time you might find one wandering in your backyard or farmstead, along roadways, or in state park campgrounds. Take it from me, it's best to give these tired, cranky, hungry, and irritable little rats the right of way, lest you become the next victim of the "Attack of the Mighty Muskrats."

RAVENS
BIRDS OF DOOM AND GLOOM?

Once upon a midnight dreary, while I pondered, weak and weary
over many a quaint and curious volume of forgotten lore—
While I nodded nearly napping, suddenly there came a tapping,
As of someone gently rapping, rapping at my chamber door.
...Quoth the Raven, "Nevermore"
—The Raven, by Edgar Allan Poe, 1845

As the cold, dreary weather and brown landscape of early winter arrives in Wisconsin, many of us mourn the passing of the warmer sunny days gone by. Most of our fair-weather feathered friends have flown south to warmer climates by now, and the leafless trees seem to be even more bare without the presence of birds to cheer us up. But not all the birds have abandoned us. Along with a few colorful birds such as cardinals and blue jays to brighten up the backyard bird feeder, juncos and grossbeaks begin to arrive from the north. We also seem to notice noisy flocks of crows and the much larger ravens found in our northern forests.

The raven is one of those mysterious birds of myth and legend that has gained a reputation of both good and evil through the ages. To some, the raven still represents the bird of doom and gloom, like the raven in Edgar Allan Poe's dark poem. But to others, including the American Indians of the Pacific Northwest, the raven was considered a god who brought life and order to the world. Even in the Bible, ravens were often portrayed in opposite roles. Before Noah sent a dove to find land after the Great Flood, he first released a raven. But the raven never returned to the ark and was forever after considered an outcast for having abandoned mankind. Yet in another part of the Bible, God is said to have sent ravens to bring food and save the prophet Elijah from starvation during his retreat to the desert.

Ravens are the largest members of the crow family, which also includes magpies and jays. You can usually tell them apart from regular crows by their larger size, heavy beak, and ruffled throat feathers. They also do not "caw" like crows, but rather produce a loud, deep-toned *corronk* call. Ravens are found throughout the Northern Hemisphere, but unlike the common crow, they have not adjusted very well to civilization. Today, they are more common in less populated areas such as northern Wisconsin, although they are occasionally found farther south, especially in winter.

Ravens mate in February or March, building their nests of sticks high in the treetops. Young nestlings are noisy and eternally hungry. Both parents spend much time and energy feeding their young several times a day. Actually, both young and old ravens have a reputation for having "ravenous" appetites. Even the word raven is defined in the dictionary as meaning "to eat hungrily or to catch and destroy." Ravens eat just about anything they can catch, and many of them depend upon road kill or carrion to survive, especially in winter. They are also known to eat small mammals such as rabbits, mice, and rats, and to prey on birds and their eggs.

Ravens also eat acorns and berries, and are fond of agricultural crops, especially corn. Because of this, ravens, like crows, were once considered vermin to be destroyed on sight. Over the years they were shot, poisoned, and even killed by the thousands with bombs until the Migratory Bird Treaty Act was signed in 1972, giving them some protection against total elimination.

Whether you consider them to be evil birds of gloom and doom or handsome majestic birds of the northwoods, ravens continue to spark our imagination. Let's hope these bigger-than-life birds of lore and legend will "nevermore" be threatened with destruction and continue to create a sense of wilderness wherever they're found.

BLUEGILLS
SCRAPPY LITTLE FIGHTERS

They're called America's favorite sport fish. Whether you're a professional angler on the walleye tournament circuit, a charter captain hunting for trophy salmon on the Great Lakes, or just an ordinary soak-a-worm weekend angler, chances are you caught your fishing fever years ago by reeling in a little bluegill. Admittedly, bluegills don't produce the same excitement as hooking a monster muskie, nor do they create the intense emotional, near-religious fervor that walleyes do in Wisconsin. Yet, pound for pound (or more like ounce for ounce), these scrappy little fighters can create some excitement of their own, especially when caught on light tackle. The current state record for a Wisconsin bluegill is a two-pound, nine-ounce whopper caught in Green Bay a few years ago.

Bluegills are abundant in nearly every lake, river, pond, and puddle in the state. With an appetite like a growing teenager, this fish always seems to be hungry, usually eager to eat most anything it can suck into its mouth. Bluegills feed on everything from algae, insects, and worms to larger prey such as minnows and small fish—even smaller bluegills. Although you can catch a bluegill most anytime of the day, they are most active at dawn and dusk. On quiet summer evenings you can hear bluegills "pop" on the surface of lakes as they feed on newly hatched insects. Bluegills can grow to nine inches in length, reaching maximum size in only a few years in good habitat. Unfortunately, in many lakes they often eat themselves out of house and home, resulting in stunted populations that may not grow larger than four or five inches.

Bluegills are members of the sunfish family, which also includes large and small-mouth bass, rock bass, crappies, and their look-a-like cousin, the pumpkinseed. Bluegills get their common name from the iridescent blue color under their jaw and gill cover, and not from the dark spot on their ear flap, which is really solid black in color. Pumpkinseeds also have the same "blue" gills, but also colorful face stripes and a scarlet spot on their ear flap. Being a "sun" fish, you'd think bluegills would enjoy the sunshine, but they much prefer the shade and shelter of aquatic vegetation, brush, stumps, or boat docks. They do, however, "like it hot," so to speak, and seem to thrive in lakes and rivers where water temperatures reach well into the upper 80s.

Late spring and into June is the best time to go after big bluegills, as they move into the shallows of lakes and rivers to spawn. I remember spending many hours as a kid, hanging over the bow of my rusty tin rowboat on a small lake near my home, just watching bluegills perform their elaborate spawning rituals. As the water temperatures approach 67 degrees, male bluegills move out of the deeper waters and claim their spawning grounds near the shoreline. By using their fins and mouth, they move the mud, sand, and gravel to create saucer-shaped depressions or nests, about a foot in diameter, on the lake bottom. They use their tail like a broom to sweep the nests flat and clean. In a good area, there might be forty to fifty male bluegills building and guarding their nests at one time, producing an under-water landscape of moonlike craters.

Once the spawning nests are completed, the female bluegills move in. Like all young males of any species, the appearance of the females creates a mad dash to attract a mate. The males show off a bit by swimming around and around the outer rim of their nests. When a female approaches the nest, the male speeds up in even faster circles, in a sort of "suck in the gut and pump out the chest" gesture to the opposite sex.

Once the female selects a mate, they swim around together inside the nest until they touch bellies and eggs and sperm are released. The spawning cycle continues for several days, with females visiting more than one nest and males attracting more than one female. One of the reasons bluegills are so successful and plentiful in nearly every body of water is their tremendous reproductive capability. One female can pro-duce some 25,000 eggs or more in a single season. After spawning, females leave the nest and their eggs in the security of their very pater-nal male partners. These house-husband males stay with the nest and fan the developing eggs with their fins to aerate and keep them clean until they hatch into fry.

There's an old saying that all fishermen go to heaven. Why exact-ly, I'm not sure. Maybe it's because of their saintly dedication to their sport, or perhaps because the passion of fishing is just such good, clean fun. On the other hand, as the wife of more than one fisherman has suggested, it might be because hell won't have them. Whatever the rea-son, you can be sure fishing will be great in the great beyond, and if there's a fish to be caught in heaven, it will probably be a bluegill. ▲

EPILOGUE

Epilogue

PASSENGER PIGEONS
POSTMORTEM FOR A SPECIES

It might have read like some obscure obituary in the local press announcing the passing of someone few knew or cared about:

"Martha Washington, aged 29 years, died of natural causes at 5 p.m. today, September 1, 1914, at her home. She had no survivors."

Yet, only a handful of newspapers bothered to print the story at all. Martha's only companions at the time of her death were her keepers at the Cincinnati Zoo, who promptly froze her body in a 300-pound block of ice and shipped her to her final resting spot at the Smithsonian Institute in Washington, D.C. Despite the lack of public interest at the time, Martha turned out to be a unique celebrity, for she was the sole relic of her race—the last passenger pigeon on earth.

The last truly wild passenger pigeons had disappeared from the landscape many years earlier. The last passenger pigeon in Wisconsin was shot near Babcock, in 1899. Many years later, in 1947, the Wisconsin Society for Ornithology honored the last passenger pigeon by erecting a large stone monument, on a high bluff overlooking the Mississippi at Wyalusing State Park. A brass plaque describes, simply but accurately, how the passenger pigeon, once numbering three to five billion birds, could have disappeared so quickly: "This species became extinct through the avarice and thoughtlessness of man."

Passenger pigeons were large, wild birds, native only to North America. As their name suggests, these "birds of passage" were in constant movement over hundreds of square miles in search of feeding and nesting areas wherever hardwood forests grew, including much of Wisconsin. Here, the massive flocks would gorge themselves on acorns, chestnuts, berries, and wild seeds. But their favorite food, by far, were the small, triangular nuts of the American beech tree. These are the attractive trees with the smooth, gray bark in which people often carve their initials. Today, beech trees are still found, scattered in small wood-lots and parks throughout the eastern part of Wisconsin.

Although many theories have been offered over the years to explain the extinction of the passenger pigeon, they all center around two reasons—over-harvest and destruction of habitat. Passenger pigeons had always been hunted for food by Native Americans and, later, by early settlers, with little effect on their populations. But, with the advent of market hunting and the demand for both adult birds and their young, appearing as "squab" on restaurant menus across the country, passenger pigeons suddenly found themselves to be a constant year-round target for market harvest. Instead of the few birds shot here and there, pigeons were being shot, netted, clubbed, and trapped by the thousands. Even the trees they roosted and nested in were not safe, as pigeoneers used poles to knock down the nests, set sulfur fires under them to suffocate the birds, or even cut the trees down to get at the birds in their nests.

At the same time passenger pigeons were being slaughtered by mar-ket hunters, their food supplies were dwindling, as beech and other nut-bearing trees were being felled to make way for cities and croplands. Although passenger pigeons caused little damage to standing crops, they did raid newly seeded fields and fed on harvested grain shocks. Because of this, farmers killed as many of them as they could, to protect their crops while earning a little extra cash. A common method of taking pigeons at the time was to soak old grain in alcohol and spread it around the fields and later club the inebriated pigeons to death.

In the 1800s, millions of passenger pigeons were also captured alive, packed tightly in crates, and shipped to big city shooting clubs for use in a new sport called trapshooting. The pigeons were put into steel spring traps that were designed to throw live birds into the air for the shooting competitions. Public sentiment eventually turned against this inhumane sport, and trapshooting evolved into its current form, using only "clay" pigeons. At about the same time, Wisconsin legislators passed new laws to protect the remaining passenger pigeons, but they were poorly enforced, and loopholes in the law protected only the adult birds. The harvest of young squab continued unchallenged. In the end, extinction came from the inability of the passenger pigeon to raise enough young to cover the losses of adult birds and to the loss of the beech tree forests they depended on for survival.

Upon the dedication of the Passenger Pigeon Monument at Wyalusing State Park, in 1947, Aldo Leopold wrote, "There will always be pigeons in books and museums, but these are effigies and images, dead to all the hardships and to all the delights. They know no seasons; they feel no kiss of the sun, no lash of the wind and weather." While stationed at Wyalusing State Park several years ago as the park manager, I often watched park visitors read the inscription on this monument and touch the well-polished silhouette of the passenger pigeon forged in brass. Although usually silent, I knew what they were thinking. "How could we have done this?"

As the last glint of life faded from the colorful eyes of Martha Washington on that hot and muggy September afternoon in 1914, little did she know that the world had at that moment changed forever. It was more than just the disappearance of the passenger pigeon, it was a wake-up call for all mankind. We learned that we could destroy an entire race of animals, but also had the power to save them from extinction. Today, hundreds of environmental and conservation organizations are working towards the common goal of preserving and enhancing wildlife populations around the world. We hope that this new global interest in wildlife, from our backyards to the most remote rainforest, will mean that we will never again have to build a monument to a lost species. ▲

Notes

Notes

Notes

Illustration Credits

Index

MORE BOOKS from Prairie Oak Press and Trails Books

ACTIVITY GUIDES

Wisconsin Underground: A Guide to Caves, Mines and Tunnels in and Around the Badger State, *Doris Green*

Acorn Guide to Northwest Wisconsin, *Tim Bewer*

Paddling Southern Wisconsin: 82 Great Trips by Canoe and Kayak, *Mike Svob*

Paddling Northern Wisconsin: 82 Great Trips by Canoe and Kayak, *Mike Svob*

Wisconsin Golf Getaways: A Guide to More Than 200 Great Courses and Fun Things to Do, *Jeff Mayers and Jerry Poling*

Great Cross-Country Ski Trails: Wisconsin, Minnesota, Michigan, and Ontario, *Wm. Chad McGrath*

Great Wisconsin Walks: 45 Strolls, Rambles, Hikes, and Treks, *Wm. Chad McGrath*

Great Minnesota Walks: 49 Strolls, Rambles, Hikes, and Treks, *Wm. Chad McGrath*

Best Wisconsin Bike Trips, *Phil Van Valkenberg*

TRAVEL GUIDES

Historical Wisconsin Getaways: Touring the Badger State's Past, *Sharyn Alden*

The Great Wisconsin Touring Book: 30 Spectacular Auto Tours, *Gary Knowles*

Wisconsin Family Weekends: 20 Fun Trips for You and the Kids, *Susan Lampert Smith*

County Parks of Wisconsin, Revised Edition, *Jeannette and Chet Bell*

Up North Wisconsin: A Region for All Seasons, *Sharyn Alden*

Great Wisconsin Taverns: 101 Distinctive Badger Bars, *Dennis Boyer*

Great Wisconsin Restaurants, *Dennis Getto*

Great Weekend Adventures, *the Editors of Wisconsin Trails*

The Wisconsin Traveler's Companion: A Guide to Country Sights, *Jerry Apps and Julie Sutter-Blair*

Great Minnesota Weekend Adventures, *Beth Gauper*

Tastes of Minnesota: A Food Lover's Tour, *Donna Tabbert Long*

Sacred Sites of Wisconsin, *John-Brian Paprock and Teresa Peneguy Paprock*

HISTORICAL GUIDES

Historical Wisconsin Getaways: Touring the Badger State's Past, *Sharyn Alden*

Walking Tours of Wisconsin's Historic Towns, *Lucy Rhodes, Elizabeth McBride and Anita Matcha*

Wisconsin: The Story of the Badger State, *Norman K. Risjord*

Barns of Wisconsin, *Jerry Apps*

Portrait of the Past: A Photographic Journey Through Wisconsin, 1865-1920, *Howard Mead, Jill Dean and Susan Smith*

PHOTO BOOKS

Wisconsin Lighthouses: A Photographic and Historical Guide, *Ken and Barb Wardius*

Wisconsin Waterfalls, *Patrick Lisi*

The Spirit of Door County: A Photographic Essay, *Darryl R. Beers*

OTHER WISCONSIN BOOKS

The Eagle's Voice: Tales Told by Indian Effigy Mounds, *Gary J. Maier*

Driftless Stories: Outdoors in Southwest Wisconsin, *John Motoviloff*

River Stories: Growing Up on the Wisconsin, *Delores Chamberlain*

Northern Frights: A Supernatural Ecology of the Wisconsin Headwaters, *Dennis Boyer*

Driftless Spirits: Ghosts of Southwestern Wisconsin, *Dennis Boyer*

To place an order, phone, write or email us.

TRAILS BOOKS
P.O. Box 317, Black Earth, WI 53515
(800) 236-8088 • email: books@wistrails.com
www.trailsbooks.com